The Lebanese Diaspora

The Lebanese Diaspora

The Arab Immigrant Experience in
Montreal, New York, and Paris

Dalia Abdelhady

NEW YORK UNIVERSITY PRESS
New York and London

NEW YORK UNIVERSITY PRESS
New York and London
www.nyupress.org

References to Internet websites (URLs) were accurate at the time of writing. Neither the author nor New York University Press is responsible for URLs that may have expired or changed since the manuscript was prepared.

Library of Congress Cataloging-in-Publication Data
Abdelhady, Dalia.
The Lebanese diaspora : the Arab immigrant experience in Montreal, New York, and Paris / Dalia Abdelhady.
p. cm.
Includes bibliographical references and index.
ISBN 978-0-8147-0733-3 (cl : alk. paper) — ISBN 978-0-8147-0734-0 (pb : alk. paper) — ISBN 978-0-8147-0771-5 (e-book)
1. Lebanese—Foreign countries. 2. Lebanon—Emigration and immigration. I. Title.
DS80.6.A23   2011
305.892'75692—dc22   2011012529

New York University Press books are printed on acid-free paper, and their binding materials are chosen for strength and durability. We strive to use environmentally responsible suppliers and materials to the greatest extent possible in publishing our books.

Manufactured in the United States of America

c   10 9 8 7 6 5 4 3 2 1
p   10 9 8 7 6 5 4 3 2 1

To my mother, Malaka Salem,
the first transnational immigrant I have known

Contents

Acknowledgments

One question repeatedly came up whenever I had to explain my research project: Why the Lebanese? It was assumed that my interest in studying the Lebanese derived from my Arab origin, but the interrogator usually wanted to know why the Lebanese from among all the Arabs. The truth is, I developed an interest in studying the Lebanese despite my desire not to study "my own people." I had wanted to avoid becoming the informant who would present an insider's view of the community. I could not do so, even if I tried. The diversity of Lebanese immigrants can hardly be captured by drawing on commonalities of language and culture that are often contested. I was drawn to studying the Lebanese specifically as a result of the diversity of the community and the contentions inherent in defining a Lebanese identity. I had hoped that somewhere within the plethora of narratives that express distinct class, educational and religious backgrounds, gender and age positions, and streams of thought and ideals, I would find my own commonalities with others and understand my own experience with migration and displacement. Fortunately I found many. The diverse personal histories of the immigrants I interviewed were only complicated by the differences in the cultural milieus they immigrated to. The distinct urban contexts were also chosen to represent different state policies and attitudes toward immigrants. I can only begin to express my appreciation for the people I encountered in Montreal, New York, and Paris. Those who agreed to participate in my research shared their life stories and personal experiences, and I was touched by their willingness to communicate their private feelings. Many of these participants assisted me during fieldwork beyond the interviews; they invited me to their homes, to parties, and to family gatherings, and they offered several referrals that made my fieldwork effortless and enjoyable despite the time constraints. A few participants in Montreal and New York also offered shelter during my field visits, and I thank them for their kindness. A number of these individuals have become dear friends, and have provided critical personal and professional advice. While trying my best to stay true to their narratives and viewpoints, I also made every effort to keep their identities anonymous.

Without doubt, the contributions of my academic mentors, Steven Seidman, Richard Alba, Ronald Jacobs, and Richard Lachmann, were critical for my graduate training in general and for this project in particular, and I feel especially fortunate to have been their student. From my first day at the State University of New York (SUNY)—Albany, Steven Seidman provided invaluable critiques, insightful advice, and pleasurable mentoring. I benefited tremendously from his theoretical and analytical rigor, as well as his friendly guidance. Steve also provided a significant source of motivation and challenge, and I hope I can continue to meet his challenges in the future. Richard Alba has generously supported me at various stages of this research project and has provided me with extensive training in sociological analysis. He has been a great mentor and was also always concerned about my intellectual development and personal well-being. Ronald Jacobs's contributions were instrumental at every stage of this project: from its initial conception, theoretical and methodological construction, and data gathering to its final completion. Ron was also the source of encouragement and friendly advice at many critical moments during the last few years. Richard Lachmann gave me indispensable ideas that helped my analysis, and also provided substantial support, advice, and motivation.

This research was supported by a fellowship from the International Migration Program of the Social Science Research Council with funds provided by the Andrew W. Mellon Foundation, and a research award from the Middle East Research Competition sponsored by the Ford Foundation (administered at the time by the Lebanese Center for Policy Studies). It was also assisted by a number of grants through the University at Albany: the Allen E. Liska Dissertation Award, a Benevolent Association Research Award, Initiatives for Women, and Research and Travel grants from the Graduate Student Organization. I am also appreciative to Philippe Fargues, Patrick Simon, and Youssef Courbage at the Institut National d'Études Démographique. They provided me with institutional support, academic consultations, and numerous connections that made my stay and data collection in Paris, a city I had never visited before, a comfortable and joyful experience.

My family is my strongest source of support, love, and understanding. The contributions of my mother Malaka Salem, sister Dina Abdelhadi, late brother Omar Abdelhadi, and father Abdalla Abdelhadi have had a direct impact on my academic training and research choices. Growing up in a transnational family shaped my interests in migration and border crossing at a very young age. At the age of four, when my parents moved to Saudi Arabia and I remained in Egypt with my siblings and dear aunt, I started learning from my parents that caring, responsibilities, and attachments extend over national borders and overcome geographic distances. When it was my turn to move to the United States and leave my family members behind, their sadness was only overcome by their willingness to help me pursue my dreams. During my years in the United States, I continued to rely on their unwavering encouragement, generous emotional and financial support, and unconditional love. Despite the distance, my family members have always been there for me, especially at critical times. The loss of my brother a year after my arrival in the United States was consequential in my life, but he continues to provide a source of passion, integrity, and challenge. The passing of my father in 2009 was also detrimental to my family, but it has confirmed my beliefs in the strength of transnational connections and furthered my motivation to finish this book. My sister, Dina, continues to provide balance and serenity, and I could not have managed through the years without her. More recent additions to my family, my nephews Yassin and Omar, only strengthened my transnational ties and confirmed to me that global awareness starts at a very young age. Having to explain my research to them helped me to elucidate my argument. When they started giving me examples of their own cosmopolitan attachments, however, I was left speechless. Yassin and Omar are a real source of joy and hope in my life, and I thank them for it. To my family: thank you for making my work meaningful.

My first colleagues at SUNY—Albany taught me much about sociology and helped me to construct a new home away from home; I am thankful for having them in my life. Amy Lutz, James Dean, Jennifer Gunsaullus, Elena Vesselinov, and the late Bridget Fitzgerald never hesitated to provide critical analyses of social and academic concerns, as well as friendly advice. Their friendship is an important source of appreciation and excitement. I also thank Tariqul Islam for his friendship and technical assistance. My friends Sheri Kunovich and Rebecca Carter were instrumental in making Dallas a home. The support and encouragement that I received from Shahnaz Rouse were also instrumental in the completion of this book, and she always provided generous support and hospitality in New York.

David Bowling came to my life during the final stages of writing this book but valued it as though it were his from the beginning. He has provided invaluable encouragement, excitement, and assistance. To my life, he continues to offer treasured joys and affection as much as motivational challenges and inspiration. I thank him for making my life richer in so many ways, and I forgive him for not helping with the index.

Finally, I thank Ilene Kalish, Aiden Amos, and Despina Papazoglou Gimbel for their amazing work at NYU Press and their support throughout the different stages of finishing this book.

Global Immigrants

Three Views on Diaspora

In December 2008 I set out to obtain an entry visa from the German Consulate in Cairo, preparing to attend an academic workshop there. I was in Cairo visiting my family and thought that spending a day of my vacation at the consulate would be better than taking the time from my busy teaching schedule in the US. After a long wait, I handed the receptionist the stack of required papers for my visa. She took one quick look at my papers and exclaimed that my application could not be processed at the consulate in Cairo, since the supporting documents originated in the United States (i.e., proof of employment, letter from the chair of my department promising that I would be returning to teach in the following semester, an invitation letter from the workshop organizers, my bank statements, hotel reservations, flight itinerary, and proof of health insurance coverage in Europe). She told me that I should apply for the visa in the United States. In a state of shock, I explained that I was not returning to the United States before the workshop and that I was holding my one and only passport that had been issued by the Egyptian government. She insisted that, in her view and that of the supervisors she had consulted upon my request, I was not Egyptian "enough."

This stunned me, as I had never considered myself American (enough). Yet here I was being defined by my American employment and residential status. Despite my thirteen-year stay in the United States, I am not even a permanent resident. I still have to apply for an entry visa, marking me as non-American every time I enter the country. I could not explain this dilemma to the receptionist. I could not tell her that I had never felt American, despite the various indicators of my successful assimilation. The reminders that I do not belong to American society are constant and numerous. Many are related to travel. With every visit to a foreign country, I must obtain an entry visa similar to the one I was seeking at the German Consulate in Cairo. Standing in line at the various consulates, I was always queued up with others of dark complexion, thick accents, and thus questionable intentions. American citizens are rarely in such lines, and my presence there marked my non-American status. The strongest reminder of that status takes place at airports, upon my reentry into the United States and standing before the officer working for the Citizenship and Immigration Services (CIS; formerly known as the Immigration and Naturalization Services [INS]). For a few years after September 11 I developed an anxiety toward international travel. I always fear that I will not be allowed back into the United States and will be deported to Egypt, or even possibly Guantanamo Bay. I have been to the back room of the Immigration Services two or three times, the place where all those with visa violations or questionable papers, or those suspected of smuggling, are taken. Although I only sat on a chair reading a book until the officers cleared whatever issue that had come up about my papers and allowed me to leave, the time I spent in those back rooms behind CIS airport counters only aggravated my anxieties—and as my anxieties worsened, any attempt to feel that I belong to American society weakened as well.

So back to Cairo, where my entire family lives, where I grew up and went to college, and where I thought I would return should everything else fail. But now I was being told that I do not belong there. The obvious question came to mind: Where do I belong?

The issue of national belonging is a source of anxiety to many immigrants worldwide, myself included. Such anxiety, however, is not the driving force behind this book. Rather, this book explains the various meanings that immigrants attach to their experiences of belonging to or being excluded from diverse societies. Being an immigrant is a process that involves creative adaptations and strategic maneuvering, and the formation of new global belongings that escape the confines of the singular nation-state. Highlighting their creative maneuvers and adaptations to the various communities in which immigrants participate, I argue for the need to rethink our notions of national membership and emphasize multiple belongings that are not simply based on ethnic, national, religious, or class similarities. The book describes how immigrants manage to forge ways of belonging and find sources of coherence and stability in spite of the harsh and difficult experiences of migration they face. Despite encounters with national/ethnic exclusion and an obvious awareness of their difference from their host societies, immigrant encounters and lived experiences are often productive of new identities, as well as sources of both communal solidarity and affirmation.

The analysis in this book is based on the concept of diaspora as best suited for understanding the paradoxical experiences and contradictory forms of belonging that define and give form to migration. The most central accounts in immigration studies emphasize the ways in which members of the immigrant community became absorbed by the main society and were assimilated through various mechanisms such as language absorption, socioeconomic mobility, and intermarriage. Generally assimilation is defined as a one-sided process of incorporating migrants into host societies. In the process of adapting to the new setting, migrants are expected to give up distinctive cultural and social attributes so as to become indistinguishable from members of the new society. To some extent, the assimilation model has been employed in all "highly-developed immigration countries" (Castles 1997). Among these countries at present, France typifies assimilationist policies and continues to offer the longest, strongest, and most ideologically elaborated tradition of assimilation in Europe (Brubaker 2005). While accounts of assimilation take into consideration that some early immigrants may hold on to an ethnic identity, the argument follows that such a tendency is only symbolic because, for these immigrants, ethnic identity carries little social, economic, or political weight (Gans 1979). Similarly, in the French context, religious, ethnic, linguistic, regional, subcultural, and other ascriptive identities do not hinder assimilation or the commitment to the national community as they are relegated to the private sphere (see, e.g., Ireland 1996). The emphasis on assimilation leads many authors to overlook the more complicated experiences that early immigrants endured.

Naff (1985) and Truzzi (1997) provide examples for the assimilation of Arab immigrants in the United States. The authors examine the experiences of early Arab immigrants in the United States who were mostly of Syrian Lebanese origin and conclude that many of them have undergone a process of complete identificational assimilation, or "Americanization." Naff (1985) describes the manner in which they adopted regional social attitudes, tastes, and accents as they followed the middle-class path up the economic and social ladder. Similarly Truzzi (1997) describes the successful business and professional endeavors of many Arabs in the United States. The author stresses that many Arabs in the United States entered politics and did well in government, as governors, representatives, or advisers to the president— but "they entered not as Arab-Americans, but rather as assimilated Americans" (ibid.:13). The experience of Arab Americans, however, cannot be fully grasped within the assimilation framework. Although Arab Americans of the earlier waves have assimilated and emerged as white within the American racial structure, Gualtieri (2009) argues that they are "in between" or "not quite white." Emphasizing their ethnic formation historically, Gualtieri goes on to argue that their earlier encounters with race at the beginning of the twentieth century marks their difference within American society and shapes their position in the post–9/11 context.

Gualtieri's analysis represents the second strand of immigration studies that emphasizes pluralism and multicultural contexts of reception in analyzing immigrant experiences. Pluralism refers to multiple paths for immigrant incorporation into the host society. "Multiculturalism," the most popular form of pluralist approaches, is characterized as the acceptance of immigrant communities as ethnic minorities. Multiculturalism emphasizes that ethnic groups retain their distinguishable character (such as language, culture, social behavior, or public sphere) from the majority population within a larger multicultural society (see, e.g., Basch et al. 1994; Castles 1997; Glazer and Moynihan 1970; and Portes and Rumbaut 1996). On one level, multiculturalists emphasize that retaining ethno-communal solidarity is an important aspect of belonging to a plural society (Glazer and Moynihan 1970). In 1971 Canada became the world's first official multicultural nation and continues to offer a model for other countries (Communication Canada 2001). Currently Canada, Australia, and the United States provide different elaborations of multicultural contexts for the reception of immigrants (see Kymlicka 1995; Castles 1997). In recent years much attention has been directed toward the analysis of transnational immigrant practices. Transnationalism often reflects incomplete assimilation and the strengthening of ethnic pluralism in host societies (Morawska 2008).

While offering significant departures in the understanding of immigrant experiences, transnational analyses are less conducive than diaspora as a framework for investigating global immigrant experiences. A number of scholars have drawn a distinction between transnationalism and cosmopolitanism in understanding "global subjectivity"—or the impact of migration on people's understandings of their position in the world. For example, Pnina Werbner (1999:19–20) defines "cosmopolitans" as those who familiarize themselves with other cultures and know how to move easily between cultures. "Transnationals," on the other hand, are people who, while moving, build encapsulated cultural worlds around themselves, most typically worlds encapsulated by religious and family ties. Thus the framework of transnationalism contributes to the understanding of immigrants' communities and identities by incorporating the cross-border attachments carried on by many immigrants but does not contribute to our understanding of new identities and communities that emerge out of experiences of migration. Diaspora provides an entry to the analysis of migration within global spaces as it delineates groups of people that span nation-states. At the turn of the new century Albrow (1997) suggested that, in the age of globalization, "diaspora may become the dominant mode of the ethnic sociality." Although such a claim may be contested in various social contexts, I believe that diaspora captures important sociological relationships embedded in the lived experiences of first-generation immigrants in today's global world. More important, diaspora provides a framework through which to understand immigrant integration that moves beyond traditional sociological models, such as assimilation and ethnic pluralism (Abdelhady 2006). As an explanatory paradigm, diaspora possesses malleable qualities, such as the awareness of simultaneous inclusion and exclusion, that apply to diverse immigrant communities (Barkan and Shelton 1998). To account for such protean qualities of diaspora in contemporary societies, I investigate the Lebanese immigrant communities in Montreal, New York, and Paris. Understanding their positions as products of global economic, political, and cultural dynamics, Lebanese immigrants exhibit forms of identification, social connections, and modes of cultural expression that take into consideration a global diasporic awareness. These identities, communities, and artistic forms cannot be understood within traditional frameworks of assimilation or ethnic pluralism. Transnationalism can only provide a partial understanding of these migratory dynamics. Diaspora, however, provides an entry into investigating global positions and dynamics.

The Lebanese diaspora is an important site for investigating immigration dynamics and the ways in which immigrants are affected by global economic, political, and cultural processes. Lebanese immigrant communities around the world constitute the largest groups of Arab immigrants. As a diaspora, Lebanese immigrant communities have historical roots in almost every corner of the world. From the mid-nineteenth-century on, people from the Middle East have been moving in large numbers to North and South America, Africa, and northern Europe. Most of these immigrants came from Mount Lebanon,[1] and the Lebanese continue to make up the largest group of immigrants from the Middle East (Hourani and Shehadi 1992). Emigration has been a prominent aspect of Lebanese society since the second half of the nineteenth century. A combination of factors contributed to the dispersion of the Lebanese people over different parts of the world. Mount Lebanon was inhabited by heterogeneous groups of different ethnic and religious backgrounds, and a range of push-pull factors varied for each group. Some were driven by push factors such as economic desperation, religious discrimination, or political oppression. Numerous accounts emphasize the primacy of economic factors in motivating early waves of emigration (see Karpat 1985; Naff 1985; Suleiman 1999).[2]

As a result of the various economic and sociopolitical factors, substantial emigration occurred between 1860 and 1914. During this period approximately 330,000 Lebanese (from Greater Syria but mostly from Mount Lebanon) emigrated. Between 1900 and 1914 the annual rate was about 15,000. The rate dropped sharply during World War I and immediately thereafter, but a net annual emigration rate of about 3,000 persisted between 1921 and 1939 (Labaki 1992). Among those who had emigrated by 1932, 123,397 were Maronites, 57,031 were Greek Orthodox, and 26,627 were Melkites (Greek Catholics) but only 36,865 were Muslims and Druzes (U.S. Country Studies 2003). Although emigration declined in the period during the two world wars owing to the global economic crisis, it resumed after 1945 despite the relative growth of the Lebanese economy during the decade of 1950–60. During the 1960s and 1970s the oil boom resulted in a significant increase in migration from Lebanon to the oil-producing countries of the Persian Gulf (from 3,000 to 10,000 annually) (Labaki 1992).

The outbreak of the civil war in 1975 significantly accelerated emigration.[3] The seventeen-year war brought about the total destruction of the economy and a "forced collective exodus of hundreds of thousands of people from their villages and towns" (ibid.:909). About half the Lebanese who left during the war settled in oil-producing Arab countries, and the other half headed to Europe, the Americas, Africa, and Australia. A net number of 990,000 Lebanese individuals (40% of the Lebanese population) are believed to have migrated in the period between 1975 and 1989. Although all religious groups were negatively affected by the war in Lebanon, analyses of its effects on migratory trends point to specific patterns. First, during the period from 1975 to 1982, the majority of emigrants were Christians. Following the Israeli invasion of Beirut in 1982, the trend was reversed toward a majority of Muslim and Druze migrants (Helou 1995). Second, given the large-scale waves of migration, Lebanese emigrants during the war came from diverse economic and professional backgrounds that include both white- and blue-collar professions (ibid.; Labaki 1992). However, 47% of total emigrants belong in the professional and skilled labor category (United Nations Development Programme [UNDP] 2004). Finally, the emigration of families, as opposed to individuals, and greater reliance on chain migration were predominant mechanisms for migration during the war years. According to the UNDP (ibid.), intensive migration during the war affected Lebanon's demographic profile, most significantly in the form of a decline in the sex ratio of the working populations (reflecting higher migration for males).

Labaki (1992) points out that four hundred thousand Lebanese emigrants left during the first year of the war (some of them returned a year later) and argues that the last years of the war brought migration figures close to those of 1975. The presumed end of the war with the signing of the Taif Accords in 1989 was followed by an eruption in fighting among the various Christian groups and led to another wave of large-scale migration. The failure of the Accords to halt the killing diminished hopes for a peaceful future in Lebanon, and more people sought stable conditions in the diaspora. The failure of the peace accords also led many Lebanese to think of their presence outside Lebanon as less of a temporary exile and more in terms of a permanent settlement.

In 1992 new elections took place and managed to achieve a broad national consensus.[4] National stability, however, only increased the waves of migration after 1992. An economic slowdown and high unemployment rates are key factors accounting for present-day Lebanese emigration. In the absence of official statistics, estimates vary, and the figure of outflows of more than one hundred thousand persons per year in the latter 1990s is cited as conservative (UNDP 2004). According to the UNDP, men and those with higher education constitute the majority of migrants from all ages. Lebanese youth (ages twenty to twenty-nine) represent the majority of those who migrated in recent years. The pursuit of economic opportunities abroad is the most important reason for migration (62%), followed by education (21%). These factors make Lebanon one of the world's most emigration-prone countries, resulting in a large diaspora whose numbers exceed that of the population in the home country (Abdul-Karim 1992).

The long history of Lebanese immigrant communities notwithstanding, their spread around the world allows for a comparative analysis in diverse national contexts. Stressing that "place matters," Nancy Foner (2005) calls our attention to the importance of studying the same diasporic group in different locations in order to understand the ways that immigrants adapt to specific locations and different contexts of integration. Immigrants of Middle Eastern origin tend to settle in urban areas. Historically the Lebanese immigrants' first destinations were New York in the United States and Montreal in Canada (Abu-Laban 1992). Since the outbreak of the Lebanese civil war in 1975, Paris has become a destination equal in popularity to the two North American cities (Hourani and Shehadi 1992). The three cities continue to serve as magnets for present-day Lebanese immigrants for several reasons. First, the three cities are major port cities and international, commercial, educational, and cultural centers, and thus form "diasporan capitals" (Butler 2001), where communities from many diasporas, not just the Lebanese diaspora, congregate. Second, New York and Montreal provide strong networks that have traditionally linked the Lebanese immigrant communities with the home country. Finally, the French milieu (as a result of colonial history), which is congenial for many Lebanese immigrants in both Montreal and Paris, facilitates their comfort with (and in) the host societies. As such, the three cities are important not only owing to the presence of the large Lebanese communities in each context but because they provide contexts for the development and articulation of diasporic identities and communities.

The three contexts of this book were chosen to highlight global dynamics as well as specific national differences of integration contexts and policies. These three settings vary in terms of the contexts of immigrant reception, where assimilation and multiculturalism take on different meanings, and result in different immigrant experiences for the diaspora. France is a nation-state that sees itself as universalist and egalitarian (Kastoryano 2002), and French national identity rejects the possibility of multiculturalism (De Groat 2001). In contrast to Canada and the United States, France is considered a model of an assimilationist nation-state, based on territorial requirement for citizenship (Brubaker 2005). Unlike the French context, Canadian multicultural citizenship is grounded in a commitment to universal values with a fundamental respect for ethnic diversity (Kymlicka 1995). Will Kymlicka emphasizes that multiculturalism in Canada typically implies that immigrants have a right to express their ethnic identity without fear of prejudice or discrimination, especially given state sponsorship of ethnic press, associations, educational programs and cultural activities. Official immigration policies in the United States, on the other hand, have always been informed by a mix of multicultural and assimilatory tendencies, operating almost simultaneously (see, e.g., Cornwell and Stoddard 2001). With the lack of official policies to assist in either direction (mostly a result of American individualism) immigrants are expected to navigate the socioeconomic demands for assimilation (even when segmented) and the cultural affinities of multiculturalism.

These differences notwithstanding, Canada, France, and the United States have similar traditions for dealing with immigrants. All three nations have brought in massive numbers of immigrants over a very long period of time. Whereas North American histories of mass immigration are well known, those of France are often overlooked. At various points during the twentieth century France brought in more immigrants per capita than did the United States, leading Gérard Noiriel (1988:21) to suggest that immigration carries more economic and social importance in France than in the United States. Furthermore, the three countries define citizenship expansively and inclusively (Freeman 1995). Unlike many nations, France, Canada, and the United States adhere to the principle of *jus soli* which offers citizenship to all individuals who are born or have settled within their borders. Both France and the United States have dominant cultural traditions that treat citizenship as essentially political—one can choose to become French or American—and both reject ethno-cultural conceptions of citizenship (Brubaker 1992). Although the Canadian conception of citizenship is based on multiculturalism that includes granting group-specific rights (specifically in the form of First Nations' territorial claims and political autonomy and Québécois' rights to cultural preservation), immigrants are still expected to actively seek integration into Canadian society. Thus all three countries emphasize citizenship as an active process to be sought by immigrants.

Consequently the three cities provide arenas where diverse dynamics are produced that expand our understanding of diasporic communities and experiences. While looking at daily lived experiences, I focus on the ways in which members of diasporic communities negotiate their cultural belonging and make sense of their daily realities. By providing a comparative investigation of the three cities, I illuminate the conception of diaspora theoretically and empirically. Further, I focus on the similarities between the three settings in order to show the common features of diasporic life regardless of the context of reception. Similarly, by highlighting some of the differences in experiences, I illustrate the ways that immigrants adapt to different national contexts. Investigating the Lebanese diaspora as a unit that extends beyond national boundaries, my analysis of Lebanese immigrant communities in three world cities opens up a global perspective in thinking about immigration, global processes, and new forms of alliance. Throughout the analysis provided in this book I draw on theoretical arguments developed within cultural studies and postcolonial criticism in order to elucidate the daily experiences of Lebanese immigrants. At the same time I present the major patterns found within these lived experiences in order to empirically ground the theoretical arguments.

What Is Diaspora?

> I have never lost hope of returning to my homeland some day.
> However, I no longer remember where I came from.
>
> —Cf. Safran 1991

The word "diaspora" is traditionally used when referring to immigrant populations that span more than one national context. The intensity of global processes in the last few decades brought a revival of the concept for understanding immigrant experiences. For example, Soysal (2000:2) declared that diaspora "captures much of our analytical and popular imagination, and claims explanatory fortitude in narrating the presence and conditions of immigrant populations."[5] The word "diaspora" is derived from the Greek verb *speiro* (to sow) and the proposition *dia* (over). It also refers to the "scattering of seeds" and thus the Greek's association of diaspora with migration and colonization (Cohen 1997), implying acculturation and assimilation while at the same time maintaining a rooted tradition. All diasporic communities establish themselves outside their country of origin, but the customs, languages, and religions they carry with them create varied senses of loyalty and nostalgia. Throughout history, the expression acquired a more sinister and brutal meaning as it signified a collective trauma as in the cases of Africans, Armenians, Jews, and Palestinians. Some authors emphasize that the term "diaspora" should only be used in reference to such groups who share a catastrophic past, and underscore diaspora as a normative concept. Chaliand and Rageau (1995:xiv), for example, highlight the forced aspect of diaspora creation: "A diaspora is defined as the collective forced dispersion of a religious and/or ethnic group precipitated by a disaster, often of a political nature."

Sinister significations waned, as in more recent years groups of people started to define themselves as diasporas even though they were neither active agents of colonization nor passive victims of persecution. Among these numerous examples are the Maghrebi, Turkish, Indian, Persian, and Cuban diasporas. The diversity of experiences referred to using the term "diaspora" only led to the ambiguity often associated with it. Nowadays the term "diaspora," or more specifically "diasporic community," seems to be used as a metaphoric designation for several categories of people such as expatriates, expellees, political refugees, alien residents, immigrants, and ethnic and racial minorities. Apprehensive that the term may lose all analytical meaning and value, a number of scholars have attempted to come up with more rigorous definitions, as well as specific approaches to its conceptualization.

A diasporic population is one that is dispersed (voluntarily or involuntarily) from an original homeland to two or more territories. Given the broad spectrum of diasporic groups, ties to the homeland are of added importance in defining the diasporic experience. The homeland forms the basis for collective memory, and for ethno-communal solidarity and consciousness; it also molds cultural, social, political, and economic life in the diaspora (Safran 1991; Sheffer 1997; Van Hear 1998). Alongside a strong relationship to the homeland, members of diasporas may also share a feeling of alienation based on the conviction that "they are not—and perhaps cannot be—fully accepted by their host society" (Safran 1991:83; see also Vertovec and Cohen 1999).

Almost all authors who discuss diasporic communities emphasize notions of collective memory, communal consciousness, homeland, and alienation. These features, however, do not allow for an understanding of diasporas that transcends an ethnic community framework—those that are formed around traditional forms of identification and solidarity. Clifford (1994:310) distinguishes between a diasporic community and an ethnic neighborhood in the way diasporas have "historical roots and destinies outside the time/space of the host nations." Unlike the discourse of ethnic minorities, the discourse of diaspora emphasizes the desire to return to a homeland as part of an ongoing transnational solidarity or, as the author describes it, "diaspora communities are 'not-here' to stay" (ibid.:311).

The myth of return is arguably the strongest aspect of a diasporic community (Clifford 1994; see also Safran 1991 and Sheffer 1997). The desire to return to a homeland and its durability over time differentiates diasporas from ethnic groups that are part of most modern societies (Clifford 1994; Marienstras 1989; Safran 1991; Van Hear 1998). Not only do members of the diaspora seek to return to the homeland, but so, too, do members of the host societies. Accounting for the "illusion of impermanence," Weiner (1986:47) asserts that,

> despite the intention of governments and the expectations of nationals, a large proportion of foreign workers [an incipient diaspora] remains indefinitely in the host country, living in a state of legal and political ambiguity, economic insecurity and as social outsiders, if not outcasts. The children who have come with them, or have been born within the host country, are in an even more ambiguous position; though more at home in their host country than in the land of their parents, they too are expected to return "home."

Despite the emphasis on return and impermanence, most diasporas persist and their members do not go "home." In some cases there may be no homeland to return to, or a homeland may exist but it may be an unwelcoming place with which members of the diaspora cannot identify politically, ideologically, or socially. In other instances it may be inconvenient and disruptive to leave the diaspora. Moreover, diasporas may construct narratives of a homeland that are far different from the actual people in the homeland, which can lead to tension and disagreement between homeland and diasporic peoples (Winland 1998). Whereas these reasons persist and may lead to a sense of alienation from the homeland similar to that felt toward the host society, the myth of return not only distinguishes diasporic communities but also serves to solidify ethnic consciousness and solidarity.

The way members of a diaspora hold on to the myth of return is fairly complex. The myth of return to the homeland serves to maintain tradition and solidarity, but unlike sojourners "who cling to the culture of [their] own group" (Siu 1952; cf. Yang 2000), members of diasporic communities realize that "they are not and will never be unified in the old sense, because they are irrevocably the product of several interlocking histories and cultures, belong[ing] to one and the same time to several homes" (Hall 1995:629). As a result, the durability of the myth of return, as a defining feature of diasporic life, presupposes the durability of the diaspora itself outside the homeland. In other words, the homeland and the desire to return to it are constructed in such a way that they serve as a basis of communal solidarity that maintains the strength of diasporic life but, at the same time, are never sought in their own right (see Abdelhady 2008).

The myth of return notwithstanding, "diaspora" more accurately refers to the establishment of social, political, economic, and cultural exchanges between and among the spatially separated populations comprising the diaspora (Butler 2001; Lavie and Swedenburg 1996; Van Hear 1998). Thus diaspora precisely represents the multiple loyalties that migrants, exiles, and refugees have to places: their connections to the space they currently occupy, their "host" country; their continuing involvement with the "homeland"; and their involvement with the larger diasporic community.[6] The multiple loyalties of diasporic populations allow them to occupy multiple cultural spaces and become entangled in social, economic, and cultural ties, which encompass both the mother country and the country of settlement (Lavie and Swedenburg 1996). These loyalties and spaces also include other members of the diaspora in different parts of the world. The multiple spaces occupied by the diaspora allow members to enjoy a flourishing communal life and increasing achievements under conditions of exile.[7]

While most theoretical attempts aim to provide a general understanding of diaspora as a concept, Vertovec and Cohen (1999) present a way to operationalize the concept and make it empirically useful for studying immigrant communities. The concept, according to these authors, can be understood as integrating three aspects of immigrant experiences. First, as a social form, or type of community, diaspora illustrates a three-way relationship between the homeland or country of origin, the host society or country of residence, and the larger diaspora community that extends over a number of nation-states. Second, as a form of identification, diaspora embodies a variety of experiences that are grounded within national boundaries but also transcend them. At the root of the process of creating a diaspora identification is fragmentation, homelessness, and displacement. Finally, as a mode of cultural expression, diaspora involves the production of new forms of artistic expression that also transcend local and national geographical locations. Vertovec and Cohen contend that understanding diaspora as a social form, a type of identification, and a mode of cultural expression is central not only for the analysis of the immigrant community itself but for that of the host society as well. More important, they emphasize that diaspora captures the existing global culture and social structures that are deepening and expanding in contemporary life. Utilizing Vertovec and Cohen's definition, I examine the identities, community formations, and cultural expressions of Lebanese immigrants. Working within the framework of diaspora allows me to consider the possibility of individuals or groups experiencing contradictory processes of assimilation as well as ethnic retention in the same context. The framework also highlights, analytically, the ways that immigrants transform the societies they participate in. Finally, diaspora focuses on historical and sociopolitical contexts through the comparative lens of global experiences.[8]

A final word of caution on the term "diaspora" is in order. Scholarly analyses of the term display ambiguities in its use and analytical emphases. In celebrations of transnational practices and global integration, for example, "diaspora" is used to represent the declining relevance of nation-states as an analytical unit of analysis (see, e.g., Tölölyan 1996). At the same time diasporas are also held responsible for engaging in extreme nationalist activities and supporting violent nation-building projects. Diasporic communities, then, are emphatically nationalist and exclusionary. In a nationalist vein, Benedict Anderson (1998) argues that diasporic communities strengthen primordial myths about national unity and homogeneity. He stresses that long-distance nationalism can lead members of the diaspora to support extremist views and violent struggles, as their actions lack political and social accountability. In the face of these contradictory understandings of the concept, a number of scholars construct ideal types in attempts to retain the utility of the concept in explaining important features of transnational practices and global attachments (see, e.g., Cohen 1997). Instead of contrasting diaspora to nation-states as units of analysis, my approach to diasporic communities underscores the relationships between the diaspora and national politics and discourses in which the community is embedded. My analysis also highlights exclusionary nationalist strategies but, unlike Anderson's approach, places these strategies within a context of diverse experiences lived in the diaspora. As a metaphoric designation, I use diaspora to refer to members of an immigrant community who share an awareness of the community's historical existence around the world and refer to their experience as diasporic. As an analytical tool, I use the term "diaspora" to delineate the multilayered forms of belonging and contradictory forms of expression that these immigrants experience.

Globalization processes have become more integral to sociological analyses than any time in the past. Immigration flows, an integral part of globalization, have always been central to sociology as a discipline. Analyses of immigration, however, have focused on frameworks bound by nation-states, namely, assimilation and ethnic pluralism. Studies that highlight the assimilation of immigrant groups to their host societies provide useful analyses of important transformations that immigrant groups undergo over time. Similarly, studies emphasizing ethnic pluralism portray the experiences of many groups to define their ethnic communities and identities within multicultural environments. Recent pluralist analyses have also drawn our attention to transnational spaces that immigrants construct and maintain between their homelands and host societies. Despite the valuable contributions of the different frameworks, the understanding of immigration must take place within a global framework that incorporates countries of origin, host societies, other regions where members of the scattered population may dwell, as well as an unbounded sense of attachment to universal cosmopolitan ideals. The framework of diaspora promises valuable contributions to such analyses, as it signifies multiple loyalties and identities that members of immigrant communities possess. In an increasingly global world, we need to understand the effects of immigration within a global space and orientation (Basch, Glick Shiller, and Szanton Blanc 1994) that moves beyond national boundaries and cultures (Kearney 1995). As distances and borders "hold limited significance in these [contemporary] circumstances: the globe becomes a single 'place' in its own right" (Scholte 1996:431). Thus an understanding of cultures and societies within a global framework has to address issues of identity, solidarity, and culture within a multidimensional, unbounded, and transitory approach. Although I shall not be focusing on diaspora as a critique of the existing theories of immigrant incorporation, I wish to illustrate ways in which diaspora communities undergo various experiences that are not adequately described by the existing frameworks. Inquiring about the ways in which ethnic communities, identities, and cultures are neither disappearing (as assimilation theory would predict) nor remaining what they were in the homeland (as in the ethnic pluralism model), my research explores new approaches to immigration and emphasizes the paradoxical and contradictory aspects of immigrant communities. Using "diaspora" as a framework provides an analysis that escapes the assimilation and ethnic pluralism binary that dominates the immigration literature. Moreover, using diaspora as a framework also allows me to examine the ways in which immigrant communities may be transforming their host societies as they contribute to its culture, social, political, and economic institutions. Furthermore, by emphasizing the global sphere of interaction in which members of diasporas participate, this analysis offers valuable contributions to the study of immigration in general and, in particular, to its sociological component.

The Lebanese Diaspora in Three Cities

My first meeting with Antoine took place at a coffee shop on the Champs Élysées shortly after my arrival in Paris in December 2002. He was exhausted at the end of a long work week at his new job for an international law firm, but I persuaded him to meet with me by choosing a place near his office. He had first e-mailed me in the summer of 2001, responding to a request for research participants of Lebanese origin that I had sent out to a list of Arab-Americans in New York City; Antoine, living in New York at the time, had volunteered. He had just finished his law degree and was actively looking for a job. He believed that he had a good lead for one of the international firms in New York City and was anticipating a job offer. A week before his prospective employer's expected response, the twin towers of the World Trade Center were destroyed in the terrorist attacks that changed his life forever, as well as the lives of many Arabs around the world. The law firm never made Antoine an offer, and he was not called for any interviews during the six months he remained in New York before deciding to leave.

During that period Antoine and the other Lebanese contacts I had in New York advised me to terminate my field research, citing the scrutiny of the Arab community as their reason. As a sociologist I felt that such a socio-historical moment should be documented, but as an Arab I also shared with my informants their sense of anxiety, uncertainty, and lack of safety. I decided to halt my interviews in New York temporarily, and, while observing the community there, I started my data collection in Montreal. During that time Antoine's finances dwindled and his visa was about to expire, so he moved from New York back to Beirut where he had grown up. Shortly after his arrival in Beirut, Antoine realized that he did not want to live in Lebanon. Despite a well-paying job, he explained that, after his six-year absence, he no longer fit in to Lebanese society. The few years he had spent away from his family and friends had made him critical of the social norms and mores to which he thought he was accustomed. Although he strongly wished to return to New York, his experience with racialization and exclusion after 9/11 led him to Paris instead.

Arriving in Paris a second time on a tourist visa, Antoine had a very difficult time for his first four months. Lacking the right to rent an apartment or open a bank account made it harder for him to look for a job. Looking back at those harsh months, Antoine lightheartedly explained that he needed a signed lease to open a bank account, but he also needed a bank account to sign a lease, and that he needed a permanent address to include on his resume but he also needed a job before he could sign a lease for a permanent address. Such bureaucratic irony, he explained, is intended to make it impossible for newcomers to settle in Paris and thus conveyed that he was not welcome in French society. Having lived in three different countries outside Lebanon, Antoine was aware of his lack of belonging to any one society, which was a source of discomfort and ambiguity for him.

> I don't feel comfortable 100 percent. It's kind of an awkward situation. In my experience, I didn't belong to Greece, I didn't belong to the States, so far I don't belong to France, and when I go to Lebanon, I feel that I don't belong to Lebanon.

Yet, such diasporic lack of belonging did not cause Antoine to give in to bureaucratic forms of exclusion. Many immigrants find ways to outwit the bureaucratic system, and so did Antoine. He eventually found a job that matched his credentials. More important, despite his awareness of the various forms of bureaucratic and legal exclusion from both American and

French societies, Antoine stressed that he never felt like an outsider in New York or Paris. Growing up during the Lebanese civil war and thinking about his lack of mobility then, Antoine noted his initial desire to leave: "I was thirsty to get to know other places." He described his initial five years outside Lebanon as a "honeymoon" period when he did not go back to Lebanon even on vacation. Despite the hardships he encountered, he looked favorably at his years in New York and stressed that he still wished to move back if conditions allowed it. Meanwhile, he was surrounded by a large network of French friends and colleagues and a small circle of Lebanese immigrants in Paris. He quickly introduced me to his French and Lebanese friends, helping me with my fieldwork and ability to gain contacts there.

Antoine's experience is similar to many Lebanese immigrants I encountered in the three cities. In fact, all eighty-seven individuals whom I interviewed shared an awareness of bureaucratic exclusion and social difference—or, in diasporic terms, a sense that they were not fully accepted in their host society. As in common understandings of diasporas and transnational practices, Antoine and my other respondents maintained a relationship with their homeland and often entertained the idea of returning there. Antoine is unique, perhaps, as he is one of very few respondents who actually returned to Lebanon when conditions in New York ceased to be favorable. His return, however, caused him to realize that "one can never truly go home." The years he spent in New York changed his perception in such a way that he found himself unable, or unwilling, to fit back in to Lebanese society. Similar to other immigrant experiences, Antoine maintained a constant relationship with Lebanon despite his long absence. His relationship with the homeland, however, was based on the construction of "home" in ways that did not necessarily match social reality. Once faced with a reality that was different from the nostalgic image that he had relied on for years, Antoine decided to leave Lebanon a second time. His eventual departure to Paris, however, does not mark his permanent abandoning of the myth of return. Being in Paris and having a stable job allows Antoine to visit Beirut more often than before. The addition of a baby niece, as he remarked, makes his trips more frequent and enjoyable.

Many respondents remarked that, following 9/11, their sense of feeling different in their host societies was heightened. In fact, in some cases, their identification as Arab was strengthened following the increased racialization they experienced post–9/11. But they also stressed their integration in their host societies and active participation in their city's social, economic, political, and cultural life. Some drew on romanticized notions of the chameleon-like adaptable nature of the Lebanese immigrants whose Phoenician ancestors are known for having excelled in maritime trade and travel. The majority, however, challenged the ambiguous position in which they found themselves and constructed identities that question the simple categories of exclusion/inclusion. Antoine's awareness of his conditional inclusion in American and French societies motivated him to seek forms of inclusion socially, economically, and politically. His diverse social network, lucrative professional position, and activities in a number of social and political groups in Paris point to his desire to participate fully in French society. Antoine's narrative stresses both his membership in the diaspora community at large as well as his global mobility. Two years after our first meeting in Paris, Antoine informed me of his potential move to Shanghai. Like other highly mobile expats, Antoine insisted on keeping his circle of friends close after his move. Although I did not communicate with Antoine regularly after I left Paris and do not consider myself a close friend of his, he still invited me to visit him in Shanghai and reminded me that I have a home there. Like Antoine, other Lebanese immigrants participate in various societies and networks, and construct identities that reflect their transitory status. I discuss these identities, networks, and forms of expression in the next three chapters. The rest of this introduction explains major patterns of Lebanese migration and outlines specific aspects that are unique to each city.

"White, but Not Quite": Lebanese Immigrants in New York

According to the 2000 U.S. Census, New York City is home to the largest population of Arabs, as with the general foreign-born population in the United States.[9] With its long history as an immigrant gateway and continuous inflows of large groups of contemporary immigrants, New York offers immigrant connections to the majority of its residents (Foner 2006). Ethnic relations in New York City may vary from the rest of the United States, but at the same time New York continues to share similar conceptions of race and ethnic relations with the rest of the country as well (see Foner 2005).[10] New York is home to large populations of many first-generation immigrants. The multicultural aspect of the city makes it attractive for many first-generation Lebanese immigrants, and its cosmopolitan nature makes it even more so for the highly educated ones.

Michel did not choose to live in New York City, but he ended up moving there when his brother-in-law who lived in a New York City suburb helped him move from Beirut. Michel grew up in the Christian (specifically

Maronite, or the Eastern Catholic sect) section of Beirut and was only nine years old when the civil war broke out in 1975. As a teenager, he was recruited into one of the pro-Israeli militias shortly after the Israeli invasion in 1982. Michel's father grew fearful for his son's future and decided to send him to the United States, where his older sister lived with her husband. After he finished his high school in the suburbs of New York, Michel moved to Brooklyn to attend a university.

As a college student, Michel came in contact with other Lebanese immigrants of different religious and class backgrounds. These differences were very meaningful to the many Lebanese immigrants who were forced to leave their homeland because of the war, which was escalated by such divisions, and who were forced to live through extreme forms of segregation in Beirut as the city was divided among the different militias and religious sects. Quickly Michel and his acquaintances became aware that, based on selective media representations, mainstream American society was largely unaware of the social and political divisions and saw Lebanon only as a war zone, especially after the bombing of the U.S. Embassy in Beirut in 1983. The general stigmatization of the Lebanese in American society gave Michel and his Lebanese acquaintances a common purpose that united them in countering existing stereotypes and educating the larger society about Lebanese culture and its nonviolent history. Similar to earlier waves of Arab immigrants, Michel gained a stronger sense of his Lebanese identity in the United States.[11] Arguably the civil war brought many Lebanese in New York together despite their different political affiliations, class positions, and residential patterns which they would have upheld in Lebanon because of the sectarian divisions. Instead of defending these divisions, Michel and other Lebanese immigrants who left their homeland as a result of the civil war chose to participate in New York's cultural arenas in order to alter mainstream images of the conflict-ridden country. They also abandoned sectarian divisions and reconstructed images of the homeland that reflected their interest in an illusory cohesion and stability. Michel founded a Lebanese organization that intended to overcome social differences that existed and continue to exist in Lebanon. Michel also hosted a weekly radio show that featured Arabic music. Both activities were intended to represent the homeland and its culture beyond conflict and disintegration, as well as define Michel's own identity as part of the cultural mosaic of New York City. Following 9/11, many of the same individuals chose to participate in public life to amend American society's views of Arabs. Among the various forms of public participation in New

York are the annual Arab-American Comedy Festival and "A Community of Many Worlds" exhibit that took place at the Museum of the City of New York in 2002.

Like other racial and ethnic groups in the United States, placing Arab-Americans within the American ethnic/racial structure has been a source of debate. According to the census classification, individuals of North African and Middle Eastern decent are classified as white/Caucasian, and 80% of Arab Americans identified themselves as such in 2000 (De la Cruz and Brittingham 2003).[12] At the same time the state and media racializes these same individuals as essentially "Other," which leads to a contradictory placement of Arabs in American culture (Naber 2000). At one level the conflation in the media of the categories Arab, Middle Eastern, and Muslim as violent, backward, and irrational contributes to the construction of an inferior Arab/Muslim/Middle Eastern culture and the perception of Arabs as nonwhite others.[13] The view of Arabs as undesirable others was most evident in the 2008 presidential elections campaigns, when Obama was continuously accused of being an Arab and his middle name often used by his opponents to discredit his suitability for the presidency.[14] Arab women, in particular, are either represented as oppressed or totally absent from media portrayals, which extends the stigmatization of Arab communities. Such media representations of popular images that emphasize the exclusion of Arabs from American society take place despite their inclusion among the majority white population. As a group, Arab Americans are left to experience stigmatization, exclusion, and frequent discrimination without the benefits of being recognized as a minority group that brings about legal and political benefits.

The identity of Arab Americans is further complicated when taking religion and national origin, among other things, into account (see, e.g., Haddad 1994).[15] Arab American anthropologist Nadine Naber (2000) observes that, like other racial/ethnic groups in the United States, differences among Arab Americans indicate that they do not fit within the American racial labeling system. For example, some Arab Americans have blonde hair and blue eyes, others have curly hair and dark skin. Despite the original debate within Arab American activist circles on the issue of classification and identity, the events of September 11 marked a new historical juncture and a change in the racial formation of Arabs in the United States (for a report on discrimination against Arab Americans in the aftermath of 9/11, see Ibish 2003).[16] Although still contested, the new racial formation led many to realize that "it is no longer possible to deny that we are people of color" (Naber 2000). The ongoing war on terrorism has increased the racialization of Arabs in the United

States. Yet the census continues to mask their difference by including them in the Caucasian racial category. The elimination of the ancestry question in the 2010 census only concealed their experiences further.

Whether individuals of Lebanese origin identify themselves as Arab is not a straightforward issue, a topic I discuss in the next chapter. The Lebanese constitute more than one-third of the total Arab population in the United States (37% in 2000). Of first-generation Lebanese immigrants, one-third arrived in the United States after 1990, and another third arrived between 1980 and 1990 (Brittingham and de la Cruz 2005). The majority of Lebanese migration has resulted from the civil war—with two-thirds of the first-generation Lebanese in the United States arriving after the war, which started in 1975. Many people left at the beginning of the conflict, and streams of migration followed with each escalation of the fighting. As noted earlier, 80% of Arab Americans identified themselves as racially white in 2000. An even larger majority of Lebanese immigrants is believed to have identified as such. Michel explained his reasoning for such identification when I met with him in the summer of 2000. He emphasized that he is simply nothing else. Referring to his fair skin color, Michel exclaimed: "I choose white because I can't be anything else. I am obviously not black, Hispanic, or Native American." While Michel's initial choice of belonging to the white strata in American society may point to a simplistic understanding of the position Arabs occupy in American culture, it also reveals his awareness of his privileged position, having obtained a graduate degree from an Ivy League university and started his career at a reputable engineering firm.

Historically Arab immigrants have fought to be included in the white racial category in the United States. Soon after the turn of the twentieth century, the Syrian-Lebanese were officially included in the Caucasian racial category and were gradually characterized as belonging to the white subculture within American society (Truzzi 1997:21). Their incorporation within the privileged racial group allowed members of the predominantly Syrian Lebanese community to utilize their "whiteness" and to become more "Americanized" (for accounts of Arab American assimilation, see McCarus 1994; Naff 1985; and Younis 1995). However, the "whiteness" of the Arab/Syrian Lebanese was often contested by members of the community and was rarely accepted by mainstream society.[17] The events of 9/11 brought to the forefront the nonwhite status of Arabs in the United States and, among them, many Lebanese first-generation immigrants. Michel's story illustrates such a transformation. Two years after our first conversation, Michel remarked on his uneasiness with being labeled white. Having once accepted his categorization as white in the U.S. racial structure, following his experience with special registration that was enacted by the U.S. government in September 2002, Michel exclaimed: "For the Lebanese [and other Arabs] national origin is more important than skin color."[18]

The experiences of Michel and many Arab immigrants in New York City with special registration brought about a sense of stigmatization and exclusion. However, their participation in the city's public life became more active and salient. Instead of capitulating to exclusion, many Arab Americans actively distanced themselves from terrorists, and many organizations issued official statements condemning terrorist acts. One such attempt was portrayed in the candlelight vigil held in the heart of Arab New York on Atlantic Avenue. Others focused their efforts on educating the public about Arab cultural diversity. For example, following reports of police racial profiling of Arabs post–9/11, organizations such as the Arab American Association of New York and the American MidEast Leadership Network stepped in to provide cultural sensitivity training programs to officers of the New York Police Department (Millard 2008). Many other groups organized voter registration, know-your-rights forums, and other activities aimed at political integration. Research on the 9/11 backlash (e.g., Bakalian and Bozorgmehr 2009) has revealed that the mobilization of the targeted populations was one of unexpected consequences. Unlike historical precedents (e.g., Japanese internment during World War II), Middle Eastern and Muslim leaders across the country rallied their constituents to integrate into the civic and political institutions at the local and national levels. Almost immediately they stood firm, claiming their rightful place in American society, and protested the backlash by the government initiatives as well as the hate crimes and bias incidents. In fact, increased racial profiling and stigmatization of Arabs in the United States post–9/11, while remaining comparatively low, motivated many Arab Americans to reinterpret the multicultural structure of American society through participating in public life to shape the ways they wish to be portrayed by others.

An Ambiguous Visible Minority: Lebanese Immigrants in Montreal

Arab migrations to the United States and Canada are extremely intertwined and ought to be viewed historically as two streams of a trans-Atlantic flow to the Americas (Aboud 2000). In many accounts of early migratory streams during the late nineteenth century, migrants from Ottoman Syria have set out to an imaginary place called "Amereeka" but ended up in Canada, South America, Australia, West Africa, Europe, or New Zealand when they were denied entry to the United States or owing to manipulation by migration and shipping agents (see Issawi 1992 and Khalaf 1987). Similar to the United States, the Lebanese are the largest group of Arab immigrants in Canada (almost a quarter of the Arab origin population). The context Canada provides, however, is considerably different from that provided by the United States. Canada's immigration policies are largely informed by the demands for economic development,[19] but the presence of explicit policies of symbolic recognition and multiculturalism is a major departure from the laissez-faire approach to immigrant incorporation in the United States.[20] Multiculturalism in Canada typically implies that immigrants have a right to express their ethnic identity without fear of prejudice or discrimination, especially given state sponsorship of ethnic presses, associations, educational programs and cultural, activities (Kymlicka 1995). Thus, for visible minorities (Canada's nonwhite groups), multiculturalism translates into demands for the recognition of their cultural differences. It also represents a desire to integrate into Canadian society and to be accepted as full members.[21]

Historically Arabs in Canada have not been able to contest their exclusion from the majority group the same way that Arabs in the United States fought for their inclusion in the Caucasian racial category. Although initially subject to the same restrictions on immigration as other members of the "Asiatic race," in 1949, following persistent pressures, Syrian Lebanese immigrants in Canada managed to widen the range of admissible dependents from among the Lebanese, Syrians, and Armenians. Members of these three groups were allowed to bring in fiancés/fiancées, spouses, children, siblings and their dependents, parents, and orphan nephews and nieces under the age of twenty-one of Canadian residents. Other "Asiatic" citizens were only allowed to bring in wives and minor children. These changes in the entry eligibility of Syrians, Lebanese, and Armenians were merely administrative, as they took the form of discretionary measures given to immigration officials but led to an increase in the population of Arab immigrants. The more significant impact of these discretionary measures, however, is that they maintained the ambiguous and ill-defined status of Arabs in Canada as belonging and at the same time not belonging to a minority position (Aboud 2000), marking their position as "in-between" as in the United States. The narratives provided by my respondents in Montreal highlight their awareness of their "visible minority" status as they stressed that they are not European and do not look like Europeans. At the same time their ambiguous status was sometimes expressed when they aligned themselves with rightist politics and conveyed their interest in limiting state provisions to new groups of immigrants.

Arab Canadians mostly live in either Ontario or Québéc, and more than half of all Arab Canadians live in either Toronto or Montreal (Lindsay 2007). Montreal provides an important context for investigating Arab Canadian immigration. According to the 2006 census, Montreal was home to the largest Arab minority in Canada and to the second largest group of recent immigrants following Toronto (Statistics Canada 2008). Many Lebanese immigrants consider Canada to be the ultimate land of settlement, a place "where children can have a decent future" (Kemp 1992:685). With its emphasis on multiculturalism and ethnic pluralism, Canada is seen as providing Lebanese immigrants with the opportunity to form communities that reinforce social attachments and political commitments to the homeland and maintain their ethnic cultural identity (Abu Laban 1992). Identified as the second largest "visible minority" group in Montreal in 2006 (Statistics Canada 2009), Lebanese Canadians make use of Canada's multicultural policies to strengthen their ethnic identity as well as public participation in Canadian public life.[22]

A survey conducted by the Canadian Arab Federation (CAF) in November 2001–February 2002 offers a broad portrayal of the Arab Canadian community and identity. The majority of survey respondents (62.6%) claimed a dual identity and rejected the idea that they were leading two contradictory lives, one Canadian and one Arab (64%).[23] A large majority of the respondents were fluent in both English and French (inside and outside Québéc). These Arab immigrants who took part in the survey chose Canada because of its human rights, its multiculturalism, and the presence of family members. In terms of community life, the majority of respondents reported involvement in mainstream (as opposed to Arab) cultural events and high levels of voting in recent elections. Although one-third of the respondents reported feelings of alienation (politically and culturally), the majority was satisfied living in Canada and with the Canadian government polities (except for the government's handling of the widening gap between the rich and poor). Although 80% of Arab Americans identify themselves as white, only 35.3% of those surveyed by CAF chose white as a racial category. The relatively large percentage still indicates the ambiguous understanding of their position as "visible minority" that Arabs in Canada possess. The group of respondents choosing the white racial category was the largest, followed by 26.1% choosing "olive," 25.7% choosing brown, and 0.4% choosing black. The Canadian census, however, unlike the U.S. census, does not categorize the population in racial terms, but individuals can be identified as members of visible minorities.[24]

Policy debates surrounding Canadian multiculturalism have been a topic of political debates in recent decades. Many argue that multiculturalism is causing a fragmentation of Canadian identity and national cohesiveness.[25] Lara, however, is a Lebanese immigrant in Montreal whose narrative illustrates the cohesiveness of Canada's multicultural society. Lara, twenty-eight years old when I met her in the summer of 2003, is a chemist who moved to Montreal at the age of seventeen. She moved in 1992 at the end of the war, as did many other respondents who grew more pessimistic when the massive killings escalated at the end of the conflict. She had a sister in Montreal, which made her choice of destination and decision to leave easier. She initially lived with her sister, but she married three years later and moved closer to the university with her husband, as both were pursuing graduate training there. Then, in 2000, she divorced and went back to Lebanon but returned to Montreal a year later. Upon her return to Canada, Lara became more accepting of her identification with Canadian society alongside her Lebanese identity. She has a four-year-old daughter who was born in Montreal, which was Lara's main reason for leaving Lebanon a second time. Lara recognizes that the opportunities for her child in Canada are broader than her prospects in Lebanon. Another primary reason for her return to Montreal was her desire to be independent, financially and socially. In addition to these strategic interests, she emphasized that the years she spent in Canada, and that she is bringing up her daughter in Canada, have made her Canadian: "I am Canadian in my lifestyle, in how I know my way within the state system, which I like . . . I am proud to be Canadian." In some ways Lara reached this understanding when she moved back briefly to Lebanon. A failed state and lack of institutional rights made her realize what she would lack by living in Lebanon. Knowing about the social welfare and civic rights that she has in Canada as a member of a visible minority, and knowing how to be granted these rights "within the state system," is how Lara defines her identification with Canadian society. At the same time that Lara identified herself as a member of a visible minority, she also saw herself as racially white. This choice of identities reflects Lara's familiarity with Canadian ethnic hierarchies and her integration within Canadian society.

Lara also stressed her "lifestyle," which for her means social and financial independence, as her way of being Canadian. Her independence, especially from family members (e.g., for child care or financial resources) is central in understanding her way of negotiating her Lebanese identity alongside a Canadian one. She emphasized that in terms of family values she is still "very Lebanese," in the sense that she gives priority to family over other aspects of her life, that she respects her elders, especially her parents, and seeks their approval and satisfaction, and that she values strong relations with her siblings and extended family members (in Montreal and Beirut). Independence, for Lara, does not contradict these values, as she is the one choosing which aspects of her identity are more valuable than others. Lara also points out that her "social principles" are Lebanese. Valuing honesty, caring for others, and being close to friends and neighbors are things she learned during her childhood in Lebanon, and thus by adhering to these values, she is also remaining loyal to her Lebanese identity. Since she spent her childhood (and most of her teenage years) in Lebanon, she affirms that, despite her Canadian identity, "Lebanese is what I will always be."

Combining Lebanese and Canadian identities was an easy process for Lara. In her view, being Canadian meant being able to be many things, not only in the multicultural sense of having different groups existing next to and more or less accepting of one another but in the sense of learning about other cultures and possibly adopting their ways and practices. In Lara's words: "Here, there are many nationalities [cultures] with which I interact, and they make me a different person every day." In this regard, she contrasted herself to other Lebanese who never left Lebanon, saying that they are "just Lebanese and do not know about anything else. Despite their [religious/ethnic] differences, they are all the same and will always be the same." Lara, on the other hand, by living in Canada, has been offered a new environment and a new identification, as well as being influenced by, and identifying with, the various cultures that Canada embodies. Thus, according to Lara, she became an "Arab" in Canada, when she made friends with people from other Arab countries and was exposed to their cultures. But she also identified with Armenians, Greeks, and Russians through the various experiences that she shared with people from these countries. In other words, Lara understands that her social experiences, as influenced by the people from other countries, makes for a *unique* individual, one who lives in Canada, possesses Lebanese origins, and enjoys cosmopolitan cultural experiences.

Lara valued her unique social position and wanted the same for her daughter. For example, living in Montreal, Lara's daughter was learning French in kindergarten, and at home Lara was teaching her Arabic. Because Montreal was a bilingual city, Lara knew that her daughter would eventually learn English as well. Lara recognized that her daughter's ability to converse in these three languages would enable her to communicate with relatives in Lebanon, participate in Canada's multicultural society, and have more options in life overall. She was aware that in the multicultural environment of Montreal, difference was always emphasized as it brought about material gains and social and political recognition. Multiculturalism also enriches social life in Montreal. Having more options in life, for Lara, not only implied having marketable skills and being able to find a good job. More important, Lara referred to having options in terms of the cultural repertoires that her daughter could draw upon and the societies to which she could belong. Since she constructed her own identities through her ability to mix and accommodate different aspects of several cultures, Lara's desire to foster her daughter's ability to communicate cross-culturally indicates the value of a cosmopolitan identification as an important part of her experience.

The Canadian multicultural system is sometimes understood as encouraging the separation of ethnic groups to minimize assimilation and instead promote the value of retaining one's distinctive cultural habits and traditions (see, e.g., Thomas 1990). Lara's narrative illustrates that state-sponsored multiculturalism in Canada provides a conceptual and cultural framework for the integration of immigrants. As Lara indicated, the ability to retain one's ethnic identity in Canadian society allows immigrants to preserve aspects of their ethnic identity which they might disavow in other contexts such as New York before and after September 11. While multicultural policies may create an environment where immigrants can more freely construct an ethnic identity that does not contradict their membership in Canadian society, the same policies paradoxically produce an environment that is less accepting of immigrants and their activities. Addressing multiculturalism, Myron Weiner (1986) notes that it has produced more political controversy than any other issue that deals with migration, as it stirs the passions of both its supporters and opponents. After more than thirty years of official multicultural policies and programs in Canada, the idea of multiculturalism appears to be less accepted among Canadians than among Americans (Heisler 1992). For instance, in the late 1980s, a smaller proportion of Canadians than Americans thought that it would be preferable for new immigrants to maintain their culture than to assimilate: three-fifths of Canadians and half the Americans questioned in a cross-border survey thought that newcomers should change their culture "to blend with the larger society" (Lipset 1990). More recently, and following the events of 9/11, Canadian institutions emerged as less supportive of immigrant cultural expressions than American ones. In the United States, as one example among many, an Arab American exhibition at a New York City museum was organized to portray "A Community of Many Worlds," educating New Yorkers about the cultural and social contributions of Arabs to city life. In Canada, an exhibition titled "The Lands within Me: Expressions of Canadian Artists of Arab Origin," which had been organized before the terrorist attacks, was postponed indefinitely post-9/11 and stirred controversy over Canadian multiculturalism till it finally opened at a later date.

Bon chic bon genre: Lebanese Immigrants in France

Paris offers a departure from the North American contexts described so far. France is a nation that sees itself in universalistic and egalitarian terms (Kastoryano 2002), and consequently French nationalism rejects multiculturalism as particularistic and antithetical to being a French citizen (De Groat 2001). Moreover, Arab migration to France stems primarily from North Africa (mostly from Algeria and Morocco and to a lesser extent Tunisia). In fact, Maghrébins (those from former French North Africa) are the largest single immigrant group in France (Hargreaves 1995).[26] Unlike the United States and Canada, more than half of France's immigrants come from Muslim countries, mostly the former colonies of West and North Africa, and thus they are visually recognizable as foreigners because of their skin colors, hair textures, and accented French (Hargreaves 1995). Despite the diverse origins of immigrants in France, a process of racialization constructs immigration as a North African problem, particularly relating to Algerians and Muslims, and their children, who are homogenized into one group: "*les Arabes*" or Franco-Maghrébins (Miles and Singer-Kérel 1991; Wihtol de Wenden 1991). Such homogenization in the French context creates a binary between an ostensibly monolithic French culture versus a uniform Arab one, and also positions Islam as the representative culprit of the Arab problem to the French nation.

Nadia, a Lebanese Sunni Muslim who lives in Paris, does not protest French society's conflation of Arabs and Muslims. A perplexing aspect of French Lebanese immigrants is their heavy investment in distancing themselves from *other* immigrants, especially North Africans, who are perceived as the "problem." At thirty, Nadia was already an established middle-class professional working as a financial controller and living in an apartment in a wealthy Parisian quarter when I interviewed her in the winter of 2003. During our interview Nadia stressed her difference from other Arabs in Paris, which was unusual at least for an outsider to French immigrant politics, highlighting that Lebanese, in France, are often not considered to be Arabs, or at least not those who are seen as the problem.

Lebanon's relatively respected status in French culture, as Nadia indicated, was reflected in the popularity of Lebanese cuisine and packaged tours to

Lebanon consumed by many non-Arab French individuals as part of their vacations and luxury travel. Lebanon is marked as a center of secularism and modernism in the Muslim Middle East region in the mind of the French citizen, which partly explains why they vacation there as well. These perceptions are based on the assumption that most Lebanese are Christian (mostly Catholics) and therefore unlike the Muslim Arabs of North Africa.[27] Not surprisingly, Lebanese Muslims like Nadia often do not correct these perceptions in order to reap the benefits of French society's view of the "good" Christian Lebanese immigrant.

In 1989, at the age of sixteen, Nadia had left Beirut with her mother and brother. Because Nadia's father remained in Lebanon, the family never thought of their initial move to Paris as permanent. Even today she maintains a transnational link to Beirut. In "The Lebanese Migrant in France: *Muhâjir* or *Muhajjar?*" Middle East expert Perg Kemp (1992) explains the ambiguous position France occupies in the worldview of the Lebanese migrants. France is positioned (geographically and mentally) between traditional lands of migration, such as Canada or West Africa, and temporary destinations, such as Cyprus or Jordan. The transitory position that France occupies in the psyche of Lebanese immigrants is illustrated in Nadia's narrative of transitory migration that split her family for almost fifteen years. Despite the lack of accurate patterns and figures on Lebanese immigration in France, Kemp offers a notable distinction on the Lebanese presence in French society. He argues that the Lebanese migrant in France is not a *muhâjir*, an immigrant seeking to settle permanently in France, but a *muhajjar*, a migrant who has been forced to leave the homeland without the decision to settle anywhere permanently.

According to the 1999 French census, 28,160 individuals in France were born in Lebanon, 79% of whom claim French nationality. The census does not provide data on third and later generations, and thus it is difficult to assess the magnitude of individuals of Lebanese origin (Simon 2003). Despite their small number and transitory presence, the Lebanese in France tend to have a strong economic presence. According to Hattab (1985), 81% of the working Lebanese in Paris are in three professional categories: industrial and commercial, liberal professional (e.g., doctors, engineers, teachers, and artists), and senior and intermediate executives. This percentage is significantly larger than the percentage for immigrants altogether (18%). The percentage of Lebanese immigrants engaged in manual labor (4%) also contrasts sharply with that of the general immigrant population (58%). Although these figures are from the mid-1980s, a time that marks the shift in the nature of the Lebanese community in France, they still explain the perception of the Lebanese community in France as an elite social group.

The social and cultural composition of the Lebanese community in France has undergone major changes during the last two decades that contradict the pattern of immigration in North America. Initially Lebanese migrants to France were mostly educated, fluent in French, and wealthy. They tended to reside in France temporarily to pursue higher education or spend vacations in their second homes in the Côte d'Azur (Kemp 1992). About half the Lebanese in France live in Paris (Abdul-Karim 1992), and reside in the *quartiers chics* (mostly in the west and southwest areas of the city) and the students stay in the *quartier Latin*. In general, the early immigrants relied on money generated in Lebanon to sustain their stay in France. Starting in the mid-1980s, the economic crisis in Lebanon reversed many of these trends. Money generated in France by the Lebanese was used to sustain their families back home, making their stay in France less transient. The pattern of migration to France also became "more democratic," as those who were less wealthy and not proficient in French were also leaving Lebanon for France. In terms of residential patterns, more and more Lebanese immigrants and businesses were starting up in the less wealthy areas and in working-class suburbs (Kemp 1992). Despite these "democratic" tendencies, the majority of the Lebanese in Paris still reside in the wealthiest areas, precisely the opposite residential patterns of North Africans in Paris (Simon 2003).

Nadia's class background is central to her understanding of her position as in-between French and Lebanese cultures but also not restricted to the two. Her French-orientated education and family vacations that she spent in the south of France (both before and after she left Lebanon) made her associate with French culture at a young age. Although it took Nadia a few years to adapt to living in Paris, she maintains that she "took the good from the bad." Initially she had difficulty socializing with other teenagers at school who commented negatively on her accent and cultural background and sometimes called her *Arabe*. These difficulties socializing continued through college, as she describes here:

> Once I borrowed a few francs from a friend of mine, and I thought, instead of paying her back I can treat her to dinner. I knew that the dinner would cost more than the money I borrowed, but in Lebanon you're not supposed to return favors in money. So after I took her out and we had a nice evening together, she reminded me that I still owed her the money. I was a little shocked, but then decided to accept it as a cultural difference.

Though initially she relied on such assertions of cultural difference, Nadia's long stay in France led her to see herself as both French and Lebanese. In her words: "I am trying to take the best from Lebanese and the best from French, and make a mixture." Nadia's emphasis on appropriating what she regards as the best elements of both cultures into her own identity is based on her sense of belonging and not belonging. This in-between status gives rise to a critical point of view that transcends the insider/outsider binary of a singular cultural framework. Taking issue with French aloofness and impersonal interactions with neighbors and friends, as well as Lebanese reliance on an inefficient government system and disregard for planning for the future, Nadia only adopts what she finds to be positive aspects of the two cultures. She told me, for example, that her joie de vivre comes from her Lebanese side and that her savings account comes from her French side. But even this example illustrates more of a mixture than Nadia herself realizes, as joie de vivre describes a French cultural attitude, even if the Lebanese have given it an added glow. The mixture of terms in Nadia's account may indicate an assumption that the two cultures are contradictory, but she stresses the similarity of both cultures in that they are both multicultural and liberal (in terms of social rights and norms). Specifically, she says,

I think we have so many things, Lebanese and French, in common, well, they stayed for twenty years in Lebanon but their cultural influence lasted longer, so I do not always find the two countries to be that much apart. It is just that everywhere you go you'll find some things you like and other things that you won't like. It takes time, but in the end it becomes very straightforward. Once you know yourself more, you realize that you can accept certain values and challenge others.

Nadia went on to explain that despite the war that was going on in Lebanon at the time, she grew up in a multicultural society where she had friends from various religious and national origins. The multicultural influence on her life carried into her experiences in Paris where many of her friends are first- or second-generation immigrants from various parts of the world. Her frequent travels, as a tourist or to visit childhood friends who are dispersed in Europe and North America, also provide her with enriching global experiences. All together, she sees her life as a product of many societies, and though she acknowledges that she may not fit in totally in any particular culture, she still values the worldly experiences her diasporic identity encompasses.

Competence in the French milieu allows Lebanese immigrants to participate comfortably in French society and occupy a favorable position in French culture, unlike the experience of North African immigrants in France. In contrast to the North Africans, Lebanese immigrants, with the exclusion of students, are politically to the right and at times support the far-rightist National Front Party (Kemp 1992). The political and social conservatism of the Lebanese (especially regarding immigration issues) places them in a more favorable position within French society, especially compared to working-class Algerian migrants. Reviewing a poll conducted in 1989, Kemp contends that,

> behind the reality of the Lebanese war there is in the French mind the idea of a Lebanese who is schematically urbane, French-speaking, a French first-name carrier, non-sectarian (albeit identified as a Christian), and striving to live decently and normally while surrounded by hostile and cynical forces. (ibid:691)

The picture in the French mind of Lebanese individuals escaping genocide and foreign intervention assisted in constructing the image of Lebanese as victims.[28] Moreover, Lebanese individualism strengthened the affection the French have for the Lebanese, especially when contrasted with other immigrant groups. As they are mostly professional and secular, and live in the wealthy quarters, they are not considered a threat to the French national identity. Although some Lebanese immigrants have taken on Arab issues as part of their public participation in French society, they do so in a manner that is largely accepted by French society. Looking at Lebanese political activism during the civil war, Kemp explains how their activities do not challenge their integration into French society:

> Even when tension in Lebanon is at its highest, protests by the Lebanese community in France remains quite civilized, and demonstrations by Lebanese nationals have a certain BCBG (*bon chic bon genre*) touch and never constitute a threat to public order. When they shout slogans, Lebanese demonstrators do so in good French, their banderoles are written in Latin script and show no spelling mistakes, and they are accompanied by this or that French politician who acts as their advocate and interpreter before French public opinion. (ibid.:693)

Although Kemp does not compare Lebanese-led demonstrations to those organized by North Africans, his assertion that the demonstrations are "civilized," "chic," and conducted in "good French" point to how Lebanese immigrants in France view themselves vis-à-vis North African (or other) immigrants.

Under the French assimilationist immigration model, membership in the national community involves voluntary commitment to the Republic and its values. Religious, ethnic, linguistic, regional, subcultural, and other ascriptive identities have been accepted as temporary features but relegated to the private realm (Castles and Miller 1993). The division between public and private is specific to France, and group identity is meant to be a private matter.[29] Minorities are not recognized in the public sphere or in legal texts, and official surveys cannot include questions about religion or ethnicity, as is permissible in the United States. Retaining ethnic identity in private and asserting Frenchness in public is the main tension in French public policies toward immigration and minority rights.[30] Many Lebanese immigrants understand the public/private dichotomy in French society and manage to navigate its dictates successfully. In Nadia's case, she asserts that her approach to dating and family matters continues to be Lebanese despite her long residence in France. While understanding that her approach may be considered conservative among contemporary French youth and may therefore limit her options in finding a partner, Nadia defends her personal values, asserting that "I can never live with someone without being married to him, I just don't know how to do that." Her traditional views toward private matters coexist with her public integration in French society, as evidenced by her professional career, her middle-class neighborhood, and her diverse group of both immigrant and native French friends.

Description of the Book

That I, as an Egyptian living and working in the United States, studied Arab immigrants may seem like a cliché. As a student of international migration, I had learned about the assimilation of groups of immigrants to American society through various mechanisms (such as economic mobility, political participation, intermarriage, language acquisition, and residential integration). I also learned about ethnic pluralism and multiculturalism, and the ways that immigrants retain (or more likely gain) an ethnic identity upon settling in a new country. However, after my first few years of living in the United States, I realized that neither approach described my own experience or those of other immigrants around me.

Nor did the literature on Arab immigrants in the United States seem to describe my experience. Much of that literature discusses many of the difficulties that the initial waves of immigrants faced in terms of not knowing the language or the customs of the new world, until they achieved high levels of success and integration into the middle class (see, e.g., McCarus 1994; Naff 1992; Suleiman 1999; and Younis 1995). Analyses of post–World War II streams of Arab immigrants, however, emphasize their high levels of education and social status that motivated them to participate in American society as Arab Americans who had a strong interest in maintaining ethnic attachments to their homeland as well as their ethnic community (see Haddad 1994; Sandoval and Jendrysik 1993; and Marshal and Read 2003). The events of 9/11 renewed the interest in Arab immigrant communities. However, the emphasis continues to be on ethnic dynamics that shape immigrant integration and are shaped by experiences with discrimination (see, e.g., Bakalian and Bozorgmehr 2009; Cainkar 2009; and Jamal and Naber 2008). Regardless of the framework used in the analysis, none of these studies provides a comparative approach to understanding the immigrant experience in order to identify context-specific dynamics.

Neither approach to immigrant integration seemed sufficient to explain contemporary experiences like mine, where global processes of extensive travel, communication, consumerism, and international politics produce intertwined subjectivities and social positions. Although globalization is not new, of course, the intensity of global processes shapes our lives, especially those of immigrants, in increasingly significant ways. In contrast to the sociology literature that emphasizes processes of assimilation, ethnic pluralism, and transnational communities, postcolonial analyses argue that dynamics of migration are best understood through notions of hybridity and diaspora. Postcolonial theories stress that, historically, global processes of immigration, trade relations, colonial expansion, political alliances, wars, and invasions have contributed to the fusion of heterogeneous elements of different cultures resulting in hybrid cultures and identities (Kraidy 1999). Regarding the effects of migration, postcolonial scholars reject the duality of either assimilation or ethnic pluralism, arguing instead that some identities emerge that neither assimilate to the new society nor remain unchanged by it (Hall 1992). These identities and the communities they bring about draw on various cultural traditions while simultaneously generating new cultural mixes and forms (Bhabha 1994; Hall 1992; Nederveen Pieterse 1994). The understanding that all national cultures are hybrids leads postcolonial scholars to frame a picture of the world as increasingly interconnected and interrelated, leading them to problematize the nation-state as the overarching framework for understanding immigrant communities. More important, postcolonial analyses emphasize the multiple options for individual identification, attachment, and forms of association.

The analysis provided in this book underscores the importance of the specific cultural and historical settings that give meaning to particular identity formations and community building. Understanding identity as situational, multivalent, and interlocking, as the following chapters show, is better illustrated by the concept and theory of diaspora. My analysis illustrates that immigrants negotiate their identities and communities beyond the duality of assimilation and ethnic retention. Instead, immigrant identities and communities are referential, contradictory, and ambivalent. The framework of diaspora allows us to integrate the multiple forms of collective lives in which immigrants participate. Ranging from national (homeland and host society) and transnational to diasporic and global, diasporic conceptions of identity and community allow immigrants cosmopolitan identification and force a rethinking of immigration as a three-way process involving the homeland, the host society, and worldwide immigrant communities. The narratives offered in this book, including those of Antoine, Michel, Lara, and Nadia, all move beyond ethnic and transnational understandings of experiences and identities. Instead, their diasporic narratives emphasize simultaneous inclusion and exclusion, finding a home within increased mobility, and establishing stability and coherence within transitory experiences. These diasporic narratives are shaped by specific national contexts of what is taking place in Lebanon and the three host societies, the Lebanese diasporic community at large, and multiple global dramas that shape subjectivities and understandings of social positions.

Although I do not focus on diaspora as a critique of theories of immigrant incorporation, I nonetheless demonstrate that diasporic immigrant communities undergo global experiences that are not adequately described by the dualistic transnational model or by the uniformist incorporation models of ethnic pluralism and assimilation. Rather, I argue that ethnic communities, identities, and cultures are neither disappearing (as assimilation theory would predict) nor remaining what they were in the homeland (as in the ethnic pluralism model), and explore new approaches to immigration that emphasize the paradoxical and contradictory global aspects of immigrant communities.

Hargreaves (1995) notes that one of the assumptions that the frameworks of immigrant incorporation share is that immigration is coterminous with the boundaries of the nation-state. Speaking of the experience of immigrants in the European Union, Hargreaves calls for an analysis of immigrant experiences that approaches incorporation beyond nation-states and within a regional framework. My analysis extends Hargreaves's request as it takes into account a global context in which immigrant identities, communities, and cultural expressions are articulated. As the transformations experienced in the three contexts indicate, new waves of immigration are challenging assumptions of national identity and old models of incorporation. Moreover, the experiences of Lebanese immigrants in the three different national contexts examined here allow us to understand how Arab immigrants are dealing with a post–9/11 anti-immigration climate in nationally specific yet global ways. Having sketched the situation of the Lebanese immigrant communities in the three contexts, the next three chapters use the in-depth interviews to explicate and explore the rich narratives of my Lebanese immigrant subjects' identities, communal lives, and cultural forms of expression.

In order to understand the multifaceted dynamics of diaspora existence, I used multiple research methods for data collection. Given the exploratory nature of the research questions, and in the interest of producing detailed narratives of migratory experiences, I relied on qualitative methods for data gathering. The primary form of data collection was semi-structured, in-depth interviews that allowed me to gather personal narratives from members of the Lebanese diaspora. Through in-depth interviews with eighty-seven first-generation Lebanese immigrants that were collected over a six-year period, from 2001 to 2007, I was able delve into the diasporic aspects of the Lebanese communities. The interviews helped me to specify the formative events in the immigrants' experiences and examine issues of identity and consciousness based on firsthand experiences. In addition to questions of identity and consciousness, the interviews also addressed issues related to social networks and cultural life.[31] Snowball sampling was used to reach the desired number of respondents. Relying on a variegated group of informants (such as academics, young professionals, religious figures, small-business owners, shopkeepers, and students) created diversity among the members of the sample. I also posted announcements soliciting participants in a number of organizations that cater to Arab immigrants and electronic list-serves of Arab immigrant communities. Purposeful sampling was sometimes utilized to guarantee the representation of the religious/ethnic diversity of Lebanese society and the immigrant community. The interviews were conducted in English, French, or Arabic, and sometimes a mix of all three languages, based on the respondents' choice.[32] I also kept a field diary to record my observations following each interview and social interaction. These notes were useful in reconstructing the narratives during data analysis.

In addition to interviewing, I relied on field observation in order to come to a more comprehensive understanding of life in the diaspora. At the beginning of data collection in each city, I participated in community events (political, religious, or social) as a way to find respondents and also observe general forms of interactions. Once I established contacts, my informants also invited me to attend organized social events through their churches, organizations, or friends. I was also sometimes invited to "hang out" in a city where I did not live permanently, which enabled me to observe informal interaction. Social gatherings, religious celebrations, political demonstrations, organizational meetings, and cultural performances are among the types of events that I attended. I was fortunate to meet respondents who supported my research and invited me to these events. More important, I believe that I was welcomed in the immigrant communities in New York and Montreal because of our shared native language (Arabic) and umbrella identity (Arab origin). In Paris, my status as a graduate student living in the United States seemed to have facilitated my entry to the field more than did my Arab origins. In general, utilizing field observation allowed me to develop a better understanding of the personal narratives, as well as form insights into the processes of community building. These observations also allowed me to account for the interaction between the diaspora communities and host societies in terms of engagement, exclusion, or exchange of ideas and strategies.[33]

Chapter 2 focuses on the narratives of immigrant identity I obtained from the respondents. These narratives varied by country of immigration, but the majority of respondents narrated their identities in diasporic ways. The chapter explores the importance of diasporic identity for understanding current immigration patterns and rethinking current models of incorporation. Emphasizing the ambivalence that Lebanese immigrants share toward their understanding of their ethnic identities, the chapter illustrates the ways that they negotiate the meanings of being Lebanese in different settings and define context-specific ethnicities. Members of the Lebanese diaspora experience simultaneous association with, and dissociation from, their homeland and host societies. Ethnicity, in the form of transnational sentiments and practices, is only a minor part of the narratives. Indeed, the majority of the narratives express diasporic identification that ponders issues of belonging and difference in two or more societies, multiple identities, fragmentation, and global positions. In addition to diasporic identities, Lebanese immigrants identify themselves as cosmopolitan citizens who feel that their experiences are integral to the creation of world communities of which they are a part.

Chapter 3 addresses community networks and attachments, specifically diasporic ones, and illustrate how they shape and reshape their homeland, host societies, and the larger diaspora through links and connections in a global world. Transnationalism highlights immigrants' involvement in both the homeland and host societies. Lebanese immigrants, however, share an awareness of and connections with other Lebanese immigrants around the world that differentiate a diaspora from a transnational community. Furthermore, their desire to effect social change in their different societies in turn leads them to group around issues and shared dispositions instead of traditional ethnic communities. In line with the narratives of diasporic identities and cosmopolitan conceptions of citizenship, respondents in my study demonstrate global forms of belonging that consequently understand their immigrant communities in non-territorial terms.

In chapter 4 I chart the ways in which diasporic identities and communal attachments are expressed by the artists among my respondents and focus on their cultural expressions as a diasporic practice and form of engagement. Just as Lebanese immigrants navigate between the homeland, the host society and the larger diaspora, so, too, do the artists among them express sentiments of nostalgia and displacement but also global feelings of belonging and cosmopolitanism. Lebanese diasporic artists express their belonging to a global community and cosmopolitan duty through their art work which emphasizes global social change, justice, and ways of thinking. My focus on artists illustrates direct engagement with the diasporic existence, as the artists emphasize expressions of memory and displacement, and directly engage in a dialogue with immigration policies in their host societies. These artists represent actual attempts to deal with the civil war as an important factor shaping the Lebanese diaspora in the contemporary world. At the same time their interest in social change encompasses their homeland, their host society, and the world at large.

The final chapter concludes by reflecting on the importance of multiple attachments and identifications as well as examining the meaning of cosmopolitanism in our contemporary global world. The chapter stresses the utility of diaspora as a framework for understanding immigration processes that is applicable to diverse populations and adaptable to different national contexts of reception. By exploring the everyday narratives of immigrants' diasporic lives and expressions, I contribute to the analytical discussions that constitute our knowledge of the patterns and dynamics of contemporary immigration in a globalized world. Contemporary immigration flows are creating common patterns of integration as more nations are receiving large numbers of "new immigrants." These common patterns are important for understanding the dynamics of a global society. More important, this book argues that members of the Lebanese diaspora understand their experiences in global, cosmopolitan terms, which calls for extending the definition of diaspora to include forms of global subjectivity. Using a comparative method that draws on Lebanese immigrant experiences in Montreal, New York, and Paris, I argue that the concept of diaspora is key to understanding processes of immigration and incorporation in the contemporary world. Given the multiple identities and forms of collective life exhibited and the global outlook that is shared by members of the Lebanese diaspora in three national contexts, this analysis argues, based on its empirical and comparative methodology, for the need to move beyond assimilation and ethnic pluralism as modes of understanding contemporary immigration.

Narratives of Identification

Between Ethnicity and Cosmopolitanism

Neither a state nor a fact
nor a moral nor a condition
to be an immigrant
is to be history
and You know something about that.

—Fares 1982

When I first started collecting research data for this book in the summer of 2001, I was invited by a Lebanese American acquaintance to a *hafle,* or ethnic party, at a Maronite church in one of New York's suburbs. I saw this as a good opportunity to observe the community that I had set out to study and possibly to recruit respondents who would agree to be interviewed. As an Egyptian, I had assumed that I would be easily welcomed into the Lebanese community in New York since I share a language and culture with its members. I also considered myself to be familiar with Lebanese history and society since I lived in Egypt during the civil war, and the media provided heavy coverage and analysis of the conflict. I had also formed friendships with many Lebanese students who studied at the American University in Cairo where I went to college, and later in upstate New York as graduate students. The *hafle* also promised to be fun, as well as a chance for me to practice dancing *dabke*—which I have learned from my friends in college—and enjoy some homemade authentic Lebanese food.

Although I did not intend to focus my research on the role of the Maronite Church in maintaining the diaspora, I knew that religious institutions are important sites where the diaspora can be studied. Among Lebanese immigrants, the Maronite Church is believed to be an important institution. Together with Sunnis and Shiites, the Maronites are assumed to be one of the three largest religious groups in Lebanon.[1] No official census has taken place since 1932, and so it is rather difficult to determine which is the largest of the three groups (see, e.g., Maktabi 1999). In the diaspora it is even harder to predict the religious makeup of those who left over the years. Existing studies argue, however, that the earlier waves of migration—those that lasted until the Israeli invasion in 1982—were predominantly Christian. Even following 1982, when all religious and ethnic groups were leaving the country, many believe that Muslim migrants were more likely to choose Arab Gulf countries as destinations for temporary settlement. Although I had no way of estimating the religious makeup of the immigrant community to ensure that my respondents accurately reflected the diversity within Lebanese society, it was important to include members of all the religious groups that exist within Lebanon, and the *hafle* promised to be an event where I might recruit some Maronite respondents.

The *hafle* turned out to be an important moment of ethnic pride where Arabic music was performed, the Lebanese flag flaunted, and religious symbolism exhibited. The event was organized in an attempt to produce a "heritage aura" where ancestry is celebrated and a sense of Lebanese-ness is constructed.[2] Besides the few first-generation Lebanese immigrants in my company, almost all the attendees were third-generation Lebanese or more and not necessarily familiar with the language or the culture. The priest explained that fact later when he agreed to share his experience with migration and religious leadership in private. This fact also explained the prevalence of tourism literature and basic information about Lebanon. Indeed, the *hafle* is best understood within the framework of symbolic ethnicity in which white ethnics can choose to participate (Waters 1999). Despite the efforts to construct a moment of Lebanese identity, there were only brief moments of *dabke,* and the *baklawa* was not fresh. More prominent at the event was the sensual reporting on religious persecution and victimization of Christian minorities in other Arab countries which was achieved by passing out petitions against some national governments in the region. More important, I had my first experience with rejection, as the few attendees who were first-generation immigrants refused to talk to me as soon as they found out that I am from Egypt. I was later told by my friend that they are former members of the Maronite Phalange Party (a popular rightist party that sees Lebanon as a non-Arab Western society). Their refusal to communicate with me was based on the assumption that I am Muslim and therefore the enemy.

Over the course of doing research, a number of other people refused to be interviewed. Most of them were contacted because of their leadership roles for a number of religious organizations. A number of Shiite leaders in

Montreal and Paris and a Maronite leader in Paris refused to be interviewed outright. The lack of participation on behalf of religious leaders and right-wing political affiliates certainly skews the experiences I illustrate in this book. However, I am also confident that my national/religious background has encouraged others to participate and share their stories. This does not mean that most respondents were raised Sunni and identified as Arab.[3] To the contrary, many respondents willingly shared their experiences with a researcher who was not a total insider and possibly objective when investigating the nature of Lebanese community in Lebanon and in the diaspora. Equally important was my identity as a graduate student, as many individuals were glad to see an academic interest in their stories. More important, in Paris and Montreal, coming from the United States proved helpful, as many respondents set out to explain their views on the difference between living in France or Canada versus North America or the United States. As I illustrate in this chapter, the ethnic makeup of each of the cities was also central in the narratives my respondents provided.

Lebanese Diasporic Identities

Lebanese immigrants have a strong sense of being Lebanese, which, for many of them, means different things. Stressing a wide range of factors from a delicious cuisine, strong family values, an appreciation of music and dance, and an entrepreneurial spirit to an experience with collective trauma induced by two civil wars, social disintegration, corrupt governments, and economic dependency, all the individuals I interviewed had an answer to the meaning of being Lebanese. Clearly none of these attributes is unique to the Lebanese or Arabs more generally. Understanding ethnicity necessitates delving into that which the immigrants perceive to be ethnic about their patterns of self-identification and sociocultural practices, not whether individuals retain or relinquish ethnic identities (Eid 2008; Nagel 1994). Claiming a narrative of ethnic identification is a characteristic of diasporic communities that is central to their maintenance over time. Thus understanding ethnicity entails investigating the ways ethnic boundaries are negotiated and transformed from one context to the other. Because ethnic boundaries can be brightened or blurred in ways that affect the integration of immigrant groups in their host societies (Alba 2005), this chapter highlights the characteristics Lebanese immigrants activate to either strengthen or weaken their difference from others. At the same time the narratives described in this chapter shed light on the ways in which immigrants believe that members of the host societies also maintain their boundaries which ultimately strengthen reactionary ethnic identities.

The first half of this chapter illustrates how Lebanese immigrants construct ethnic identities and boundaries that provide connections between the individual's past and his or her present social, cultural, and economic relations (see Mohanty 1991; and Rutherford 1990). The rest of the chapter addresses the more common processes of identification among Lebanese immigrants, which are characterized by mixture and plurality and draw our attention to the fluidity, and sometimes contradictory, aspects of immigrant cultural identities in the contemporary world (see Werbner 1997). Illustrating how Lebanese immigrant identities are negotiated in particular contexts and through various processes, I believe that "ambivalence" rather than ethnicity or multiculturalism is a more accurate concept for understanding these cultural identities. As opposed to the emphasis on boundaries, the concept of "ambivalence" allows us to perceive the construction of identities through the negotiation of difference instead of assuming the coherence and predetermined nature of such difference (Papastergiadis 1997). For example, in a study of second-generation Arab youth in Montreal, Paul Eid (2008) argues that, when applied to immigrant identities, "ambivalence" directs our attention toward the strategies migrant youths employ to move away from both their host society's and ethnic community's ethno-national boundaries and construct nontraditional ways of identification that are based on their reinterpretation of ethnicity and nationality. As a result, immigrants' processes of identification redefine the position of the immigrant in society and transform the host society's culture as well. Emphasis on ambivalence also draws attention to the ways that immigrants negotiate processes of assimilation and ethnicity. In the example provided by Eid's study, second-generation youth construct ethnic identities as Arab Canadian. Their identities, however, move beyond the boundaries of ethnicity, as they are based on the negotiation of norms and traditions to which the ethnic community adheres. At the same time ethnic identities are sometimes emphasized to subvert derogatory representations of Arabs in Canada. At other times, however, ethnicity is downplayed to ward off prejudice and discrimination that may hamper assimilation into Canadian social institutions.

The conception of negotiated, ambivalent, and contested identities further allows us to understand the ways in which global processes impact processes of identification. Globalization is generally understood as producing multiple possibilities and new forms of identification (see, e.g., Hall 1992; and Nederveen Pieterse 1994). Stuart Hall (1992) argues that in a global environment, immigration is associated with identities that are "poised, in transition, between different positions." As a product of migration and displacement, the diaspora's identification connotes a cultural condition that comprehends issues of belonging and rootedness as well as exclusion and alienation. Scholars of diaspora, however, typically link belonging to the homeland and estrangement from the host society as key to the process of identity formation (e.g., Vertovec and Cohen 1999). Others such as Kim Butler (2001) view the diasporic experience as based on the awareness of the distinction between those who have migrated and those who remain in the homeland. For Butler, the diasporic search for belonging is not synonymous with identifying with the homeland and an ethnic community. Similarly Lavie and Swedenburg (1996) understand diasporic identification as a process involving an active search for one's rootedness and a heightened awareness of being transitory. In other words, members of a diaspora are constantly involved in processes of association and disassociation in both the homeland and the host society. This process of identification is more than simply moving between opposite frames of understanding identity. Diaspora refers to a position where individuals feel a sense of difference with others in the homeland and the host society. At the same time members of a diaspora may claim membership in a variety of ways that include their homeland, host society, diasporic community, and the world at large. Such understanding is made possible through a conception of global positioning and experiences. In this regard, "ambivalence" provides a means for understanding the ways in which these forms of membership and the identities they inform are negotiated and contested. Using "diaspora" as a particular category of social formation, I take it to mean a process of constructing immigrants' identities that reflects multiple connections and disconnections with others in various social spheres. In this chapter I focus on processes of identification in which Lebanese immigrants engage given their particular experiences and positions within the social, cultural, and economic relations they construct and by which they are constructed.

Strengthening Ethnicity

Immigrants' perceived inability to forego memories of their homeland and its culture or language is the basis for much anti-immigration sentiments and resentments. Over the years a number of scholars and public figures have warned against the influx of immigrants to the United States who would weaken the national fiber of the nation as they are incapable of shedding their foreign ways. In this section, however, I show that ethnic identity is relational and layered, and at the same time serves particular social and political interests. Although all my respondents emphasized ethnic aspects of their identification, most did so alongside other forms of identification and explained an understanding of their identities as having multiple sources and manifestations. A small group of respondents (seventeen out of eighty-seven), however, narrated their identity by embracing their ethnic origins and stressing a unitary and fixed understanding of "who they are." Eight respondents in Montreal and nine in Paris indicated that they identify themselves as Lebanese and have no desire to identify with their host societies. None of the respondents in New York understood their social positions in terms of ethnic identification that excluded their association with the host society.

All seventeen respondents who describe their identification solely in ethnic terms contend that they have had no experiences with prejudice or discrimination.[4] To the contrary, they constructed narratives where processes of ethnic identification were more informed by a context of reception that emphasized ethnic acceptance and approval, not prejudice and exclusion. Both Montreal and Paris, where Lebanese respondents referred to unitary ethnic narratives, were repeatedly portrayed as settings where being Lebanese was supported and appreciated. For example, Farah, a married woman and mother of three who moved to Montreal in 1993, told me that French-speaking immigrants are always welcomed in Montreal. She described her feelings when she first arrived in Canada:

> People were so hospitable to us when we first came here, it felt like everyone was saying "welcome." In two hours, we felt that we have everything we need. We felt so much at home, it was like we never left.

Instead of the negative constitution of mandatory identities, my respondents' choice of ethnic identification was centered on their historical heritage, as well as their economic achievement and social and political involvement in the host society. Many Lebanese immigrants, including all seventeen respondents in this group, emphasized their Phoenician heritage and the contributions of their ancient ancestors to world civilizations.[5] As a marker of distinction, the Phoenician linkage was drawn upon as a source of ethnic pride and coherence. Similarly the ethnic origin of many Lebanese immigrants who became prominent figures because of their economic, political, or artistic achievements was also used to mark pride and difference among my respondents.

The two contexts where ethnic narratives were expressed—Paris and Montreal—are cities where a Lebanese identity particularity served the specific social and political goals pursued by immigrants living in these cities. In "Constructing Ethnicity," Joan Nagel (1994:155) points out that individuals choose an identity based on their perception of "its meaning to different audiences, its salience in different social contexts, and its utility in different settings." Consequently it is important to explain the different ways in which Lebanese immigrants constructed their ethnic identity based on the various contexts. Ethnic identification is a process that involves choosing a unitary category and source of identity. In Paris, for example, religion was central in defining Lebanese ethnic identity. Despite the French public interest in secularism, Paris provided a context where religious identity was closely linked to political interests and thus religion and ethnicity were closely intertwined in the process of Lebanese ethnic identification. In contrast, Montreal provided a context where religious identity challenged communal belonging among the religiously diverse Lebanese immigrants. Instead of religion, stressing the importance of family values and ties was a strong source defining Lebanese ethnicity in Montreal. In this regard, ethnic identification can be seen as part of a strategy to gain personal or collective political or economic advantage (see, e.g., Hechter 1987). More important, ethnic narratives are based on processes of "selective appropriation" (Somers 1994) whereby individuals emphasize historical and cultural difference from others. Ethnic identification, then, can also include a refusal to identify with the host society's mainstream values, norms, and culture.

Ethnic narratives define Lebanese ethnicity contextually. In Montreal, immigrants who are engaged in affirming a Lebanese identity want to belong to an established immigrant community where the Lebanese constitute the largest Arab immigrant group. In the multicultural environment of Montreal, difference is always emphasized, as ethnicity brings about material gains and social political recognition. Ethnic identification is encouraged by the state and is sometimes taken for granted by the members of "visible minorities." Given Canada's emphasis on multicultural citizenship and the possibility of attaining special recognition and resources for ethnic groups (Kymlicka 1998), being a member of an ethnic group is an important vehicle for success for Lebanese immigrants. The Lebanese constitute the largest group of Arab immigrants in Canada (Hayani 1999) and thus define the ways that mainstream Canadian society perceives Arabs. Lebanese immigrants in Canada, and especially in Montreal, are a very diverse group in terms of class and religious background.

Such diversity was often underrated in the narratives of my interviewees in order to maintain the coherence that they sought by constructing ethnic identities. Understandably religious identification is not a strong reference point for Lebanese Canadians, as it would point to divisions within Lebanese immigrants and thus challenge the coherence of the group as a social unit.[6]

In Paris, where the French government and public have always been sympathetic to Lebanese political conflicts, immigrants who identify ethnically sought political support from French society and the mobilization of other immigrants so that they could impact homeland politics. As I discuss in the next section, ethnic identification in Paris is articulated along two opposing themes. As the French public and government sided with Maronites during the civil war, a group of Maronite political activists stressed their ethnic identification through religious particularities and dissociating from Arabs/Muslims as an important mechanism for articulating political identities. Contrarily, other non-Maronite immigrants in Paris constructed their identities through ethnic particularities that emphasized Arab identity and culture. For the latter group, Arab unity was an important political and cultural goal. Despite the different ways of expressing their ethnic identity, the respondents who identify ethnically understood their ethnicity in terms of the particular interests they sought to affirm individually and collectively as Lebanese in a host society.[7]

While the group of respondents who expressed their identities in unitary terms constructed narratives of Lebanese-ness that are relevant to their contexts, they all share one important feature. All the respondents in this group stated that it would be impossible to return to Lebanon, although they wished that their stay in the diaspora was only temporary.[8] The desire to return to a homeland is an important feature of diasporic communities, and therefore it is important to keep in mind that the narratives constructed by this group of immigrants are emphatically diasporic. Despite an articulation of an ethnic identity that took into consideration the particular social and political environment in the two cities, the group of immigrants discussed in this section also believed that their understanding of their Lebanese identities is common to all Lebanese people (albeit there were exclusions as to who the Lebanese people are). These ethnic narratives were centered around what are perceived to be uniquely Lebanese family values, political aspirations based on religious membership, and a multicultural understanding of Arab identity.

Family Values

Among those who identify ethnically in Montreal, the family unit provides an important social institution, and maintaining it is an important goal that is sustained by drawing ethnic boundaries between "Lebanese" and "Canadian." Expectedly, ethnic identification foreshadowed gender differences. Although Canada is considered by this group of respondents as offering an environment that is conducive to raising a family, it is specifically around family values that the men in this group establish their moral distinction from the rest of Canadian society, and, as a result, their Lebanese ethnicity. These immigrant men draw on traditional Lebanese family values to distance themselves from Canadian society and contend that they do not want to become Canadian. Emphasizing that family plays a more important role in Lebanese culture, that individuals primarily identify through their family responsibilities, and that family is the main institution through which one feels integrated in society, Said, a married man in his forties and a father of two, explains that family in Lebanon has more authority over one's life:

> What is missing from our lives here is the social connections that you'd have with people in Lebanon. I am getting older, and my son is getting older, and I worry that he may leave me and move out when he turns eighteen. This is unheard of in Lebanon. [There] children stay and take care of their parents, but here they learn to become independent and leave . . . Family is very unstable here: couples fight, get divorced, and move on to other marriages.

Like other immigrants, Said specifically chose to live in Canada as it provided a good environment for raising a family. Before Montreal, Said had lived in the United States and after marrying a woman from Lebanon spent two years in New York with his wife but could not afford to have children. Although he considered Montreal to be a better environment than New York to start a family, Said still constructed the difference in family life as the main element that differentiates him from other Canadians. Said's strong Catholic beliefs made him frown upon the possibility within Canadian society of divorce, premarital sex, and children's social independence. Although sharing a religion with many members of the host society could allow immigrants to blur the boundaries that might separate them from the mainstream (see Alba 2005), Said's example shows that different levels of adhering to the same religion can be an element for strengthening the perception of difference for the immigrants themselves. Concerns about family life and children are not negotiable for Said, and they therefore rule out the possibility of adopting a Canadian identity. Said was an active member of a Lebanese social organization in Montreal, and he was well aware that the Canadian government offers recognition and financial support to ethnic organizations. Despite their appreciation of the multicultural environment that Montreal offers, which allowed them to engage in a Lebanese community, Said and other men in this group stressed that public life (in schools or social activities) work against their efforts to socialize their children with Lebanese traditions and values. Children's independence at a young age and the possibility of divorce (which is strongly prohibited in the Lebanese Catholic community) mark a loss in status for many men who reap more benefits from a patriarchal family structure. Accordingly, these men lament the weaker family ties in Canada compared to those in Lebanon. The respect for the patriarchal family in Lebanese culture is the main axis along which this group of men draws their distinction from Canadian society and emphasize their ethnic identity.

Women in Montreal also emphasized their families as an important marker of their ethnic identification but did not share with male immigrants a strong interest in differentiating between family ties in Lebanon and Canada. Instead, these women recognized that they had left their families behind to come to Canada, and thus broke with an important Lebanese tradition that would make their ethnic identification more difficult. Instead of expressing the loss of strong family ties to describe their lives in Canada, this group of women claimed that the main reason for their migration was the pursuit of their families' well-being. For example, female respondents often stressed access to good-paying jobs, education for their children, as well as health care and retirement benefits as opportunities that they would not find in Lebanon. Farah is a mother of three young children who moved to Montreal shortly after she married. Her husband works as a taxi driver, and she is an office assistant. She explained her reasons for moving to Montreal:

> The kind respect for humanity that you get here, the acknowledgment for your basic right, to an equal treatment, to health care, and good education to your children, these are things that we know we won't get in Lebanon since we do not have the right family background or the right connections.

For Lebanese immigrant women like Farah, the pursuit of these otherwise unavailable material gains for their families marked the differences in experiences from members of their host societies. Farah still had family members living in Lebanon who struggled to obtain basic health care, a proper education for their children, or well-paying jobs. She was reminded daily of her privilege compared to those relatives in Lebanon and, as a result, of her difference from other Canadians who, according to her, only know of social welfare and equal opportunity.

Unlike the ethnic narratives of men, married women and women with children were more likely to note that Canada's multicultural environment is supportive of their family goals. For example, Farah's narrative highlights the differences in the context of reception between Canada and the United States to emphasize that she felt particularly lucky for having chosen Canada to start her family. In Farah's views, unlike the United States, Canadian society does not expect immigrants to relinquish their ethnic differences but encourages the maintenance of ethnic languages and religious practices, and she wants her children to grow up knowing these. One of Farah's children was about to join a high school that offered Arabic language classes, and she said that only in Canada can children of immigrants have such an opportunity. Farah also referred to her newly married sister who lives in the United States and pointed out that she was trying to convince her sister and brother-in-law to move to Canada, not only because she wanted her sister to be closer to her but also because she was convinced that Canada offers a better environment for immigrants and their families. Most women in this group emphasized that Canada is a multicultural society where their ethnic particularities are respected and strengthened. Moreover, these women also claimed that, for Lebanese immigrants in particular, familiarity with the French language and the socioeconomic success that the community has achieved allow for the favorable reception and positioning in Canadian society.

Religious Aspirations

In Paris, Lebanese immigrants deal with specific circumstances that are shaped by the historical colonial relationship between France and Lebanon.[9] Thus, unlike Lebanese immigrants in Montreal who identified ethnically by emphasizing their difference within Canadian society, ethnic narratives in Paris stressed the similarities between Lebanese and French cultures. Ethnic identification was narrated in terms of differences in social and political practices but not in cultural values. Similar to Lebanese immigrants in Montreal, however, ethnicity was utilized as a source of coherence for those immigrants who do not have the option of returning to their homeland.[10]

Ethnic narratives in Paris emphasized political reasons instead of economic ones as the grounds for migration. Alain is the only official political refugee I interviewed, who, while working as a journalist in Lebanon, was beaten up and imprisoned twice because of his opposition to the political establishment in Lebanon. Georges referred to his status as "self-imposed" exile, as he left Lebanon when Maronite political leader General Michel Aoun was exiled in France.[11] Chady, though motivated by the lack of economic opportunity in Lebanon, also asserted that he moved to Paris when he reached a dead end in his political career in Lebanon. All three immigrants chose Paris, because they believe that it provides an ideal center for continuing their political activity and organizing other Lebanese immigrants in the diaspora toward changing the political environment in Lebanon.

Similar to Kemp's (1992) observation that the majority of the Lebanese in Paris were migrants who were compelled to leave their homeland but have no intention of settling anywhere, my respondents in this group drew on their transitory and sometimes transnational status to explain their ethnic identity. Asserting their Lebanese identity, this group of respondents did not see themselves as "immigrants" and emphasized that Paris was a transitory place that would allow them to continue their engagement with Lebanese issues until their return. For example, Georges asserted that:

> To be in Paris is not unnatural for Lebanese, because they speak French mainly, and France is the first country they think of going to. But going to France is not really immigration. To really migrate, *to leave the country*, one has to go across the Atlantic Ocean, maybe to Montreal or Buenos Aires.

Georges went on to explain that he did not consider coming to Paris as a form of migration because of the proximity to Lebanon, not only in terms of distance but also culturally. Specifically, Georges claimed (wrongly) that most Lebanese people are Francophone and Catholic, and thus share the same cultural milieu. The history of French involvement in Lebanon, brought about by missionaries, travelers, and political figures, also contributed to the similarities in Georges's opinion. These similarities rendered identifying himself as French a meaningless endeavor, since he already felt French through his ethnic Lebanese identity. More important, Georges referred to the large number of Lebanese immigrants and travelers in Paris which allows him to "live day by day what's going on in Lebanon." The Lebanese that Georges refers to are not all immigrants but political, economic, and cultural figures who frequently visit Paris for various reasons. These frequent visitors make Paris a strategic base for political organizing, which was an important goal for Georges, Chady, and Alain.

For the five Maronite immigrants in Paris who said that they do not identify as French but only as Lebanese, the starting point for defining "Lebanese" was that being Lebanese did not include being Arab. The negation of being "Arab" was expressed differently by each, mostly by drawing on various historical constructs. For example, as Georges explained:

> I am part of the Arabic-speaking people, but not Arab. If you talk about ethnic Arab, it's a lie. It's a historical and geographical lie. It's fact. But as we are Lebanese, Arabic speaking, you are Arabic speaking, and so on for others.

In his statement, Georges negated the meaning of Arab ethnicity but did not negate ethnicity itself as a social reality, since ethnicity was meaningful in his experience. Insisting that "I would accept being French more than being Arab," Chady explained his reasons:

> First of all, what is Arab? Is it a language, religion, or civilization? If it is religion, I am a Maronite and not Arab. If it is civilization, Lebanon has a longer history and civilization that preceded the Arab one. For Lebanese, there is no need for an Arab identity.

Chady's assertion that being Arab did not meet an interest shared by Lebanese immigrants illustrates the process of constructing an identity through negation to meet strategic goals. The importance of rejecting an Arab identity seemed to be a very deliberate process for these five immigrants as they spoke of the importance of forming a coherent Lebanese identity. Their narratives focused on Lebanese cultural uniqueness and sometimes superiority when compared to the Arab ethnicity. They also echoed French colonial constructions of Lebanon as modern, Catholic, and non-Arab. Like other identities, "it is precisely through processes of exclusion and othering that both collective and individual subjects are formed" (Gupta and Ferguson 1997:13). Inventing a Lebanese identity in the diaspora takes place within structural relations of power and inequality, and, at a time when being Arab evokes a wide range of negative stereotypes, the exclusion of this identity seems convenient for this group of immigrants. Like other Lebanese immigrants in Paris, all five respondents in this group referred to the assumption held by French society that "Arab" specifically meant North African. Differentiating themselves from this stigmatized immigrant group, they emphasized that Lebanese immigrants were positively received in France, and hence the importance of drawing lines of distinction between "Arab" and "Lebanese." For example, Georges justified the prejudices against North Africans in France and stated that Lebanese immigrants were different:

> I understand it because of the way the North African people immigrated to France: it's messy. Integration here has social roots and they have to expect it, and not bring so many people at the same time. You have to integrate people. And they have to understand how to integrate. So I understand the problem. When they [the French] know that you're Lebanese and especially Maronite or Christian Lebanese, then they realize that there is no difference. They know that we are not going to create a ghetto or demonstrate against them. The Lebanese community [here] is distinct from other Arab communities.

Georges' distinction between Arab and Lebanese immigrant communities drew on official French policies and rhetoric that emphasize the importance of integration and the problems associated with the formation of ghettos and ethnic mobilization (see Guiraudon 1996). Notably Georges did not see the activities of his political group in the same light, despite his assertion that the group's main goals were raising awareness and mobilizing the Lebanese around the world toward influencing change in Lebanon. Alain drew similar distinctions to stress that Lebanese immigrants did not face the kinds of hostility that "Arabs" face in France and the United States. Although religion seemed to be the central factor rendering "Arab" and "Lebanese" as mutually exclusive categories for this group of immigrants, Alain's distinctions were extended to differentiate between "Lebanese" and other Arab non-Muslim groups. During our second meeting, Alain referred to the Egyptian "Coptic ghetto" in Paris and pointed out that there was no such thing as a "Lebanese ghetto" since he believed the Lebanese were well integrated in France. Ironically Alain owned an ethnic Lebanese restaurant that was an important organizational site for many of his political activities. However, since his restaurant was in the student Latin quarter (where he met many Lebanese students who recently arrived in Paris), he did not think of it in terms of ethnic exclusivity implied by his reference to the "Coptic ghetto." This form of distinction, while foregoing a possible alliance based on religion, strengthens the more strategic claims of negat-

cal project and a larger political climate (see, e.g., Maktabi 1999). It is thus understandable that members of religious groups, and especially those sects that lack political power, may hold opposing understandings of a Lebanese identity. Four Lebanese immigrants interviewed in Paris narrated a form of ethnic identity that is based on their national as well as religious identification that also encompasses being Arab. Of the four, as noted earlier, two are Shiites, one is Greek Orthodox, and one is Jewish. They all belong to religious sects that have relatively less political power within the Lebanese political structure. In explaining the sources of their Lebanese/Arab identity Ali and Fares, the two Shiites, spoke of their strong links to the Shiite community in Paris and that they drew on their similarities with co-religious immigrants in Paris who included many from other Arab countries. Ali and Fares referred, specifically, to the recent political gains of the Shiites in Lebanon and stressed that their religious and national identities reinforce each other.[13] Both asserted that their identification has not been altered by living in Paris. They simply explained that, having grown up in Lebanon, they were used to being in a multiethnic society that always reminded them of their religious identities and social differences. I met Ali and Fares at an ethnic restaurant where they both worked. The restaurant was located in one of Paris's immigrant neighborhoods and thus was less successful than the more famous Lebanese restaurants in wealthy and tourist neighborhoods. The marginalized position of the restaurant also reflected the marginal position of Shiites in French public life. Both Ali and Fares were aware of this marginalization but stated that the advantage of being in the immigrant neighborhood was their proximity to other Arabs—some of whom were Shiite.

In contrast to Ali and Fares, who said that their identification process had not been altered with their migration, Samir and David said that their identity as Lebanese and Arab was strengthened while living in France. Samir, a Greek Orthodox businessman in his late fifties, moved from Lebanon with his wife and three children in 1989, given the deteriorating conditions of civil unrest. Samir maintained that his identity was that of an Arab, more than Lebanese or French. Having matured in the 1960s, Samir stressed that he still shared the views of that era, the political views of Arab unity and identity. Samir's religious identification as a Greek Orthodox also reinforced his Arab identification. He explained that members of the Greek Orthodox community did not share the separatist tendencies and rejection of Arab culture that members of the Maronite community have.[14] Articulating the views of Arab nationalism, Samir emphasized that being Arab is a secular, post-colonial, and futuristic identification with which he strongly agreed. With his move to France, Samir's views were only strengthened through his inter-action with other Arab nationalists from various parts of the Arab world. For Samir, Paris is a cultural center that is home to many Arab nationalists who left their countries of origin following their dissatisfaction with Arab regimes. As such, Paris provides a context for strengthening Arab identities, as it allows Samir and his friends to exchange their visions on the future of the Arab world. In this sense, Samir did not see a conflict in being Lebanese and Arab living in France as his political interests were left unchallenged. Further, belonging to an Arab diaspora reinforced his ethnic identification and did not contradict his integration in French society.

David's narrative is the most complicated, since his religious identification as Jewish is often contrasted to his national identification as Arab. David, a lawyer in his fifties, left Lebanon just as the civil war was starting. With reli-gious strife in Lebanon rising, he decided to move to Paris temporarily until the political climate stabilized. Unlike Samir, he was not socialized into the discourse on Arab identity, as he believed the discourse was mostly anti-Jew-ish. Instead, he enjoyed the multicultural aspect of Lebanese social life and had no real political interests until his arrival in Paris in the mid-1970s. He initially thought that his religious identification would enable him to partici-pate in Parisian Jewish life and ethnic community. However, he quickly saw that he was expected to give up his Lebanese identity in that environment. David grew to believe that the prewar Lebanon where he grew up was a truly multicultural society, more so than France and especially its Jewish com-munity. Notably David found more acceptance of his religious background among other Arab nationalists in the city, individuals who, like Samir, believed that Arab political identity is emphatically secular and postcolonial, and thus devoid of religious particularities. Though not necessarily shar-ing the same political views of most contemporary Arabs, both Samir and David represent a particular understanding of Arabness as it first emerged in the 1950s and 1960s and was heavily intertwined with socialist politics and regional ambitions. This understanding aimed at unifying a region that was recognizably diverse into a secular, socialist, cultural identity.

Like other forms of identity, being Arab is a political process chosen for particular purposes and in specific contexts. The four immigrants who stressed their Arab identity in Paris illustrate ways through which this form of identity was strengthened given the particular experience of migration. Unlike those who chose to deny that they belonged to an Arab culture, those who affirm their Arab identity drew on the coherence it offered to their expe-rience with displacement. For these four immigrants, being Arab offered an avenue for belonging to a wider social group in France while maintaining their difference from French society. Stressing that "Arab" is an umbrella identity that can mean different things (such as religion or political position) in different contexts, this group of immigrants saw their identity as malleable and transitory. For these immigrants, there is nothing essential about being Arab. Yet an Arab identity is meaningful to them, as it expresses their social and political positions in an environment that they do not wish to fully accept. Despite the various forms of allegiances that Lebanese immigrants may have, a transnational Arab identity can be activated and discarded depending on the political, historical, and economic conjunctures, as well as on subgroup and individual dispositions (Eid 2008).

The (Im)Possibility of Return

In this section on ethnic identity, I describe various mechanisms employed by members of the Lebanese diaspora to form unity and coherence outside their homeland. The contours of ethnic identity vary by given contexts of immigration and by the particular goals that the immigrants seek. As a result, the narratives provided do not point to a simple reinvention of ethnic and religious particularities but rather to a process of forging an identity within the complexities of global immigration. For Lebanese immigrants in Montreal, personal interests and experiences defined their Lebanese identities based on family traditions. For those in Paris, political orientations informed the articulation of Lebanese identities toward desired political changes. The narratives in this section discern that ethnic identification brings about specific social, political, and cultural consequences sought after by the immigrants themselves. The adoption of an ethnic identity by immigrants in this group is understood as a way to gain personal or collective social, cultural, political, or economic advantage. More important, ethnic identification provides a marker for distinction when individuals narrate their differences from their host societies. When immigrants are constantly reminded of their difference, as in the narratives provided in Montreal, ethnic identification offers a sense of coherence to immigrants' position in society. Similarly, when immigrants wish to preserve a favorable position of acceptance, as in the narratives of immigrants based in Paris, ethnic identification is strengthened.

Ethnic identification, however, is more than a direct result of processes of differentiation in host societies. Through their various narratives, these immigrants emphasize that they "are not here to stay" but, at the same time, "cannot and will probably not go back," which illustrates a form of diasporic identity that centers on temporality and the desire to return. Given the impossibility of return, however, ethnicity provides a second best source of coherence. As the narratives illustrate, Lebanese immigrants define their ethnicity as that aspect of their social practices that they are not willing to change. Rendering these practices ethnic preserves their sense of uniqueness when they have given up on returning to Lebanon. Regardless of their level of integration, all immigrants who narrated ethnic identifications stress their temporary presence outside Lebanon and express their desire to return to their homeland. Despite that, all immigrants in this group believed that they would never be able to return to Lebanon permanently owing to economic and political conditions.[15]

In Montreal, ethnic narratives were associated with a working-class background. The awareness that their class background would prevent them from having the same standard of living as they have in Montreal made members of this group realize that their nostalgia for returning to Lebanon would not materialize.[16] The deteriorating economic and social conditions in Lebanon, and that they have children in some cases, adds to their realization that Lebanon will not offer the same kind of future that they want for themselves or their children. Although these immigrants have accepted that they are not likely to return to Lebanon, they are also unable to accept membership in Canadian society, given the constant reminder of their difference. Ethnic identification thus provides a mechanism by which they can negotiate their belonging to Canadian society based on their perceived difference. Despite their participation in mainstream Canadian institutions and their awareness that their children are likely to grow up as Canadians more than Lebanese, immigrants in this group held on to their ethnic identities to preserve their space within Canadian society. The ethnic narratives provided, however, are negotiated along diasporic lines whereby issues of belonging, return, and homelessness are dealt with and articulated.

While immigrants who utilized ethnic narratives in Paris draw on their sense of temporality and desire to return to Lebanon that is shared by the group in Montreal, they illustrate a more active form of engagement with the homeland and the diaspora that takes shape within a particular French context and immigration dynamics. In Paris, ethnic identification was shaped by political interests that reflect religious background. The impossibility of returning was still a common theme in their narratives. The group of Maronite immigrants who rejected being French reasoned that they cannot return to Lebanon unless the political establishment is transformed, which meant abandoning sectarian confessionalism which, in their opinion, constricts the power of Maronites.[17] Although their political engagement made them optimistic about the possibility of returning, ongoing instability and economic deterioration also make them realize that their return is less than likely. Other immigrants in this group were more aware that their stay in Paris was permanent. Samir believed, for example, that he was integrated into French society given his French nationality and the fact that his children were brought up to be French. But, despite this, he did not identify as French given his transnational interests and practices. Samir owned an export-import company that trades in manufactured goods between France and Lebanon, and he frequently travels to Lebanon on business. Ethnic identification, for Samir as well as other immigrants in this group, was the result of negotiating his desire to return to Lebanon, his inability to return, and economic and political practices. Like other ethnic narratives, the impossibility of returning permanently strengthens ethnic identification as a way to maintain a connection with the homeland. Ethnicity, especially as it is expressed in transnational sentiments or political alliances, is only one form of identity that a few immigrants in my sample shared. Inquiring about diasporic identification allowed immigrants to express multiple forms of identification. I now turn to the discussion of the second type of identity narrative, one that highlights the respondents' awareness of the multiple and negotiated forms of identification. These identities also take on a strong sense of diasporic existence and global positioning.

Multiple Identities

> Unlike the sudden shift of exile or forced deterritorialization
> that clings to the dream of return and gradually evolves into
> the larger diaspora, the displaced émigré can be defined by
> contingency, indeterminacy, and moveable identity.
> —Sullivan 2001:1

Contrary to ethnic forms of identification by which respondents emphasized unitary coherent identities, a larger group of immigrants pointed out that they understood their social position in multiple and sometimes contradictory ways—what I refer to as a transcultural narrative. I use the word "transcultural" to imply the mixing of different identities and cultural repertoires. In the context of Lebanese identity narratives, transculturalism refers to blending cultures that are all intermixed in a global world. Lebanese immigrants who transculturally narrated their identities emphasize that migration was an enriching experience that allowed them to add on different forms of identity and mix cultural idioms to express their unique position at the intersection of various cultural spheres. The majority of Lebanese immigrants interviewed in the three cities narrated a form of transcultural identities that resulted from their various experiences of living in different parts of the world and the multicultural aspects of each of the individual societies. In this section I illustrate ways through which immigrants in each of the three cities are engaged in creative forms of appropriation, as well as rejection, of different cultural milieus to produce new understandings of their identities within a global context.

Compared to the group of immigrants who identify ethnically, three main features differentiate this transcultural group. They emphasized that the Lebanon they knew was a multicultural space and sought avenues for inclusion in their homeland. Likewise, focusing on the multicultural aspects of their new social settings, this group of immigrants emphasized that Montreal, New York, and Paris provide contexts where they can seek acceptance and integration. Finally, these Lebanese immigrants did not relinquish the possibility of returning to Lebanon but continue to postpone it to some point in the future. These differences from ethnic narratives notwithstanding, the defining aspects of transcultural narratives are recognizing their worldly upbringing and outlook, perceiving a lack of belonging to both homeland and host societies, and searching for commonalities with others.

Worldly Outlook

Lebanese immigrants who narrated transcultural processes of identification saw their identities as the product of two or more cultures. In explaining the multiple sources of their identity, many of the Lebanese immigrants I interviewed referred to the works of the Lebanese-French author Amine Maalouf as a vivid expression of their own experiences. In the autobiographical essay *In the Name of Identity: Violence and the Need to Belong*, Maalouf (2000:1–2) narrates his transcultural identity:

How many times, since I left Lebanon in 1976 to live in France, have people asked me, with the best intentions in the world, whether I felt "more French" or "more Lebanese"? And I always give the same answer: "Both!" I say that not in the interest of fairness or balance, but because any other answer would be a lie. What makes me myself rather than anyone else is the very fact that I am poised between two countries, two or three languages and several cultural traditions. It is precisely this that defines my identity . . . So am I half French and half Lebanese? Of course not. Identity cannot be compartmentalised. You can't divide it up into halves or thirds or any other separate segments. I haven't got several identities: I've got just one, made up of many components in a mixture that is unique to me, just as other people's identity is unique to them as individuals.

Like Maalouf, this group of immigrants emphasized the unique sources of their identity as well as the enriching aspects of migration instead of seeing their experience as a form of banishment and exile. They also shared with Maalouf an awareness of their multicultural origins. All immigrants in this group recognized that Lebanon is a country of many religions, ethnic groups, and cultural influences. To many, being Lebanese entailed being influenced by all the different cultures that constitute Lebanon. French colonization and the educational system it implemented made many of my interviewees aware of the French influence on their narratives. Similarly many narratives referred to the history of Lebanon as a trade center which brought in peoples and cultures from around the world.

Many respondents emphasized that their worldly outlook was an attribute that they gained while growing up in Lebanon and not a direct result of their experiences with migration. Many others said that their familiarity with the cultures of their host societies had been gained through their Western style education, proficiency in more than one language, and frequent travel with family members to Europe and North America. Such an early introduction to global cultural processes created strong desires to explore various experiences and interactions. For example, Khaled, who lived in New York when I met him, told me that while growing up his parents had many friends and visitors from different parts of the world and that he had traveled to the United States when he was younger to visit his aunt who lived in Washington, D.C., at the time. More important, Khaled stated that his proficiency in Arabic, French, and English shaped his knowledge of the world. According to Khaled, being able to consume cultural products in three languages allowed him to understand the world from different perspectives and identify with multiple cultural repertoires. He described the mixing of the multiple influences on his identity and his identification with multiple lexicons:

In Lebanon, with my close friends, we move from English to French to Arabic in one sentence. And this is familiar for me; it is not odd or bizarre. We do not do it to show off. It's just certain words we can express better in these languages.

Khaled's remark reveals that mixing different languages in his speech was not an act of arrogance but an expected and accepted result of his Western education and outlook. Khaled had earned his college degree from the American University of Beirut, and so his interest in graduate studies in the United States was "a logical extension." Similarly, growing up in a Sunni family that participated in elite social circles in Lebanon where French was used extensively and also in public events where proficiency in Arabic was emphasized allowed him to move comfortably within the distinct social worlds and languages. Khaled's use of language as a marker of his distinction was common to many respondents, who took pride in their proficiency in three or more languages whenever I asked them what language they wished to be interviewed in. As a result, many of the interviews were conducted using a mix of the three languages. Although most of my interviewees are highly educated professionals, some attributed their membership in a global cultured class to the fact that they had a distinct sociocultural background. Similar to Khaled, many respondents who spoke of the multiple influences on their upbringing stressed the cultural impact on their lives of being educated in the West, frequently traveling outside Lebanon, and having friends from European countries.

Most of the younger respondents, who grew up during the war and experienced a lack of mobility while knowing of their parents' life experiences traveling abroad, were inspired to leave Lebanon and ultimately decided to emigrate. Maya noted, for example, that her father had lived in a number of European countries before she was born and that the stories he told her at a very young age gave her "a thirst to get to know other places." Maya lived in Paris and had no intention of returning to Lebanon, contrary to her family's wishes. Speaking with me over dinner after a shopping trip in a fashionable Parisian quarter, Maya simply blamed her father for raising her to have an adventurous spirit. She did not travel as a child because of the civil war and the accompanying lack of mobility. But when she was accepted at the university in Paris, she jumped at this opportunity to emigrate. However, after completing her university degree, she had difficulty finding a job in Paris. This led her to challenge her parents and her class norms, and for a few months she lost her legal status. All this Maya shared with me confidently and with a sense of pride. Her decision to stay in Paris, despite her illegal status, marked her independence from her family, which she eagerly sought upon emigrating from Lebanon. Maya never worried that she might be deported, as were many undocumented immigrants. Her comfort with French society and culture, which facilitated her ability to "pass" as French, gave her sufficient confidence to ultimately get a job and legalize her status. Similarly Sherif's French education and his knowledge of Western history and philosophy made him eager to "see the places [he] has read about." During his first five years living outside Lebanon, Sherif did not return to visit even for a short vacation, as he moved from Beirut to Paris to London and then finally arrived in Montreal. Sherif's world travels were always exciting, and was an experience he actively sought, which explains his worldly outlook and cosmopolitan attachments:

My idea was basically that—it's still my idea—I would like to travel a lot and live in many countries. I want to gather as much experience, not only professionally but also human experience, as much as possible. And the best way to know a place is not by being a tourist and going to a city, you'll end up not knowing anything about that city. You have to live in it and work in it to learn about the people, the culture and the history. So this is the basic idea.

When I asked Sherif what he meant by "human experience," he replied:

You know, when you meet people and you meet different populations and different cultures. It's very enriching. And, as you know, Montreal is a melting pot. You have all ethnicities, all cultural backgrounds, all religions, you can't ask for more. So this is another thing that made me choose Canada.

Similar eagerness to know about the world and experience diverse cultures and societies led many respondents to perceive of themselves as distant from others around them who had no such desires. Although all the Lebanese immigrants I interviewed pointed to the deteriorating economic conditions in Lebanon as an important factor in their decision to leave, many of the younger respondents spoke of their worldly upbringing, their pursuit of knowledge, and their different social experiences as equally important influences. Their class resources also contributed to their relative success, as they did not have to struggle to find jobs or make friends when they first arrived in their host societies. As a result, these younger respondents were more likely to highlight the enriching aspects that emigration brought to their lives and stress its importance in their identification process.

Lack of Belonging

The worldly upbringing of many Lebanese immigrants led them to perceive differences between themselves and others around them. Drawing on these differences, in both the host society and the homeland, they understood their experiences with migration as further dissociating them from the societies they cross in their daily lives.

Carl, thirty-two years old when I met him, had left Lebanon at the age of twenty to get his master's degree in Paris; after working in Greece and the United States, he returned to practice law in Paris. Having lived in three different countries outside Lebanon, Carl is well aware of his lack of belonging to any society, and this is a source of discomfort and ambiguity for him. During our meeting at a trendy Parisian restaurant, Carl conveyed his lack of belonging despite his social and economic integration into French society:

> In many ways, I can be considered French. I speak the language, I know the culture, and I am very successful living in French society. But I am not French. I don't consider myself French and they [the French] do not consider me French either.

Khaled's narrative also illustrates this sense of not fully identifying with the various societies to which one belongs. I met Khaled, a twenty-eight-year-old graduate student who had moved to New York in 1994, at Lincoln Center for the Performing Arts in the summer of 2001, after we had seen a Lebanese film that was part of the Human Rights Watch Film Festival. Following the film and the question-and-answer session, I engaged in further conversation with those who participated in the discussion. Khaled was one of two who agreed to talk to me after the film, but he asked that the interview take place right there and then. Later he agreed to another meeting, where he elaborated upon his experiences. Despite his seven-year stay in the United States, Khaled did not identify with American society. Nor did he feel fully integrated into Lebanese society. Narrowing his cultural repertoire to only one culture where he would fully belong meant, in his view, social and cultural death:

> For instance, I go to Lebanon every year for three months, because I need to feel that I'm connected there. I am one of those people who feel like I don't belong here, I don't belong there. I am kind of in between, and that's exactly what I am. I don't feel I am fully Lebanese; I will die if I completely

abide by all the social rules of that culture, and I will also die if I abide by all the social rules of this culture.

As illustrated in the narratives of both Carl and Khaled, the feeling of not belonging to the societies these immigrants cross is a desirable and somewhat liberating position. Indeed, many believed that their worldly outlook was central to their general difference from others and thus their lack of desire to conform to one society.

Lebanese immigrants who emphasized multiple and shifting identities, instead of stressing the impossibility of returning to Lebanon, as did those who relied on unitary ethnic identities, emphasized their lack of desire to return and challenged nostalgic forms of remembering and belonging to a homeland. Their general lack of belonging became manifest when they attempted to mark their racial and ethnic differences and were confronted with experiences of prejudice and discrimination. Many referred to specific markers of difference. Specifically, most Lebanese immigrants who articulated the multiple sources of their identities also expressed their awareness of their racial and cultural differences, experiences of direct discrimination, and problematic association with Lebanon, all of which are discussed in the following sections.

Racial/Ethnic Differentiation

Lebanese immigrants were generally aware of their precarious racial/ethnic identification in the societies in which they lived. Given that racial/ethnic politics varied dramatically in the three settings examined here, differences in how each articulated racial/ethnic identities were easily identified. In the United States, Arab Americans are officially classified as belonging to the Caucasian racial category, and 80 percent of Arab Americans identified themselves as such in 2000 (De la Cruz and Brittingham 2003). Although many Lebanese Americans in New York City follow such a classification in many official surveys, identifying as white is not an uncontested act. Michel—whose narrative was presented in the introductory chapter—identified himself as white because of his inability to select an alternative from the given choices. Like Michel, all Lebanese immigrants I interviewed did not unquestionably take on the white identity. For many, questioning a white identity also involved their reservation to take on a specifically American identity. Contesting whiteness, however, was a more central narrative to Muslim immigrants in New York. Although most respondents in this group stressed that they either do not believe in or do not practice religion, religious background is relevant in understanding their racialization in American society. For example, Abeer is a New Yorker who elaborated multiple sources of identification. She came from Lebanon in 1992 to pursue her degree in medicine. Abeer identified herself as an atheist and refused to indicate her family's religious background, stressing that it was irrelevant to her experience. During the interview, however, I had reasons to believe that Abeer's family is Sunni. She explained to me that, given her appearance, people assume she is white, and this drives her to dissociate herself from the majority position and emphasize her difference:

> I make a point to differentiate myself from whites. When you think about the white majority, I think about white people who just want to have their own little America, with Caucasian, white, blonde, with colored eyes, pointing that this is their own America. And so I, if I share the skin color, it doesn't mean that I share that mentality. I definitely do not want to be considered just like another American. I want to have my own identity and I am Lebanese after all. I mean, I'm Lebanese at heart, no matter how integrated I am in the society here, I want to be different, I don't want to be within the white majority. That's why I do not consider myself as white, I'm whatever, other, and I'm Lebanese.

Like Abeer, many Lebanese Muslim immigrants did not specifically mention their religious background as a source of their racial/ethnic difference. However, more Muslims than Christian immigrants in New York spoke of their unwillingness to take on a white label.[18] In their views, whiteness is a category that includes religious practices. As a result Christian Lebanese, relying on similar religious practices and beliefs, can more easily integrate into the white mainstream society. Muslim Lebanese, on the other hand, regardless of their level of belief, cannot participate in these religious practices, highlighting their unmistakable differences from other whites. For example, Khaled, who was raised in a secular Muslim family, told me that religion was significant in shaping his experiences in New York only insofar as he felt rejected based on his Muslim/Arab identity in social settings where people were unknowledgeable about his culture.

Regardless of religious differences, most Lebanese immigrants in New York City pointed to political differences as more meaningful in marking their cultural difference in American society. Abeer explained, for example, that her interest in Middle Eastern politics and her political views surrounding the Palestinian/Israeli conflict differentiate her from her white American friends:

What concerns me is the Middle East situation, and that it is not portrayed truthfully. It's very biased, it's very pro-Israeli, and that makes me mad. There's no awareness in the American public about what's going on. They only see one side of the story, and they don't see the other. A lot of people don't even know where Lebanon is. They ask me where's Lebanon and then they go: "Oh, you had a war there."

For Abeer, the lack of political awareness that was common to most Americans with whom she interacted was central to her feelings of being different in her host society. While aware that she was seen as part of the white majority, she still emphasized the different outlooks that place her in opposition to such status. The events of 9/11 led many respondents to engage in a more pronounced rejection of whiteness. Clearly, rejecting a white identity is a product of individual choice as well as social constraints imposed on the immigrants. For example, state policies of special registration forced all male respondents to confront their otherness in American society and rendered white identification a less attainable option.

Unlike Lebanese immigrants in New York, those in Montreal did not reject a white identity based on their religious background. In Canada, people of Arab origins are identified by the state as members of "visible minorities." Because this classification is more ethnic than racial, Lebanese immigrants in Montreal accept that they are clearly marked as different from white Canadians and yet have a special place within Canadian society. This understanding of minority status was shared by all respondents in Montreal. For example, Sherif explained that his Otherness in Canada was not based on his skin color:

Even though my skin is white, and my eyes are light brown, I can't put Caucasian [on application forms]. I don't really like this question. Sometimes, if there is Middle Eastern, I check it. Usually I just put Other.

As indicated by Sherif, identification is not a process solely based on skin color. The "Other" category was a comfortable place for Sherif, as he questioned every form of identity available to him and presented various rationales for not identifying with any one group (Arab/Muslim/Middle Eastern). Sherif went on to explain that he is not Arab, as his identity was also informed by European and North American cultures and experiences. Though raised Muslim, he identified as an atheist and so was unable to choose the "Muslim" label. Finally, challenging the coherence of "Middle Eastern" as a regional identity embodying various cultural and ethnic groups, Sherif explained that he also could not adopt that label and was thus content being classified as Other.

Other respondents in Montreal, though not rejecting all forms of identification, emphatically asserted their otherness. Lara, for example, the twenty-eight-year-old chemist discussed in the introductory chapter, saw herself as both Canadian and Lebanese. She also believed that in the multicultural environment of Montreal everyone is expected to have a dual identity. Thus, for Lara, navigating Lebanese and Canadian identities daily was a straightforward process, as she felt that mixing Canadian and Lebanese cultural resources was facilitated through Canada's social structure and state policies. Unlike Lebanese immigrants in New York, those in Montreal were not inclined to view Canadian identification as strictly white or Christian or both. Instead, Canada's explicit multicultural policies and identification of Lebanese immigrants as members of visible minorities allowed my respondents to take on a Canadian identity with more ease than those in New York could take on an American identity.

Lebanese immigrants in Paris, unlike those in New York and Montreal, did not confront their racial/ethnic otherness daily. Unlike some other groups of immigrants, their understanding of their ethnic difference in France was ambiguous. Given Lebanon's colonial relationship with France, and the French education and cultural influence that most respondents acknowledged, few narratives stressed contesting a French identity. French national discourses of membership and assimilation also appeared in the identity narratives of Lebanese immigrants in Paris, as they informed these immigrants' identification with French society and culture. Most narratives, however, illustrated an awareness of the immigrants' foreign status within French society. For example, Alfred, whose family is Greek Orthodox and who was a graduate student when we met, drew on his educational background and explained that "Arab" is a historical and political identity that emerged to mark a specific colonial background and a shared political standpoint. He went on to describe that it was not necessarily the identity he embraced while in Lebanon. Explaining that "Arab" is an umbrella identity that is used strategically to mark one's difference, Alfred stated that his Arab identity is an opposition to a French one:

> I noticed that I am not the only one—I talked about it a lot with many friends. My Arab identity was affirmed—confirmed—by opposition. Because it is a mark of difference, and you need to mark your difference.

So in Lebanon you feel Christian more than Lebanese, and maybe you don't like Arabs. You tend to reject that identity. In France, I felt Arab by opposition. Although, I may be closer to the French by culture, I know French better than Arabic, I read in French, I write in French, everything is French about me, [but] I am Lebanese and Arab, my issues and priorities are Lebanese and Arab.

Thus, for Alfred and other Lebanese immigrants in Paris, difference was marked more by political and historical positions than by racial or cultural attributes. In this regard, Lebanese immigrants in Paris were not different from those in New York and Montreal in terms of choosing processes of identification that result from political positions. Given the different political contexts in the three cities, articulating these positions takes different forms and results in different narratives of identification.

Direct Discrimination

Unlike narratives of identification that emphasize ethnicity, those that stress discrimination are more central in shaping multiple forms of identification. Experiences of discrimination contributed to my respondents' sense that they did not belong in their host society. It should be noted that most respondents denied having directly experienced discrimination themselves, but most knew of others who had suffered at least one prejudicial incident. Unlike when immigrants mark their racial or cultural difference *from* the host society, with experiences of discrimination it is the host society that marks the immigrants' difference. When respondents spoke of personal experiences of discrimination, their narratives emphasized that their lack of belonging to the host society was not a matter of preference but rather a result of mutual distancing through various social interactions. For example, the experiences of prejudice that Abeer encountered, specifically ridicule about her foreign accent, did not allow her to identify with the white majority:

From what I saw from whites dealing with me as a foreigner, I felt very ostracized, just because I speak with an accent. People would shout at me, hang the phone on me or not answer me. They would make believe that they don't understand what I'm saying.

In this way experiences of prejudice and exclusion marked immigrants' distance from the host society and heightened their sense of belonging to a negatively stereotyped minority group. Instead of seeking a coherent social position by embracing an ethnic identity, immigrants who spoke of multiple identities were also aware of their detachment from traditional ethnic identities, resulting in feelings of ambivalence about their social position.

Men were more likely, overall, to experience discrimination than women were. Some men stated that the racism that results from the combination of their gender and ethnicity was a product of stereotyping that occurs in the media and in official state policies. Michel, for example, spoke of the media's negative representations of the Middle East and specifically about the media identifying all Arab men as terrorists:

When you live more here, you start to know the unfair portrayal of the facts about the Middle East. The one-sidedness of the U.S. media toward the problem of Palestine, which directly links to the problems in Lebanon and Syria, leads to people seeing me within a negative lens. There is always an emphasis on those Arab terrorists with their stereotypically Arab features which ends up affecting all our lives. For example, at work, if I grow my hair a little bit more or if I grow a beard a little bit, they call me a terrorist. They jokingly ask if I was becoming a terrorist, but we all know that it is not just a joke.

Michel expressed this view before the events of 9/11. After going through the process of special registration in post–9/11 New York, Michel became ever more aware of his exclusion within American society. His experiences with exclusion, however, did not translate into his simply adopting a unitary ethnic identity (whether Arab or Lebanese). Instead, Michel and others sought multiple forms of integration into their host societies with the goal of instigating social change, which is discussed in the following chapter.

Gendered interactions also affected the experiences of Roy, a thirty-four-year-old graduate student who lived in New York City for two years before migrating with his family to Montreal in 1991. Initially Roy, one of his brothers, and his parents came to attend his older brother's wedding in New York City in 1989—two of his brothers were already living in New York at the time. Shortly after the wedding, the airport in Beirut was shut down and shooting intensified in various areas in Lebanon; the family realized that they could not go back to Lebanon. The family's illegal status made their situation worse, as they could not find stable jobs or feel secure about their position in the United States. Eventually the entire family decided to migrate to Canada as war refugees, and the process was a success. Roy's first reaction to the new setting was that it affirmed his Arab and Lebanese identity. He described how, during the first few years after leaving Lebanon, he responded to the rejection he encountered with the need to affirm his ethnic identity:

> It's a normal reaction I think, when you are in a strange country, and you feel alienated from the society at large, the normal reaction is to get back to your identity as the past beckons. In Lebanon, I never cared that I was Lebanese. The idea didn't mean anything to me. I didn't care I was an Arab. It didn't mean anything as well. It's only in the time I came to the United States and to Canada, when people started describing me as such, in a pejorative manner. As a reaction, there was a period when I was very involved in affirming my identity. I am not like that anymore. I think the whole idea [of identity], the whole notion is silly.

Roy's experiences of prejudice and discrimination also prompted him to distance himself from the host society, both the United States and Canada, as he had experienced derogatory comments in both places:

> There are two instances that stuck in my mind. During the [first] Iraq war, I was working out at a gym. I left one of the weights lying about. And the attendant came and asked me to remove the weights. Then, he turned his back and said, "Those fucking Arabs." So I went to the reception, wrote a complaint, voided my membership, and got my money back. In Canada, after September 11, I was walking in the mall, about two hours after the planes struck. And some guy who was walking by looked at me, and started screaming at me: "Bastards, these bastards are gonna win." I didn't beat the crap out of him, which I could have done easily. I let it go. But it struck me. You feel accused in certain instances, accused without doing anything, accused in a transcendental manner; your state of being is one of being accused.

Both incidents that Roy experienced are gendered. In Roy's view, the gym is a masculine space and the attendant's comment was meant to assault not only his ethnic origins but his masculinity as well. And although the mall is gender-neutral, his attacker identified him as Arab because of his gender. Roy asserts that unless an Arab woman is veiled, and is thus marked as Muslim, she is less likely to be identified as Arab. For men, however, given the constant media portrayal of Arab/Muslim male terrorists, men with dark hair and an olive complexion are more frequently targeted as well as feared.

One's religion also was an important axis for marking one's difference and one's perceptions of discrimination. Notably the perception of religious-based discrimination was not specific to Muslims, who belong to the religious minority in their host societies. Lebanese Christians were aware that since Western media conflates Arab/Middle Eastern/Muslim categories, they were also implicated with the same fortune that falls on their Muslim co-ethnics. For example, Antoine attributes his hardships and his inability to find a job either in New York or Paris to covert discrimination. In New York, as noted earlier, he was expecting an offer from a law firm when, just a few days after the events of 9/11, he received a rejection letter from the firm. He noted that, although his name is "very French," his resume showed that he had earned his bachelor's degree in Lebanon, which defines him as Lebanese. According to Antoine, Americans hardly knew that any Lebanese Christians existed, which engendered their assumption that all Arabs are guilty of the terrorist attacks on 9/11. Because of these negative experiences, Antoine soon left the United States. Antoine had already started working for an international law firm in Paris at the time of our interview. In fact, it was his office experience that influenced his ideas about discrimination in the French job market. Antoine related one specific incident:

> They didn't say it directly to me, but I heard some human resource people saying: "Yeah, this candidate is very qualified. But, in his profile there was one mistake: he was born on the wrong side of the Mediterranean." They were talking about an Algerian guy. But if they say that about Algerians, why wouldn't they say that about me? Even Belgians would have a handicap in the [French] job market.

Although the discrimination Antoine perceived was related to his ethnicity, such discrimination is often conflated with religion. Antoine had a strong Christian identity, and even though he was not a practicing Christian, he believed that, given his religion, he would have had an affinity with mainstream society in any of the three countries he lived in during the last few years. Antoine recognized, however, that, given his Middle Eastern origin, he would never be fully accepted in Western culture:

> I enter wrongly in the logic way of thinking of Western countries. Because they think that all this area [the Middle East] is one religion, which is not true. I enter wrongly in their logic and I feel frustrated because of my difference.

Antoine's identification process did not contest prevailing attitudes toward Arabs and Muslims. The discrimination he experienced in the American labor market following 9/11, in fact, led him to indirectly blame Muslims for the unfairness. In Antoine's view, the world needs to be educated about the existence of Christians in the Middle East in order to lift the responsibility of terrorism off their shoulders. Indeed, he held Muslims responsible for these attacks and the intolerance that followed. Thus Antoine himself reiterated the same discourse of exclusion when it came to Muslims and Arabs, and only questioned his own inclusion in the subordinated group instead of contesting the process of exclusion itself.

Problematic Relationship with the Homeland

Various experiences with prejudice and discrimination were referred to as marking my respondents' distance from both their host society and their homeland. Although the literature on diaspora relates negative experiences in the host society to the strengthening of diasporic consciousness (see Vertovec and Cohen 1999), this group of immigrants equally related negative experiences in Lebanon as central to their identification. The discrimination these immigrants witnessed, as well as the general prejudice against Middle Easterners, translated into their feeling of not belonging to Western society. At the same time they also felt estranged from the Arab/Middle Eastern/Lebanese culture. These immigrants constructed their difference from Lebanese society through specific mechanisms. Distance from Lebanon was established within the first few years of immigration, as many respondents did not return to visit Lebanon for a long time after leaving home. They often attributed their lack of desire to go back to Lebanon to cultural differences. For example, Carl, who is a Maronite Christian, said that he did not have a sense of belonging to the Middle East or the Arab world since he was not Muslim, and that Islam is a central force in constructing such identities:

> It's kind of a controversial situation for me because I belong to that part of the world which is discriminated against, and I don't belong to it at the same time because of my religion, because unfortunately, today, the Middle East is associated with one religion. Since I don't belong to this religion, then I don't feel part of it. I feel excluded . . . Yes, my sense of exclusion takes a religious aspect. And that's why I say that I don't belong to the Arab world because now that world has assimilated to one religion, and I'm not part of this religion. Sometimes I feel frustrated as people here try to assimilate me into this religion.

Whereas Carl cited religion to explain why he felt distant from Arabs, Khaled pointed to general cultural differences to account for that feeling of not belonging to Lebanese society at large. Specifically he viewed Lebanese people who never left Lebanon as apathetic and provincial:

> I feel that the difference is growing more and more. When I'm in contact with people who stayed in Lebanon, I feel that we don't have the same way of thinking. We don't have the same interests. We don't have the same way of life, and we don't have the same perception of things. I give more value to some things while they don't. I find them extremely lazy, not dynamic. And I realize it's related to what I know, because I have had the experience of another way of living, I realize their perception, but I don't share it anymore.

Asserting their growing cultural distance from Lebanon, both Khaled and Carl also maintain that they are not likely to belong wherever they go. In Carl's case, a move from New York to Paris brought him closer to Lebanon (geographically and culturally), closer to his family and friends, as well as to the Mediterranean in general. Still, he stated that with this move his perception of the distance is greater than ever, as he is more aware of the transitory position he occupies wherever he lives. Although Carl's transitory position was at the intersection of different cultures (Arab, Muslim, Lebanese, French, Catholic, and American), at the same time it did not allow him to belong to any one of these cultures. The perceived lack of belonging to either the host society or the homeland led many of the immigrants with whom I spoke to avoid choosing one society to settle in permanently, reflecting their desire to maintain multiple influences on their identities and daily experiences.

The Lebanese civil war impacted the lives of all the first-generation immigrants I interviewed in various ways and was often related to their sense of not belonging to Lebanese society. Some respondents left soon after the war started, others left during the last few years when the fighting escalated and it seemed that the war would never end, and still others left after the war had ended when the hope of reconstruction started to fade. Sherif, the environmental engineer in Montreal introduced earlier, left after the war ended, but his frustrations with postwar Lebanon were not economic, as his education enabled him to find the kind of job he wanted in Beirut. Rather, Sherif left because he was unhappy with Lebanese society in general. As he described it:

> I reject the idea of belonging to the Lebanese society because of the war that happened, and I blame them [the Lebanese] for that. I blame them

because I was too young; I did not have a stake in the war, so I cannot blame myself for that. In the big picture I blame the Lebanese for the war that happened, for me not having a normal childhood, and for all the misery that fell on so many families . . . So, I left Lebanon. I did not think I really belonged there. I mean, I get along with my friends that are Lebanese very well. But I don't really belong there.

Because Sherif was born in 1974, a year before the war started, his early memories of Lebanon are mostly of bombs and shelters and so, understandably, he would want to distance himself from the fears and anxieties he experienced. His emigration from Lebanon was a move away from harsh memories and a lost childhood. More recent conflicts in Lebanon led Sherif and many others to distance themselves even more from Lebanese society, as they believe that sectarian strife, political power struggles, and social divisions are likely to cause the further disintegration of Lebanese society.[19]

For most respondents who narrated their difference from Lebanese people and culture, a cosmopolitan identification took its place and became the basis for their feelings of not belonging. Although these respondents agreed that Beirut is a cosmopolitan city not unlike Paris and London in terms of its culture and quality of life, they still believed that a parochial mentality governed political and social lives in Lebanon, a view they share with other immigrants. It was this parochialism that informed these immigrants distancing themselves from Lebanese society, especially for the short term. Their sense of difference from other Lebanese was not only a result of their rejection of Lebanon but also derived from the fact that people in Lebanon labeled them as "foreign." For example, Abeer described how people in Lebanon remarked on her foreign accent, which was compounded in her case since, you will recall, people in the United States made similar comments. Abeer's ambiguous state of not belonging to either society was evident when she recounted her first and only visit to Lebanon:

> People thought that I'm very Americanized in my gestures, my values, the way I dress, the way I behaved myself and the way I started speaking. For them, I speak Arabic with an accent, which I cannot see but they see it, so I don't know why. But for them, I'm like their American friend. When I'm here, they know I'm a foreigner, and when I go there, they know I'm a foreigner. So that's a very silly state.

The "silly" state Abeer described might be considered transitory, given her decision to remain permanently in the United States. However, Abeer asserted that not belonging to Lebanese society would never translate into her belonging to American society. Instead, she turned her attention to social issues that were of more concern to her. Instead of worrying about identity issues, for example, she became involved with the issue of homophobia in Arab and American societies, and sought relationships with young gays and lesbians in an effort to help them construct positive understandings of their sexuality in either society.

Creative Appropriation

It is clear now that Lebanese immigrants, and especially those who lived in a number of societies, had multiple identities and markers of difference in the places where they lived. Thus this group of immigrants were able to carve out a unique position in the world that contested traditional forms of identification. Unlike those who provided ethnic narratives that reflected a coherent understanding of their social positions, those who described transcultural identities emphasized their uniqueness as an important aspect of their identification. Instead of rejecting identification with the host society or emphasizing their differences within it, these individuals sought commonalities with the different groups of people with which they interacted. Khaled describes, for example, his move to New York City, where he felt more at home after advancing to a Ph.D. candidacy in a small town in upstate New York:

> I am more comfortable with myself now. And I am less interested in rejecting or accepting American culture, I am beyond that point right now. I think slowly now. I found some sort of balance between living in America and being from Lebanon. I bring the two together.

At one level, Khaled accepted that he belonged to American society: his partner of five years is Anglo-American; he identified with the white majority; he finished two master's degrees and was in the process of completing a Ph.D. at an Ivy League university; and he had a teaching position at a high-ranking university in New York City. Because his acceptance of and by American society was facilitated by his class background, social status, and skin color, Khaled challenged the description of his experience as assimilation or Americanization, recognizing that, in fact, he did not share any commonalities with most Americans. In response to my question as to whether he felt more integrated in American society because his partner was American, he responded:

No, to the contrary. There is always a lot of explaining to do. Generally speaking, there are a lot of cultural neuroses and specificities that people just don't get. And I got that when I first came to the United States. I was ostracized, I always felt like a complete alien. I didn't know how to read people. So I would be acting in a certain way, expecting a certain reaction, but I would get the opposite reaction. I've had that happen several times with Americans, my partner included. All of a sudden he would snap, and I wouldn't understand what did I say wrong, why did I provoke him in that way.

When Khaled tried to integrate himself into a gay community in New York (by going to gay clubs and participating in gay community organizations), he realized that he also did not identify with the American gay subculture. He complained that he was commonly perceived as an "exotic other" by many gay men he met at the clubs or community organizations he attended. Given Khaled's olive complexion, green eyes, and foreign accent, the men he encountered ignored his knowledge of American and Arab cultures (and also his knowledge of French culture, as he had had a French education before leaving Lebanon), and saw him merely as an "ethnic" individual in the United States. In Khaled's view, the gay community in New York City, and the mainstream society in general, was parochial and lacked any understanding of a complex identity. Accordingly, most of Khaled's friends are French speakers in New York; he has more in common with people who are interested in World literature (his research topic); and his interests are based more on his class background than his ethnicity. In his words: "The problem is not so much cultural differences, . . . not the fact that I'm Lebanese and someone else is American. There are also intellectual differences, class differences, all these things matter."

While refusing to accept that he had been "Americanized," Khaled also did not want to be defined as "Other" within American society. Unlike Sherif, for whom the category of "Other" was a comfortable identity in Montreal, being "Other," for Khaled, implied identifying with something that is opposite to "America" or the "West." This he saw as fictitious, since both East and West had always been intertwined historically and culturally. Given his Western-style education (both in Lebanon and the United States), Khaled knew that his identity as an Arab and a Lebanese was mixed with a Western cultural tradition: "Even my understanding of Arabic culture and my position within it goes through certain European texts and frameworks."

All the immigrants who expressed their transcultural identification contest their given identities and cultures. Some in this group maintain that they are distant even from the forms of identity that they may adopt. A common feature in these narratives is the immigrants' awareness of their precarious position, owing, perhaps, to their disadvantaged class or nationality as in Carl's case discussed earlier. Others who came from a privileged background described, instead, a process of creative appropriation. Recall that Khaled's proficiency in Arabic, French, and English enabled him to mix the three languages together, even in a single sentence, as a way of demonstrating his familiarity with several cultures and histories. He explained:

> One of the things I never made an effort to change is my accent in English, and I know a lot of people who made the effort. And I know I could have done so easily. Instead, when I speak, I throw in a lot of Arabic words in English [sentences] and I force my friends to ask me what they mean. I do so to create a familiar kind of spoken environment. So all of my friends here, they know at least thirty or forty Arabic words, like *khalas, taiyyeb, yalla, ma'lesh.*[20] I think it's important for me to . . . feel that I am not just taking the language that is foreign, just abiding by certain rules of communication.

This unwillingness to abide by given rules, whether in communicating or in other interactions, was a popular strategy among those respondents who wanted to differentiate their identities in various settings. Instead of emphasizing his difference to detach himself form his social environment, Khaled made a point of creating connections that brought him closer to his surroundings. For example, while a general sense of dissatisfaction and detachment led Khaled to move to the United States, living away from Lebanon caused him to appreciate various aspects about his homeland that he admitted to having overlooked in the past. Similarly, after initially rejecting an identification as an American, Khaled had come to find a comfortable space that he could accept. Explaining that being a product of multiple cultures did not mean that one has to accept them, and that sometimes it might result in recognizing one's detachment, Khaled illustrated his view on negotiating a form of belonging: "But there is one set of social rules in every culture at least one . . . where I see that I fit there or here. I constantly have to go back and forth."

Appropriating particular aspects of each culture to define his own position, Khaled also explained that the process of forging an identity was not momentary and meaningless but rather a deliberate process that involves self-reflection. Identifying with any culture, in his view, is a process that takes place regularly. Although immigrants may initially assume a lack of belonging to their host society, most Lebanese immigrants find that accepting certain aspects of a culture, rejecting others, and having mixed feelings about most is a playful exercise that makes the experience of globalization and immigration more enriching and cosmopolitan.

Describing diaspora as a phenomenon that both enlarges and does away with a dual identity (e.g., Arab Jew, African American, or French Maghrebi), Lavie and Swedenburg (1996) contend that diasporic existence is not simply one of migrating between two opposing poles depending on varying contexts and sociopolitical interests. Jonathan Friedman (1995:78) has analyzed the effect of globalization on identities, maintaining that globalization may entail a transcultural process of identification, one that is a product of mixed or supranational forces "that is not in between but above . . . [that is] betwixt and between without being liminal. It is shifting, participating in many worlds without becoming part of them." Transculturalism is differentiated from multiculturalism by means of emphasizing a process of mixing different cultures and breaking the boundaries between them instead of reinforcing these boundaries to maintain the distinct features of a group or culture within a larger society.[21] All transcultural articulations of identity among the Lebanese immigrants I interviewed shared the construction of multiple, negotiated, and contradictory identities. Like Abeer, Khaled, Carl, and Sherif, many Lebanese immigrants emphasized multiple influences on their identification process, but their narratives stressed the creative ways in which these multiple and sometimes contradictory sources are mixed and contested to form their unique position in the world.

Cosmopolitan Identification

Although the unique process of mixing identities may enrich the lives of those respondents who had this experience, these individuals do not have the sense of coherence enjoyed by those who narrated unitary ethnic identities. Mixing different identities and lifestyles in his daily experience, Fareed acknowledges the ambivalence associated with forging an incomplete sense of belonging. During our conversation in the summer of 2001, he described his experience living in Tennessee and the District of Columbia before moving to New York City. Living in three cities after leaving Beirut, Fareed recognized that he did not completely fit in with any of the three settings. And yet this ambivalence about his social position motivated him to seek coherence in his experience through social involvement and community organizations. For Fareed, identity meant a collection of experiences that all left a mark in his life, and he cited the many labels that he wore: "American," "New Yorker," "white," "Arab," "Muslim," "atheist," "Lebanese," "gay," "immigrant," and "professional." At the same time he spoke of the need to move beyond unitary identities as defining one's experience and instead to draw on multiple connections to bring about desirable social changes:

> It is so confusing, but I'm not totally that concerned about that. I think that your humanity has to precede all of these labels. I mean, if anything, I really use those labels just as tools to push the right buttons. But I'm not really that hung up on it. I think that growing up in the world today, with borders falling left and right, because of technology and communication, the whole concept of labels and nationalism is becoming rather tired; unless you want to use it for your political motive, you know what I mean?

Fareed's notion of the declining importance of national identification as a result of global processes highlights his understanding of identities as transitory and strategic. Although he acknowledges that some of the multiple identities he uses are contradictory, his ability to use them strategically and creatively is more important to him than the false sense of coherence that immigrants traditionally seek.

Many other Lebanese immigrants agree with Fareed that more essential than seeking coherence is to use their unique position in the world as a way to effect social changes in the various societies they associate with. Nagi, a forty-two-year-old admissions officer at a Canadian university when we met in Montreal, provides a good example. Because he had lived in a number of countries throughout his life, he decided to utilize his experiences to benefit those around him. Expectedly, Nagi's desire to challenge the societies he belongs to did not lead to his acceptance in these societies, but he understood that he could not seek the acceptance of all those with whom he interacts. When we spoke over lunch at a famous Lebanese restaurant in downtown Montreal, I saw that Nagi was clearly well connected in the Lebanese community, as he greeted more than half the customers during the busy lunch hour. He later explained, however, that although he was popular in the Lebanese community in Montreal, he was not fully accepted because of the challenges he had brought to discussions regarding the nature of the Lebanese Canadian identity. In addition to the political differences that ensued as a result of his lack of acceptance in Montreal's Lebanese community, that he is not religious also added to the distance between him and others in Lebanon:

> They don't understand that. They'd tell you, *yalla nerouh a'kanisah* [let's go to church] and you say, no, I'm tired. They'll say, you're no longer tired, sleep, in an hour we can go to church. Then you tell them, I don't want to go to church. And when they don't get that message, you have to say, I don't like the priest, I don't like the people who go to church, and I am just not going. Then they get shocked. Maybe this would get them to understand that not everybody has to be religious.

Nagi's example shows that he was not interested in passively appropriating the different cultures he shared but instead wanted to challenge them. The separation of church and state had been an important ideal that he learned in Canada, and so he tried to make people in Lebanon aware of the consequences of having a strongly religious society and a system of government based on religions sectarianism. He also used examples from Lebanese history that, in his opinion, would contribute to improving Canadian society. For example, a major issue in Canadian society that he sees as problematic is that of race, residential segregation, and religion; in his view Canadian society needs greater awareness about these issues to avoid the conflicts that occurred in Lebanon. He believed that his involvement with these problems made him "a good citizen," as he encouraged people to seek more knowledge so as to improve the situation. Because he worked for a university, Nagi was also able to participate in educational activities with students.

Migrating between different cultures, Nagi explained his un-rooted reality by distinguishing between "immigrant" and "settler." He understood his position in his host country as an *immigrant* who had no desire to *settle* in a new society, given that his origins were elsewhere and that his future outlook focused neither on Canada nor Lebanon. With no intention of returning to Lebanon, remaining in Canada, or moving elsewhere, but rather moving between societies, Nagi saw the immigrant condition as diasporic by definition. For him, his diasporic experience did not revive a feeling of ethnicity or nationalism; instead, he believed that his experience with migration exposed him to different worldviews that allowed him to place particular local events, in Beirut, Montreal, Paris, or Johannesburg, within a global context. Like Nagi, Sherif contended that experiencing migration can only lead to questioning belonging altogether. After pointing out that being Lebanese was not the strongest aspect of his identification, he added:

> I'm not saying I belong more here, but I don't think I belong anywhere. This is a problem for immigrants. They will never belong 100 percent in their new country. For example, when I meet people here, it's always funny to meet people in Montreal and they identify themselves as Irish and Italian and then, from the conversation, I find out that they are second- or third-generation Canadian. And this is really puzzling for me. I often wonder: at which point does one start identifying oneself as Canadian?

According to both Nagi and Sherif, one does not have to identify as Canadian to contribute to society and culture. Whereas Nagi's experience with migration allowed him to place local events in a larger global context which enabled him to apply knowledge gained from one society to another, Sherif's professional background allowed him to benefit his social setting and the whole world more generally. Their interest in mixing global experiences and knowledge provides them with an important sense of coherence despite their ambivalent identification, as I discuss in the next chapter.

Conclusion

In his analysis of ethnic group identity, Fredrick Barth (1969) elaborates upon the "contextual" nature of ethnicity whereby ethnic identity can take different forms depending on which culturally shared items are utilized by individuals in their quest for meaningful self-definitions. Ethnic identity, then, becomes a flexible structure that can be modified depending on the context in which actors socially interact. With the understanding that globalization provides a framework for multiple narratives of identification, this chapter explored the varied and sometimes contradictory outcomes of experiences of migration and displacement. The different forms of identification offered by Lebanese immigrants in Montreal, New York, and Paris illustrate the ways that some identities may be expressed in terms of ethnic retention whereas others are transitory and ambivalent, demonstrating that diasporas, as Werbner (1999:6) asserts, "are both ethnic-parochial *and* cosmopolitan."

The socioeconomic status of Lebanese immigrants gives them various choices: assimilation, repatriation, or upholding a transnational community. Linguistic adaptability and proficiency in English and French, high educational levels, and family background contribute to Lebanese immigrants' sense of agency in making these choices. The variety of identity narratives, however, is based on the particular contexts of immigration as well as on individual attributes. For example, age at migration and length of stay in host societies are important indicators of the narrative that immigrants may choose to construct, whereby younger respondents and those who left Lebanon at a young age were more interested in mixing different cultural repertoires to construct their identities instead of focusing on one form of identification. Experiences with diverse groups and lifestyles, whether in the homeland or in host societies, also affects the ways in which immigrants shape their identities. Because many respondents grew up in a multicultural environment in Lebanon, their understanding of their identities as formed at the intersection of different cultures was often given as their reason for migrating and not necessarily a product of it. Similarly, the possibility of returning to Lebanon and direct experiences with discrimination shapes immigrants' sense of exclusion and, in turn, the kinds of identities they construct.

Among those who described their identities in ethnic terms, differences between immigrants in Montreal and in Paris can be identified. In Montreal, expressions of ethnicity take place within a context where Lebanese comprise the largest group of Arab immigrants, and thus the question of an Arab identity is not addressed. In a context where the Lebanese are not the largest group of Arab immigrants, such as in Paris, public opinion and prejudice toward North Africans who are defined as Arabs lead some immigrants to reject an Arab identity in order to successfully meet their goal of mobilization and raise awareness of Lebanese issues. In New York, although the Lebanese still form the largest group of Arab immigrants, ethnic expressions of identity only took forms alongside other forms of identification. Similarly, ethnic identities were expressed differently based on gender and class differences. Men and women defined their ethnic attributes differently in Montreal versus Paris. None of the women in Paris identified ethnically. Gender differences, however, were revealed in all the narratives provided, as women generally seemed less interested in returning to Lebanon than the men did, and thus expressed various degrees of accepting their belonging to their host societies. As diasporas are heterogeneous social formations (Werbner 2000), highlighting the ways the Lebanese diaspora is internally divided, along religious, class, and gender lines, is an important task. A common feature, however, is the ideology of return that shaped the diasporic longings of ethnic narratives.

Ethnic identification notwithstanding, members of the Lebanese diaspora also construct identity narratives that accentuate multiple cultural repertoires gained by unique experiences in more than one society. In "The Question of Cultural Identity," Stuart Hall (1990) formulates a notion of diaspora identities that moves beyond ethnic forms of identification. "Diaspora identities are those which are constantly producing and reproducing themselves anew, through transformation and difference," writes Hall. The different experiences that individual immigrants go through affect their understandings of their position in the world. These differences produce multiple narratives of identity that are sometimes contradictory and intersectional. These identity narratives explicate and demonstrate the making of global identities, the chief characteristic of diasporic immigration.

The multiple sources of identification observed in the three settings addressed in the book meant various expressions of identity. In Paris, Lebanese immigrants emphasized the similarities between French and Lebanese society, and thus affirmed that a transcultural identity that mixes the two sources is almost inevitable. The multicultural setting that Montreal and New York provide was also conducive to mixing American or Canadian and Lebanese identities. Both cities are seen as worldly, which allows immigrants to integrate multiple communities in their daily experiences. Compared to immigrants with ethnic narratives, transcultural immigrants did not seek a coherent experience and the question of return was not as central. Almost all the immigrants in this latter group were aware of their lack of belonging to the many societies they crossed, or at least to Lebanon and their host societies. Experiences of exclusion or prejudice sharpened, if not ossified, this lack of belonging. Instead of searching for total belonging to any society, immigrants in this group accepted their partial identification with their various societies as well as their sense of fragmentation. Referring to this ambiguous existence for contemporary migrants, Edward Said (1990:359) recounts that:

And just beyond the frontier between "us" and the "outsiders" is the perilous territory of not-belonging: this is to where in a primitive time peoples were banished, and where in the modern era immense aggregates of humanity loiter as refugees and displaced persons.

Among the Lebanese immigrants interviewed for this book, seventy found themselves in the territory that Said describes as "not-belonging." The narratives these immigrants provided, however, demonstrate that a sense of displacement from the homeland and host societies does not translate into a feeling of banishment that is as perilous as Said contends. Rather, as a territory of choice, not-belonging is taken as a marker of difference that is comfortable for many of these individuals. Although some may cling to a desire to settle on firmer grounds, these immigrants do not seek the illusory comforts of traditional forms of identification. Instead, they realize that their ambiguous status is an enriching process that they seek and appreciate. In place of a "thin" sense of cosmopolitanism that escapes a grounding in communal forms of belonging (see Calhoun 2002), the experiences of Lebanese immigrants in this group are better understood through their sense of commitment to specific issues and the emphasis they place on their duties toward social change, which I discuss in detail in the next chapter.

Unified ethnic identities and transcultural ones can somewhat be explained when investigating transcultural practices and sentiments that are shared by many contemporary immigrants. Transnationalism would allow for an understanding of the ethnic boundaries that are set up and maintained by those who constructed ethnic narratives of identity as their outlook; social, political, and economic practices maintain an immigrant's strong interest in the homeland. Similarly, transnationalism could capture the basic mixing of two cultures that inform the transcultural identities that most of the respondents described. Important aspects of immigrant identities, however, such as ambivalence, lack of coherent belonging, and creative appropriation of different cultures, are not adequately captured when one only looks at transnational practices. Diaspora, on the one hand, given its focus on fragmentation, lack of permanent settlement and worldly outlook, provides an understanding of immigrant identities that is otherwise incomplete. As most of my respondents suggested, diaspora consciousness is an aspect of being an immigrant, regardless of their transnational involvement, ethnic retention, or integration in the host society.

In *The Other Heading*, Jacques Derrida (1992:72–73) poses the question, "Is 'cultural identity' a good word for 'today'"? and answers in the negative:

> Whether it takes a national form or not, a refined, hospitable or aggressively xenophobic form or not, the self-affirmation of an identity always claims to be responding to the call or assignation of the universal. There are no exceptions to this law. No cultural identity presents itself as the opaque body of an untranslatable idiom, but always, on the contrary, as the irreplaceable *inscription* of the universal in the singular.

In this chapter I illustrated forms of identity narratives that resonate with Derrida's conception of cultural identities. Although the ways in which Lebanese immigrants make sense of their experiences varied within the three contexts examined here, all the different narratives are shaped by global positions and understandings of these realities. Contending that negotiations and ambivalence about their position in the various societies they belong to is the overarching narrative that most of the respondents share, diasporic consciousness is taken to be one of constant critique of cultural norms and social traditions as well as the creation of multiple forms of attachments and spheres of engagement.

The Power of Community

Beyond Homeland and Host Society

> On an empowered day, I describe myself as a diaspora(s) daughter
> with multiple migratory and ancestral reference points in Nigeria,
> Ireland, England, Guyana, and the United States. On a disempow-
> ered day, I am a nationless nomad who wanders from destination
> to destination in search of a singular site to name as home.
> —Jayne Ifekwunigwe, "The Critical Feminist
> Auto-Ethnographer"

Investigating Community in a Global Era

Like many of my respondents, I learned the meaning of being Arab in the
United States. Growing up in Egypt, I studied Arab nationalism and the
construction of a pan-ethnic Arab identity that was based on shared historical struggles and political interests. Aside from official narratives of coherent Arab ethnicity told in our history books, the decades of the 1970s and
1980s were fraught with fragmentation and conflict among Arab nations,
and most people around me did not see themselves as Arabs.[1] Arriving in
the United States, however, I sought out other Arabs, as this seemed a logical
approach to forging friendships and communal belonging despite my lack
of socialization into an Arab identity. One event, in particular, provided a
significant introduction to the Arab American community. In October 1999
I attended the Association of Arab American University Graduates conference that took place in White Plains, New York. The conference focused on
educating the attendees on issues related to the politics of the Arab world
and Arab American political relations. Prominent specialists on the Arab
world were invited to speak, and the events proved to be very informative.
In my experience the conference was more significant as I came in contact with many Arabs in the United States—either first-generation immigrants like myself or others who had been born in the United States and are
more accurately described as Arab Americans. The discussions I had with

these individuals on the meaning of being Arab in the United States and the ways to bring together two cultures to forge unique positions in a new social environment provided meaningful anchors for Arab American identification. For me, as someone who did not readily identify as either Arab or American, however, the discussions on Arab American identity, culture, and community were notable as manifestations of the ways in which communal identities and boundaries were being constructed and challenged before my eyes. As the conference participants debated issues specific to their own experiences with the communities where they lived, issues such as gender inequalities, nationalism, religious intolerance, and homophobia, they also contested the coherence of an Arab American community as an entity with shared beliefs and values. Yet they all shared an interest in maintaining a stable level of awareness of their membership in that community. Studying the ways members of the community contest established norms and beliefs about Arab culture and identity while at the same time retaining their identification with that community emerged as an important aspect in understanding the dynamics of diasporic community attachments.

As I was designing my research project, I chose to study the Lebanese first-generation immigrants, as it seemed easy to identify those who were born and raised in Lebanon before they decided to migrate elsewhere. Choosing a national identity promised to offer an easy way to identify the members of the community—as opposed to choosing a larger ethnic category such as Arabs which is more often challenged than accepted. As illustrated in the previous chapter, however, the meaning of being Lebanese varied by the context of immigration as well as the individuals' economic and religious backgrounds. There were also age and gender differences. As with other forms of identity, the meaning of being Lebanese is regularly constructed and contested. Delving into community attachments also poses the challenge of defining the community itself.

During my fieldwork I asked some of my interviewees about their perceptions of the Lebanese community in the city where they live. Each answer described a social group that exists "out there" but to which my respondents did not belong. They had various reasons for their lack of participation in the communities and provided numerous critiques of the community's members and activities. To most interviewees, the Lebanese community was to be found in specific churches or mosques and in a few organizations that focused on Lebanese or Arab social and political issues. Again, most of my respondents emphasized that they do not really belong to these organizations, which can be assumed as the full assimilation of these individuals to their host societies. To a large extent, my respondents have assimilated to their host societies by numerous indicators (professional status, high level of education, language proficiency, and in some cases intermarriage). Yet, given the narratives of identification that they constructed (and discussed in the previous chapter), my respondents have made no indication of their full assimilation to a mainstream society nor did they unconditionally identify with their host societies. Even when my interviewees attended Lebanese churches and participated in Lebanese organizations, they still hesitated to present themselves as members of a Lebanese community. A few explained that, as part of the essential character of Lebanese people, they are likely to adapt to a given environment and underplay their cultural difference.

Instead of accepting their initial hesitation toward belonging to an ethnic community or their essential notions of their innate identity, I decided to seek alternative analyses and look deeper into Lebanese immigrant communities and social networks. As a result, I approached the study of the Lebanese diasporic community at two levels. First, I examined the social, economic, political, and cultural institutions in which immigrants participate. Second, I looked into the structure of meaning that the individuals give to their immigrant communities. In other words, I used the stories my respondents shared about their participation in the various institutions to get to the meanings they associate with such forms of participation and the images of communities that they construct. In this chapter I present the various images that my respondents provided to conceptualize a community. In doing so I draw on the three identity-narratives illustrated in the previous chapter to investigate the kinds of communities in which members of the Lebanese diaspora participate. I also argue that the identification processes that Lebanese immigrants employ are shaped by their engagement with specific communities including their homeland, host societies, the diaspora, and the world at large. That my respondents participated in multiple communities and saw their identities and social positions as framed by their ability to navigate multiple social and cultural spheres were the reasons for their denial of belonging to a Lebanese community in their cities when I presented them with such question. As a result, in the process of conducting interviews, I learned that Lebanese immigrants would refuse to acknowledge any participation in any single social sphere, for they saw themselves as constantly crossing societies and social boundaries.

Social anthropologist Fredrik Barth conceives of ethnic groups as "categories of ascription and identification by the actors themselves" (1969:10). Such an active process of constructing ethnic group membership takes place within the socioeconomic context in which the actors are enmeshed. According to Barth, members of ethnic groups selectively draw certain defining character-istics from a pool of commonly shared symbolic resources. Once these char-acteristics are "socially activated," they become available symbolic material for the group's identity construction process. Thus, as Barth explains: "Socially relevant factors alone become diagnostic for membership, not the overt objec-tive differences (ibid.:5)." In the contemporary world, globalization provides a socioeconomic context in which immigrants' ethnic groups and identities can be understood. At the same time global processes inform the symbolic resources available for immigrants' definition of their identities and commu-nities. In this chapter I illustrate the ways in which Lebanese immigrants in Montreal, New York, and Paris construct their memberships in various groups by defining specific "socially relevant factors" that shape the forms of social solidarity they maintain. As globalization processes complicate the building of ethnic communities, Lebanese immigrants engage in transnational communi-ties that encompass both Lebanon and their host societies, as well as a Leba-nese diasporic community. More important, in a globalized world, Lebanese immigrants favor social relationships that are based on shared lifestyles and dispositions instead of traditional attachments that are based on ethnicity and nationality. Stressing that subjective choices inform the ways that individu-als define their group membership, I demonstrate that Lebanese immigrants choose to draw on their global experiences to define their position in the vari-ous communities to which they belong. The relationships that Lebanese immi-grants form construct global communities that are "consciously and continu-ously reinvented" (Kennedy and Roudometof 2002). While the material goals that members share continue to be important in the invention of a commu-nity, globalization processes accentuate cultural and informational concerns to become more likely bases for community ties (ibid.).

Invoking Barth's argument on ethnic boundaries and their maintenance, John Armstrong (1976:394) stresses that "the mobilized diaspora . . . has often constituted for centuries a separate society or quasi-society in a larger polity." The assumption of a separate society has been upheld in many analyses of diaspora communities (see, e.g., Safran 1991; and Tölölyan 1996). Yet Roger Brubaker (2005) points to the tension in the literature on the importance of boundary maintenance in analyzing diasporic communities. He reminds us of Stuart Hall's popular statement that "diaspora experience . . . is defined, not by essence or purity, but by the recognition of a necessary heterogene-ity and diversity; by a conception of 'identity' which lives with and through, not despite, difference; by *hybridity*" (1990:235). In this chapter the narratives of Lebanese immigrants illustrate such experiences that live "with and through" an awareness of difference. And yet these differences provide a way in which belonging is negotiated in the various communities. Believing that immigration extends the diversity of discourses and communities within which individuals position themselves, this chapter focuses on the different ways that immigrants forge their belonging to the various communities they choose. Specifically I address immigrants' continual interest in the homeland and the tensions involved in their transnational belonging. David Hollinger (1995:2–3) proposes the term "postethnic" to understand communal attachment that "favors voluntary over involuntary affiliations, balances an appreciation for communities of descent with a determination to make room for new communities, and promotes solidarities of wide scope that incorporate people with different ethnic and racial backgrounds." In light of Hollinger's argument, my analysis addresses the ways in which immigrants engage in "postethnic" communities that transcend traditional ethnic attachments to forge new ties shaped by their transcultural and cosmopolitan identities. The "postethnic" framework allows me to illustrate the contextualized and globalized affiliations that Lebanese immigrants have in the three cities examined here, and I discuss this in the second half of the chapter. First, in the next section, I address the transnational ties that Lebanese immigrants construct to maintain their involvement in the homeland as well as their participation in their host societies. Such transnational attachments cannot be understood simply in terms of "divided loyalties" that are shaped by fragmented identities. Instead, immigrants' involvement in multiple societies is shaped by their understanding of their identities as a product of multiple cultures that are mixed in such a way as to produce a unique position in the world and a unique engagement with social issues. To illustrate this argument, first I sketch out the way Lebanese immigrants maintain their relationship with their homeland and host societies, and then illustrate the forms of transnational involvement they employ.

Between Homeland and Host Society

> The exile knows that in a secular and contingent world, home is always provisional. Borders and barriers, which enclose us within the safety of familiar territory, can also become prisons, and are often defended beyond reason or necessity. Exiles cross borders, break barriers of thought and experience.
>
> —Said 1990:365

In order to understand the Lebanese diasporic community, I asked my respondents about their social relationships, political orientations, as well as social and economic practices. The kinds of social relationships diaspora signifies are created by experiences of migration and maintained by collective memory, communal consciousness, and a desire to return to the homeland (see, e.g., Safran 1991; Sheffer 1997; Van Hear 1998; and Vertovec and Cohen 1999). In the case of Lebanese immigrants, regular interest in the homeland is preserved through elaborate networks that permit and encourage exchanges of money, political support, and cultural influence among the host society, the homeland, and other segments of the larger diaspora (i.e., members of the diaspora community in other countries around the world). Frequent visits to Lebanon strengthen connections to the homeland and steady communication with Lebanese friends and family members, whether in Lebanon or elsewhere, reinforce not only social ties but political and economic concerns as well.

Arrival and Re-Creating a Home

Expectedly the experience of migration is a turning point for all the first-generation immigrants I interviewed. Many spoke of their memories upon arriving in their host societies, describing their initial sense of alienation, excitement, and bewilderment. Nadia, a thirty-year-old banker in Paris, left Beirut with her family at the age of sixteen to live in Paris. She described her first interactions with schoolmates:

> Even though I spoke French very well, people here were different. They talked differently, everything was different. When you go to school when you are sixteen, you have all your friends [whom] you've known since you were still young. People knew each other at the school I came to and I was a stranger. A foreigner coming from I do not know where, as if I was coming from another planet. Some people were very nice to me, but I was a bit distant.

Nadia soon learned to adapt to her Parisian school. Her feelings of distance also motivated her to learn more about her Lebanese origin so that she could describe to her classmates Lebanon's history and social environment. Her experience, like that of many other immigrants, brought her closer to Lebanon once she became an immigrant. The awareness of difference and a sense of alienation are feelings shared by many Lebanese immigrants. Often the initial sense of alienation drives immigrants to engage in practices that make them feel at home in their new settings. Although these practices vary from idiosyncratic behavior to active engagement with creating or participating in an ethnic community, they are all meant to provide a sense of familiarity for the new arrivals. In Nadia's case, reading Lebanese literature and watching Lebanese movies were her way of maintaining a familiar cultural environment in her initially foreign setting. In *Inventing Home*, Akram Khater (2001:85) argues that early waves of Lebanese immigrants in the United States "could not be allowed to hover indeterminately between the 'modern' and the 'traditional.'" Faced with assimilationist forces that undermined their cultural background (similar to Nadia's example in France), they had to engage in processes of self-affirmation and positive reconstructions of "home." "'Home,' as it emerged, was a concoction of romantic memories stoked by distance, new realities that required a place, and plenty of gaps in between" (ibid.:87–88). In Khater's analysis, the early waves of Lebanese immigrants who arrived in the United States during the late nineteenth and early twentieth centuries were farmers or artisans, relatively poor, and poorly educated. They were expected to give up their foreign ways and learn to become American. Unlike members of the early waves of Lebanese immigrants to the United States, Nadia was familiar with French culture before her migration. French culture is based on the Republican model which requires that all individual particularities (such as religion) be confined to the private sphere. As a result, the process of constructing home, for Lebanese immigrants in France, takes place privately through activities such as reading, listening to music, watching films, or decorating the home.

Attempts to concretize the homeland are emphatically gendered. Among my respondents, Lebanese immigrant women experience and remember their homeland through physical practices and in reference to specific locations and family members. Lebanese immigrant men, on the other hand, perceive of their homeland through relationships that they form with people around them. This gender difference is also reflected in the works of Lebanese immigrant writers. In a study of Anglophone Lebanese fiction, Syrine Hout (2005) discusses the works of two authors, Nada Jarrar and Rabih Alameddinne, and illustrates the different constructions of home and exile they express. Although not accounting for gender as a relevant factor in shaping these reconstructions, Hout emphasizes that the two authors present oppositional views and attitudes toward memory, war, and exile. Jarrar views home as "location, usually a house, associated with actual or substitute family members and serving as a storehouse of childhood memories from which selfhood is derived" (ibid.:221), and these views were shared by women in my sample. Similar to my male respondents, Alameddine's work illustrates home as "peace of mind that can be enjoyed anywhere" (ibid.) and that is brought about through relationships with people.

Women's emphasis on creating images of their homeland in their domicile relates to historical constructions of a "proper Lebanese woman." In *Inventing Home*, Akram Khater (2001) illustrates the efforts taken to domesticate Lebanese immigrants to the United States during the late 1800s. Despite their mostly rural background, early immigrant women were discouraged from participating in public life, especially work, in an attempt to bring them closer to their middle-class American and Lebanese counterparts. While contemporary Lebanese immigrant women in my sample are likely to contest limits on their participation in public life, their relationships with the homeland were presented within the domestic realm as an affirmation of their middle-class status. The shaping of physical space to mirror what the immigrant remembers from home is a common strategy employed by immigrant women to create a sense of comfort and to remind them of "who we are." For example, Marlin, a homemaker who was in her fifties and lived in Paris when I met her in 2003, explained the Lebanese decorations in her apartment that were mixed with French classical paintings:

> Because we are a mixture between East and West, we have both, and we want to remember that. This [Lebanese decorations] reminds us that we are from there. We cannot forget. We see both cultures, but you have to keep your roots before you can add another culture.

Marlin's expression of her ties to both societies through house decorations also served as a reminder of her difference within French society as a product of different cultures and transcultural identification. During our interview in her apartment in Paris, Marlin emphasized her proficiency in speaking English, Arabic, and French, and said that her identity is informed by all three cultures. The French paintings on the walls of her apartment alongside the Lebanese tapestries, her location in the wealthy Parisian quarter, and the sounds of American Jazz in the background as we drank our Lebanese coffee were all important expressions of Marlin's feelings of home. In contrast May, a thirty-one-year-old lawyer working in New York City when I interviewed her in 2002, sought to create a familiar physical environment in a different way. She was unwilling to abandon her habitual behavior carried over from childhood in her new setting:

Whenever I have an apartment, I always furnish and decorate it, and stock up my fridge. People who come to my house are always surprised, because in New York people always order out, they always go out, but in my family's house there were always full pantries and I always try to make my new apartment [my] home.

Unlike many of the respondents I met in Paris who invited me to their homes and expressed generous hospitality, my interviewees in New York, including May, always preferred to meet me in the busy coffee shops of Manhattan. May suggested a possible reason for this difference when she told me that her apartment is a "typical New York apartment" with barely enough room for one person. She contrasted her small apartment in the lower east side of Manhattan to her childhood home in Beirut, pointing out that her small dwelling is a major departure from the vast dwellings she was accustomed to in Lebanon. Despite the small space and almost nonexistent kitchen, May's sense of security depended on keeping a full pantry. She went on to explain that having a full pantry was a necessity while growing up during the civil war given the insecurities regarding food and mobility, and that she sought a similar security in her unfamiliar environment in New York. Both Marlin and May underscore the importance of physical space in constructing a sense of belonging in their homelands and in their various communities.

Cut off from their homeland and facing constant challenges in their effort to belong to a new society, "the stranger is perpetually required to make herself at home in an interminable discussion between a scattered historical inheritance and a heterogeneous present" (Chambers 1994:6). Re-creating a familiar environment in their new settings does not serve as a form of nostalgia for May or Marlin, as their activities do not necessarily take them back to specific memories or particular places. Instead, their activities are based on choices they made to re-create a familiar environment in their new surroundings and thus make it appear friendlier and more adaptable.

Whereas women sought a sense of home within their dwellings, male immigrants in my sample were more likely to seek that sense of home with reference to community events. Re-creating a sense of home was the main reason why many individuals I interviewed stated that, despite their lack of religious beliefs or desire to belong to a religious community, they still participated in Lebanese religious festivals, attended church for Easter and Christmas, or observed Ramadan. These events reminded them of life in

Lebanon and were also opportunities to "stay in touch" with the culture and traditions that they had left behind. Participating in religious activities, similar to May's need to fill her pantry, did not always make sense or resonate with the respondents' lifestyle and personal beliefs. These practices, however, provided a sense of shared subjectivity that made my respondents feel part of a larger Lebanese society.

A desire to feel at home also drives immigrants to seek relationships with others who share the same ethnic background. For example, Ruby, a forty-three-year-old nurse who had lived in Paris since 1989 while her husband remained in Beirut, told me that as soon as she arrived in Paris she had to find a Lebanese grocery store, beauty salon, doctor, and lawyer as they made her feel at home. In a similar vein other respondents, having left Lebanon to pursue their studies elsewhere, organized Lebanese associations in the universities they attended. For example, Alfred, a graduate student at the Sorbonne when I met him in Paris, had been the head of the student union in his former college in Beirut and had started a political party for the youth before he left. He continued his student activity shortly after arriving in Paris, as it gave him a sense of continuity. The initial focus of his group was to present a positive image of Lebanon to French students and to society in general. By organizing exhibitions, lectures, discussions, and film presentations on Lebanese culture, Alfred and his group members sought to inform other students about the different aspects of Lebanese society. Similarly Michel, who worked as an electrical engineer in New York, explained that shortly after arriving in New York in 1983 he started the "Friends of Lebanon Society." The group emphasized the need to organize cultural activities in order to sustain members' collective memory and knowledge of Lebanon's traditions and heritage. Membership in the group was open to all Lebanese of any ethnic/religious background as well as non-Lebanese individuals, and thus it provided solidarity based on an interest in Lebanon. Michel noted:

> It held us together. We weren't all of the same mentalities, but at least it helped just by meeting each other, although we didn't feel it then, but now looking back, it was a feeling of comfort. We had a common goal. We had a common thing we were working toward, just to promote the culture of Lebanon. And this was enough to keep us together.

As seen in the examples of Alfred and Michel, membership in a formal organization provided a common goal and common interests which are integral to constructing solidarity and communal belonging. Organizing cultural activities, such as exhibitions, lectures, seminars, and festivals, is a popular strategy to connect immigrants to the homeland. Philanthropic activities also aim to increase public awareness of Lebanese issues as well as providing material assistance to some groups in Lebanon that are in need; thus a sense of community is provided based on material as well as cultural goals.

Analyses of transnational communities illustrate the ways in which immigrants' political, social, or economic lives are shaped by their interest in the homeland. Interest in the homeland has different meanings among the various immigrants. For some, it involves maintaining continuous communication with family and friends or keeping themselves informed about political, social, or cultural events in the homeland. For many others, interest in the homeland strengthens their involvement in public activities that are related to Lebanon or the Middle East. Organizations that directly relate to Lebanon, such as the Friends of Lebanon Society, reflect the "desire to endure" a diasporic sense of community (Chaliand and Rageau 1995). Transnational cultural practices also illustrate the ways that events such as religious festivals, national holidays, and traditional celebrations are transported to the host society. These events are important vehicles through which communal solidarity and consciousness are maintained. Examples of these forms of holding on to cultural traditions abound in the lives of the Lebanese immigrants with whom I spoke in Montreal, New York, and Paris. For example, many respondents were keen on their annual participation in religious festivals and gatherings organized by the Lebanese organizations. Similarly, many participate in Lebanese film festivals, artistic exhibitions, and national celebrations. These activities were considered important for identifying with, and feeling attachment to, their homeland. Even immigrants who had no interest in visiting Lebanon or had no family members or friends still living there were keen on attending such activities, as it allowed them to stay connected to Lebanese society both in Lebanon and in the diaspora.

In an attempt to define home in the context of mobility, Nigel Rapport and Andrew Dawson (1998:9) wrote that

> "home" . . . "is where one best knows oneself"—where "best" means "most," even if not always "happiest." Here, in sum, is an ambiguous and fluid but yet ubiquitous notion, apposite for charting the ambiguities and fluidities, the migrancies and paradoxes, of identity in the world today.

The authors' notion of home as ubiquitous is relevant to the understanding of Lebanese immigrant narratives that stress the re-creation of home through physical or relational practices in their new settings. In these narratives, Lebanese immigrants do not stress home as a specific physical territory to be found in Lebanon, in their old houses, or among old family members and friends. Instead, home is something that is sought, imagined, and recreated in the new settings and everyday practices.

In the journal *Diaspora*, Khachig Tölölyan (1991) contends that members of a diaspora must perceive themselves as belonging to a collectivity whose specific identity is clearly differentiated from the host society. Such a collectivity is constructed through communal institutions that mark social boundaries between the host society and the diaspora. More important, as Tölölyan (1996) illustrates in the case of the Armenian diaspora, social and political involvement define the difference between symbolic ethnic identity and diasporic attachments. Lebanese immigrants seek the marking of their national community in ways that also strengthen their ethnic identities beyond symbolic forms (see Gans 1979). Participation in Lebanese organizations (such as those based on region, village, or family affiliation) provides the sense of ethno-communal attachment that Tölölyan, among others, believes is essential for a diaspora community to endure. However, the involvement of Lebanese immigrants in ethnic organizations is not always the result of feeling alienated in the host society—a popular argument in diasporic literature (see, e.g., Safran 1991). More significant, participation in specific communities and organizations related to the homeland does not preclude forging attachments with the host society.

New Localities for Involvement

Although immigrants' initial public involvement is mostly based on homeland issues, interest in their host societies soon follows to mark these immigrants' social, cultural, and political incorporation into their ethnic communities. Public involvement takes place through civil society organizations and initially has two related aims: to effect changes in Lebanon and to change the host society's perception of the Middle East. For example, Fareed, a thirty-nine-year-old graphic designer in New York, spoke of his motivation to be active in the Arab American community: "I want to be remembered as someone who helped the community and worked to better the image of Arabs as a whole and the Lebanese specifically."

Many immigrants such as Fareed, Michel, and Alfred regard themselves as representatives of Lebanese society and believe they need to set good examples for the host society. This desire to appear as the "good immigrant" motivates them to succeed in the host society. Presenting themselves as role models gives immigrants a sense of purpose and achievement that enhances their interest in Lebanese issues as well as their involvement in a Lebanese community. In most cases, however, this pioneering role also means a movement beyond homeland interests and an involvement in communities that are based in the host societies.

Referring to first-generation Pakistani and Indian Muslims in the United States and Canada, Karen Leonard (2000:26) argues that given the established Judeo-Christian tradition in North America, many of these first-generation immigrants attempt "to place themselves both inside and outside 'the West.'" Indian and Pakistani Muslims in Leonard's study are critical of the North American culture in which they find themselves but are historically related to it. Finding that they are at a disadvantage, these immigrants seek "common grounds" by highlighting the similarities between Islam, Christianity, and Judaism. Similar to Pakistani and Indian immigrants, Lebanese immigrants also seek "common grounds" to counter their disadvantageous position in their host societies. Many of my respondents, Muslims and Christians alike, are engaged in introducing their host societies to Arab culture and negotiating a space in public life. Michael Suleiman (1994) reports a similar process of political engagement with regard to Arab Americans. Based on a survey of politically active Arab Americans, Suleiman observes that a larger number of younger respondents are entering the political process primarily because of ethnic concerns: "they feel the need to either defend their community and its causes or else enhance its position in U.S. society, or both" (ibid.:55). Ethnic concerns, however, compel Arab Americans in Suleiman's survey as well as the Lebanese immigrants in mine to become active participants in their host societies. While Suleiman's analysis does not look into the kinds of concerns that Arab Americans may be involved with over time, my respondents emphasize that their participation in their host societies moves beyond their ethnic concerns as they begin to see themselves as transnational and cosmopolitan individuals. Similar to the Pakistani and Indian immigrants in Leonard's study, they seek "common grounds" with members of their host societies. For my respondents, however, these grounds are expressed in the form of shared concerns about their host societies as opposed to a similar religious worldview.

Analyses of transnational immigrant communities stress immigrants' growing tendency to maintain close ties with their home countries after migration. The continual interest in the homeland is the core of a diaspora's ethno-communal consciousness and solidarity, which also forms the basis for what Vertovec and Cohen identify as "a tension of political orientations given that diasporic people are often confronted with divided loyalties to homelands and host countries" (1999:xviii). This tension emerges as immigrants participate either individually or collectively in the domestic politics of their home and host countries as well as in the international political arena. The notion of divided loyalties has been contradicted in recent transnational accounts, however, whereby assimilation into the host society and transnational connections to the homeland are understood as reinforcing each other (see, e.g., Smith 2005). Although many immigrants participate either individually or collectively in the domestic politics of their home and host countries, they do not shift their loyalties from one country to the other (Levitt 2001). Instead, transnational immigrants are integrated into their host societies as well as their homelands, and many are active in international politics. Soysal (2000) illustrates, for example, that during the last elections in Berlin, Turkish immigrant organizations pushed for their local voting rights and demanded to vote in European elections. At the same time, the same groups pressured the Turkish government to advance their voting rights in the Turkish national elections. Thus these groups see themselves as belonging and participating in multiple civic spaces—in Berlin, in Europe, and in Turkey. This is an increasing trend among other immigrant populations in other parts of the world. For example, in *Diasporic Citizenship*, Laguerre (1998) provides an illustration of the Haitian immigrant community in the United States and argues that these immigrants see themselves as citizens of the home country, as Americans, and as both. These immigrants participate fully in the social and political lives of both Haiti and the United States, and constantly migrate between their dual identities while understanding that they are both and neither at the same time.

The multiple loyalties expressed by members of the Lebanese diaspora are a result of active choices that my interviewees made. Participation in the host society is considered an important source of belonging to the place where the immigrants decided to live. Shortly after arriving in their new settings, many Lebanese immigrants with whom I spoke found that they were fully immersed in their host societies as their social networks, personal goals, and regular activities resembled those of members of the mainstream. In some cases, my interviewees rejected the notion of belonging to an ethnic community that is not integrated into the mainstream society. For example, Fareed took issue with a lack of integration and stated that many Lebanese Americans do not really see themselves as part of American society:

You can meet somebody [who has been here for] twenty and thirty years, and they still think of themselves as not part of the American [society]. For them there's always "American," and then there's "us." And that's a problem, because as long as they don't think of themselves as Americans, then clearly they're not going to be active in the system which is necessary in order to effectively make change.

The kind of change Fareed spoke of is one that mostly relates to Arab Americans and their position in American public culture. He went on to point out that members of the Arab American community tend to complain about this issue more than any others. His own interest in change differed, however, as he stressed universal issues such as equality and justice for the poor, for women and children, and for gays and lesbians. Fareed's criticism of an Arab or Lebanese ethnic community was shared by many of my respondents. Initially, when I asked what they thought about the Lebanese or Arab community in the cities where they lived, they all understood what that community was, and most said they did not participate in it. That many in fact did participate in ethnic community events regularly—indeed, I sought participants for my research at these events—indicates that they saw their participation as momentary and not definitive of the communities in which they see themselves as members. In Fareed's opinion, belonging to a Lebanese ethnic group or the larger American society is a choice an individual makes. Choosing the larger American multicultural society, in his view, is important not only for a sense of belonging but also for being an effective member of the American community as well as the Arab ethnic community within that larger sphere.

Similar to the multicultural environments of North America, France also provided a context where immigrants could participate in ethnic practices and at the same time become involved in their host society's issues. Mona, a forty-two-year-old social worker in Paris who was primarily interested in Lebanese issues, said that this interest motivated her participation in French society and politics.

I left Lebanon because of the war. They made me leave. I participated in a group statement against the war. Two days later they threatened to harm my brothers. This is why I decided to come here. I was still involved when I first came here. I wrote articles, and many letters. My involvement in Lebanese issues got me involved in other things as well. I try to show people here that Lebanese are good role models and that they can be successful in anything they do.

Once Mona felt settled in France, which occurred upon adopting a Lebanese son, she felt the need to fully participate in the society she had chosen to be her new home. But Mona's desire to exemplify "a good Lebanese" was not the only motivation for her involvement in French social and political issues. She also believed that it was her duty to be engaged in French issues, as she saw herself as a French citizen. Thus she felt she had an important role to play in both societies. When I inquired about her political activities in Paris, Mona described the transformation she experienced after deciding—with her French husband—to adopt a child from Lebanon. Mona wanted a Lebanese child so that he would resemble her and have her olive complexion. But when she and her husband decided to live in Paris and therefore raise their child to be French and speak only the French language, Mona began to seek a French nationality, which she had not pursued until then. She explained that initially, even after she married a Frenchman who did not wish to live in Lebanon, she had hoped that one day she would return to Lebanon. However, the decision to raise their son in France was motivated by the awareness that he would have better economic opportunities in France compared to Lebanon. Once Mona realized that she was in France to stay, she became more committed to French society and to a French nationality. She was also inspired to engage in French politics in ways similar to her engagement with Lebanese politics before she left Lebanon.

> The fact is, if I wanted to live here in Paris I have to be French, to be allowed to vote. It is very important for me to vote. And so if I couldn't vote, I would never be effective in France. So when I had my son I said to my husband, "Okay, now I am French. I want to vote, and I am interested in French politics." Now I belong to a political party and I am very active politically, but I never forgot Lebanon.

Mona's engagement in French society and politics did not negate her involvement in issues focusing on Lebanon. She still organized campaigns dealing with public health issues in Lebanon—the first was an anti-smoking campaign and she was in the process of organizing an Alzheimer's awareness campaign. She also planned to raise funds for Lebanon's first center for the elderly. All these activities, in her opinion, did not contradict her engagement with French politics and public life. In addition to being a party member, she was a member of the board of directors of two different organizations in France. Both Fareed and Mona explained that belonging to their host societies is not based on legal status or nationality. Mona pointed out that her right to vote goes hand-in-hand with her being French, not because it marked her legal status but as a mechanism whereby she could voice her opinion and concerns. In her view, being a citizen entails being concerned about the society you live in and being engaged with its issues and goals in order to effect positive change. Fareed's views were similar. He believed that many nationals and residents in the United States were not real citizens, since they were not active in society. Although their participation in their host societies may have been influenced by their interest in Lebanon, both Fareed and Mona emphasized that such interest did not contradict their engagement with either the United States or France.

In *Migrancy, Culture, Identity*, Iain Chambers (1994:82) notes that,

> to refuse the mechanisms of this binarism [between self and Other] and its techniques and technologies for separating out and subsequently positioning cultures, arts and . . . individuals, and to choose to move in the traffic between such worlds, caught in the sights, sounds and language of hybridity, where there is neither the stability of the "authentic" nor the "false," does not mean that there are not real differences of experience, of culture, of history, of power.

Chambers's observation resonates with the narratives of many Lebanese immigrants who, though refusing to exclude themselves from the mainstream society in their host countries, continue to delineate the experiences that they do not share with many around them. For Lebanese immigrants, the "differences of experiences, of cultures, of history, of power" are integral in shaping their experiences of migration and settlement, and they are reminded daily of their immigrant status—as the narratives in chapter 2 portrayed. Realizing these differences motivates some immigrants to engage in activities to educate others about Lebanon and Lebanese culture and history in the hope that they might persuade their host societies to appreciate and value Lebanese immigrants. Nonetheless, many immigrants recognize that education is a two-way process and that being accepted in their new settings also depends on their ability to let go of these differences. Choosing to live in a new society, which often heightens one's awareness of one's differences, requires learning new norms and values so that one can achieve a level of belonging that makes life in a new environment agreeable. Abeer, a thirty-four-year-old physician who has been living in the United States since 1992, provides an example of accommodating to the host society. When she first arrived in the United States, Abeer lived in Boston before moving to New

York City in 1994. Moving twice was a harsh experience, she told me, but after a few years of feeling alienated and isolated, she actively familiarized herself with American social norms and practices and as a result felt fully incorporated in American society:

> Now I understand Americans better and their social values and how they meet with other people. In Lebanon we are used to having no privacy, no boundaries, nor much personal space. Everybody is meshed with each other which provides strong cultural, social, and family support. When suddenly you're separated and you go somewhere where it's very hard to make contact with other people and establish relationships, you feel lost. With time I was able to build friendships and relationships, and now I understand how Americans live, and at the same time I'm able to find my own little niche, and that's why I'm happier now than I was before because, well, I was just sort of an isolated person and now I have sort of an entourage.

Abeer's sense of isolation upon arriving in a new country is shared by many Lebanese immigrants I interviewed. However, like Abeer, most end up adapting to their new environments and learning its ways. Learning the new society's norms and values is a prerequisite for membership in the new social setting. Membership in the new society is important for Lebanese immigrants' sense of belonging and has to be actively sought. Demanding inclusion and moving beyond addressing ethnic issues were expressed by Ziade:

> Through my group [an Arab American literary group which Ziade co-founded], people can understand and support my arguments. I am not only interested in other Arabs around, although they are very important to have on my side. I am also interested in American politicians and opinion leaders. They have to hear me too, and I make them.

Ziade was thirty-eight years old when we first met in Greenwich Village in the summer of 2001. At the time he worked in banking and was a member of a music group. The Arab American literary group that he co-founded would organize cultural events (poetry readings, speakers, and musical concerts) that, although influenced by Arab culture, did not target an Arab American audience. In Ziade's account, he readily moved away from the confines of ethnic attachments and instead took part in the host society's publics. His interest in engaging with politicians and leaders illustrates a form of participation that is not based on legal membership but challenges traditional notions of citizenship and at the same time focuses on the state as a site for bringing about desired changes (see, e.g., Trouillot 2003).

Moreover, as in Ziade's view, participation in the host society is not easily granted to immigrants. Rather, it is a right that has to be claimed. Bassam, a thirty-nine-year-old writer in Montreal, expressed ways in which he demands inclusion and a voice in the host society:

> In a multicultural society like ours, talking about Lebanon does not somehow link to Canada! Even when it comes to immigrants, they still want to hear the exotic thing: the poor immigrant who had it tough over there and he came here and he was saved . . . People are receptive, though, and they listen to what I have to say. You keep trying and eventually someone would listen which eventually allows you to say more and participate more.

As Bassam explains, participation in the host society is not easily granted to immigrants. Rather, it can be achieved through immigrants' social activities. The views expressed by Ziade, Mona, Fareed, and Bassam, as well as other respondents, point to immigrants' active interest in forging attachments to the host society. Although these views may be easily misunderstood as a form of immigrants' assimilation to the host society, Lebanese immigrants' emphasis on their desire for inclusion challenges given social and ethnic structures in their new settings instead of passively accepting these structures. Moreover, their views share diasporic elements that are present in other immigrant communities. For example, Cross and associates (1994) explain that many Franco-Maghrébins (North African immigrants, and their children, in France), especially the younger generation, neither wish to return to their homelands nor establish an ethnic (North African or Islamic) enclave in France. Instead of emphasizing their exclusion from French society, Franco-Maghrébins favor a negotiated form of integration that would not lead to their total assimilation in the sense of totally abandoning their Arab culture. These Franco-Maghrébins "seek to negotiate integration on their own terms while maintaining their right to be different" (ibid.:14). In a similar fashion, Lebanese immigrants move beyond traditional interest in the homeland or the adoption of a fixed ethnic identity. Their awareness of their diasporic existence urges them to participate in the host society as well and negotiate their belonging to various communities. In many of the views expressed by my interviewees, belonging to a community is not something that is granted to individuals. Instead, individuals have to individually choose and consciously seek membership in a community. My respondents emphasized that, despite the various motivating factors that led to their (or their parents') emigration, they have actively chosen to live in their host countries. As a result, they also have to actively form ties and be involved in communities in the places where they dwell. Their involvement in the host society, however, is more than a way to strengthen their dual ethnic identity. They spoke of ways by which they sought to move beyond the traditional ethnic labels and forms of solidarity to fully participate in their host society's politics and social issues. Such participation does not negate Lebanese immigrants' transnational involvement in homeland issues. For Lebanese immigrants, contesting a dual identity is a form of rejecting "divided" loyalties and existence. Instead, informed by their transcultural and cosmopolitan identification, they understand their communal attachments in terms of belonging to multiple societies. In the next section, I illustrate the transnational forms of community life that members of the Lebanese diaspora construct in addition to their involvement in the homeland, ethnic communities, and host society. I then move to the discussion of cosmopolitan attachments in the last section of the chapter.

Transnational Involvement

The desire of Lebanese immigrants to maintain social involvement in their host societies while preserving their interest in the homeland leads to their constant migration between the two worlds. Interest in the homeland, however, does not contradict their involvement with the issues of their host society. Indeed, participating in the host society's social and political spheres is an important mechanism whereby effective involvement in the homeland can be achieved. Alongside their desire for integration into their host societies, Lebanese immigrants believe that their membership in the diaspora can allow them to be effective in addressing problems in Lebanon, both politically and socially. In fact, belonging to the diaspora was seen as an added advantage for effecting change in Lebanon, as Fareed explained:

> That's one area that I'm happy with, which is the area of effecting change [in Lebanon] from here as Americans. I think that I have no problem getting involved and I do and I think all of us should do it. A, it's much safer. B, it's effective, it works, and we've seen it work. We had a letter-writing campaign because we had a raid by the Lebanese police against an Inter-

net provider who was accused of posting up a gay Lebanese website. And even though the owners of the service have no clue what—they can't really control what happens on the server—some of them actually were thrown in jail, and it was a whole mess . . . I mean, this is all just to say that we as Lebanese and Arab Americans in general can be much more effective than we ever even think about, working from here to effect change there. I think our countries, especially the countries that have good relations with the United States, are more likely to listen to pressure or to complaints from the United States than anything internal. I mean, internally, you can jump up and down and nobody gives a shit, they'll throw you in jail. But you get a letter of complaint from the U.S. State Department or a U.S. organization, and you get a couple of write-ups in *Time* magazine or whatever, and suddenly they'll take action because it's like: "Oh my God! We're being exposed."

Fareed is the same respondent who rejected the tendency of some immigrants to separate themselves from mainstream American society, claiming that one should identify as American to be effective in bringing about changes in American society. Fareed also describes how being outside Lebanon grants more power in effecting change in the homeland. He realizes that being in the United States gives him more clout, given the American influence in the region. So, although he has no official position, he knows that a mere letter from a U.S. organization can be more effective in challenging Lebanese state oppression than political activism inside Lebanon. He also illustrates ways in which a traditionally taboo issue, in this case homosexuality, can be addressed and contested.

In a similar fashion, engaging in philanthropic activities is also intended to address critical issues in Lebanese society. Referring to "The Friends of Lebanon," Michel cited a related example:

One time we collected money and we sent [it to Lebanon] . . . This was during a real bad period in the war in Lebanon. We sent money to not-for-profit organizations in Lebanon. We sent it to one Maronite, one Orthodox, one Sunni, one Shiite, and one Jewish [organization]. We sent an equal amount to each. And we were students then. I think we raised a thousand bucks, so we sent two hundred bucks each, and we found a person that could deliver . . . We delivered three of them to Lebanon directly, two of them for people in the United States who sent them to people.

The desire to escape religious divisions in Lebanese society was Michel's motivation to donate the money to the different sects. Many respondents stressed that addressing sectarian divisions is of paramount importance in effecting change in Lebanese society as well as among members of the diaspora itself. Michel explained that such an activity was meaningful as it would never be attempted in Lebanon, especially during the civil war. Like many of my respondents who left Lebanon during the war, Michel had issues with the sectarian divisions within Lebanese society and felt that he was more capable of challenging them, at least symbolically, through his participation in the Friends of Lebanon in New York. Michel also pointed out that the makeup of the organization itself, with the membership comprised of Maronites, Druze, Sunnis, Shiites, and Greek Orthodox, was a challenge to Lebanese sectarian norms and traditions. The members had envisioned a Lebanon free of sectarian strife and constructed a community in New York based on their vision.

Religion and class-related issues are important reasons for some of my interviewees, especially the younger ones, to "pick a quarrel" with Lebanese society, as well as with other Lebanese immigrants in the diaspora. Alfred, Simon, and Nora were in their twenties and had all moved from Lebanon to Paris is search of better careers. For these three respondents, class divisions is the worst aspect of Lebanese society, and they find it difficult to tolerate when they go back to visit. All respondents, however, understand that class issues in Lebanon are intrinsic to sectarian divisions and, as a result, focus on combating sectarian divisions within Lebanese society. The majority of respondents emphasized that being outside Lebanon allows them to analyze the divisions from a distance and gain a different perspective compared to the one they had while living in Lebanon. Alfred described what he sees as the main problem:

> In Lebanon all concerns are rather passionate and irrational. It's about factions, it's about old stories, it's really religious, or social divisions—between rich or poor, or Arabs and non-Arabs, or Muslims or Christians. I don't see a prospective for rational debate, for building the state or citizenship in Lebanon. We need to introduce some conception of citizenship or some principles of debate, or some tolerance principles.

In Alfred's view, conflict based on religious beliefs, class background, or ethnic identity is intertwined in Lebanon and produces passionate reactions that do not allow those who are afflicted by them to analyze the conflicts and seek rational solutions. Being outside Lebanon allowed Alfred and others to better understand the problems within Lebanese society and become more engaged in processes of change. Engaging with specific issues such as class equality, religious freedom, gay liberation, or gender socialization was, to many of my respondents, attainable and effective given their immigrant status. Many of the Lebanese immigrants I interviewed expressed critical views of Lebanese society and spoke of their desire to introduce processes of change, as they felt that they were in a "discontinuous state of being" (Said 1990:360) or in a continuous quarrel about where they come from.

Research on Arabs in North America refers to the post–1970 wave of immigrants as one that rejects secularism and Westernization while being more committed to ethno-religious culture and community than earlier cohorts of Arab immigrants (Haddad 1994). According to Yvonne Haddad (1983), this new cohort is mainly composed of Muslim Arab migrants who wished to transfer their strong religious traditions to their new Western environment. As a by-product of the post-1970 Islamic revival, religious identities (both Muslim and Christian) in the Arab World have prevailed over national or Pan-Arab identities (Eid 2008). Thus the new Arab migrants tended to assign a more devotional role to mosques and religious organizations compared to their secular American-born, ethno-religious peers of the second and third generation, whose implication in religious networks and mosques, if any, often assumed the social role of community binder (Haddad 1983). My research suggests that contemporary Lebanese immigrants (who form the largest segment of Arab immigrants in the United States and Canada) may be part of a new wave of immigration, one that challenges the rising religious particularities of the Arab world and wishes to engage with issues of sectarian divisions while abroad. As a diaspora, contemporary Lebanese first-generation immigrants complicate traditional imagined unities that are based on religion and national origins.

While presence outside Lebanon allows many of my respondents to experiment with new ideas about social and political problems in Lebanon, some stated that the issues they had with Lebanese society influenced their decision to leave and search for a better society. In the new setting many respondents found different problems, and they continue to struggle with aspects of their host society. Although religion and class are important sources of criticism of Lebanese society, gender and sexuality are contentious issues in both the homeland and the host society. For example, Abeer expressed her initial sense of alienation in both Lebanese and American societies given her ethnicity and sexual orientation. She maintained that Lebanese society was not accepting of homosexuality in general, and yet her experience with a gay community in New York revealed that it was not accepting of her Arab heritage:

> Among Arabs, I am not accepted since I am a lesbian. And among lesbians, I am not accepted since I am Arab and proud of it. Arabs want me to give up my lesbian identity. I tried. I used to dress and act like the girl they want me to be, especially among family members. I did not do a good job at it, so I stopped. Among lesbians, they don't like the fact that I am proud to be Arab. They emphasize that Arab culture is oppressive to women and queers. They are right, but they do not understand that I am proud of this part of my identity. I am both lesbian and Arab, yet I am not accepted in either group.

Abeer found that the community she could best relate to was that of gay Arabs, but even within this group, gender differences led to the separation between gay men and lesbians. The separation of the two groups did not affect the way Abeer related to the community in general:

> To me it is very important to be able to relate to other gay Arabs, because I share more common grounds with them than other gays and other Arabs. It joins two identities for me that were practically incompatible before. I think the community has to know that there are gay Arabs. It is also important to provide support to people who are very afraid of coming out or afraid of recognizing their own sexuality.

Abeer considers her disagreements with Lebanese society, the gay community in New York, and, to some extent, the gay Arab community foci of social involvement in the three societies of which she considers herself a part.

According to Castles (2002), transmigrants' need for political stability, economic prosperity, and social well-being in their places of residence compels them to accommodate to multiple social settings and to excel in cross-cultural competence. Thus the notion of primary loyalty to one place is misleading: "It was an icon of old-style nationalism that has little relevance for migrants in a mobile world" (ibid.:1159).

Analyses of diaspora communities highlight the fact that group members must continue to relate to their co-nationals in the homeland and elsewhere in the diaspora and that their collective consciousness is significantly defined by these relationships (see, e.g., Safran 1991). Instead of assuming affinity with other Lebanese based on national origin, most members of the Lebanese diaspora were found to challenge social divisions that characterize Lebanese society, which in turn lead them to emphasize their difference within Lebanese society. Moreover, Lebanese immigrants hold on to a problematic vision of their homeland as a source of disunity and divisions, and their diasporic collective identification is based on the desire to challenge these divisions and bring about changes in Lebanon. Despite the various forms of public involvement in which Lebanese immigrants engaged, they mostly shared a desire to be active participants in social change. The various examples suggest that they seek to be effective in Lebanon as well as in their new settings. Their awareness that they exist between the two societies also allows them to challenge given traditions and constraints. Combating sectarianism, political corruption, and violations of personal freedoms are important aspects of their involvement in the homeland. Demanding full participation in the host society allows them to gauge a basis for inclusion and participation. These concerns, while motivating participation in the host society, also triggered a cosmopolitan sense of belonging and more global forms of involvement—a point I discuss in the following section.

Diasporic Solidarity

In their analysis of cultural changes in the global era, Gupta and Ferguson (1997:7) stress that communal ties are constructed within a wide set of social and spatial relations and suggest that "it is fundamentally mistaken to conceptualize different kinds of non- or supra-local identities (diasporic, refugee, migrant, and so forth) as spatial and temporal extensions of a prior, natural identity rooted in locality and community." The authors warn against seeing non-spatial identities as extensions of those founded on nationality and geographic region. According to the authors, globalization expands and speeds up the movement of people resulting in these non-spatial forms of identity becoming more ubiquitous in the contemporary world. The kinds of social relationships in which Lebanese immigrants engage illustrate the supra-local nature of their understanding of their experiences. Regardless of their involvement in homeland issues or host society politics, almost all the respondents demonstrated membership in multiple communities as they maintained some form of connection to Lebanon and were active participants in the host society. They also emphasized their belonging to larger communities that sometimes embraced generalized identities to serve particular goals (such as Arab, Muslim, Catholic, or professional). Generally, however, in terms of social relationships, they emphasized their belonging to multiple groups and diverse networks that often included the Lebanese diasporic community at large.

In *The Transnational Villager*, Peggy Levitt (2001:7) argues that "the communities and organizations that emerge from transnational migration offer migrants a variety of ways in which to distribute their energies and loyalties between their sending and receiving countries." In the case of Lebanese immigrants, the communities and organizations that they formed facilitated their participation in both Lebanon and their place of residence. Ethnic activities and organizations that were established in the host society allow Lebanese immigrants to maintain their attachment to Lebanon and facilitate their integration to the mainstream host societies as well.[2] More important, Lebanese immigrants also maintain solidarities that extend beyond their transnational alliances to include Lebanese immigrants in various regions of the world. Participation in the larger diasporic community, independent of contacts with the homeland, is granted political, economic and social importance in the lives of the individual immigrants I interviewed.

Engagement with the diasporic community is especially important for political activists among Lebanese immigrants in the three cities examined in this book. Political activists illustrate "a continuous involvement in a triadic relationship between the diaspora, the host country and the homeland" (Sheffer 1996:8). For example, Chady spoke of the importance of maintaining ties with people in Lebanon, since "they are the ones who are living there and they keep us informed of the reality of the situation." He also stated that "people outside are also important since they have the money and the influence, and they are the only reason Lebanon has survived during the last thirty years." Chady, a thirty-one-year-old banker in Paris, once held a political office in Lebanon. He moved to France in search of a better political career and economic opportunities. He was active in a number of organizations in Paris, mostly those with a Lebanese emphasis, and he stressed that his activities were targeted toward Lebanese people worldwide, as his political career in Lebanon had made him aware of the importance of the diaspora in affecting economic and political lives in Lebanon. Similar beliefs were shared by Georges, a fifty-two-year-old political activist and writer in Paris. Georges's family members were all in Lebanon, and he referred to his situation as a "self-imposed exile," as he could no longer participate in Lebanese politics domestically. He spoke of the importance of the diaspora at large and the need to mobilize different members of the diasporic community:

Beyond political goals, the diasporic community provides an important source of attachment for many Lebanese immigrants, an attachment that is maintained by various mechanisms. On-line media provides an important arena where diasporic solidarity as well as consciousness is formed and expressed. The increase of online media is another form heavily utilized to maintain ethnic cohesion, and compellingly "changes the dynamics of diaspora, allowing for qualitatively and quantitatively enhanced linkages" (Karim 1998:12). Many of my respondents told me that online media allows them to stay in contact with many friends and family members around the world. Exchanges of news, pictures, and conversations were conducted regularly, enabling my respondents to participate in cross-border networks and keep the homeland alive. The ability to share important events as well as routine daily details equally reinforces ties with friends and family in Lebanon or in the diaspora. In general, advanced communication technology makes possible a tangible perception of a diaspora as opposed to an imagined one. For example, during my meeting with Marlin she remarked that it was approaching dinner time in Paris, which meant that her parents were finishing their dinner in Beirut and that would be a good time to call them and see how their day went. Marlin pointed out that one of the advantages of living in Paris, as opposed to New York or Montreal, was that she lived in a time zone closer to that in Beirut. The geographic proximity of Paris and Beirut was not important to her, but living in similar time zones meant that she could communicate with her family and friends in real time without having to actually see them regularly.

At the same time, many respondents criticized the tendency of "other immigrants" to be "too connected" to those they left behind as well as members of the diaspora who only cared about Lebanese ethnic and national issues. Many respondents said that their ability to stay connected, through global technologies that made daily communication easier and cheaper, was a desirable feature that reduced the distance between them and their families and friends. However, the same global technology can distract immigrants from participating in the societies in which they live, as it may focus their attention on, and social involvement in, the places they left behind. For example, Alfred explained that when he first arrived in Paris he still had a girlfriend in Beirut and that he spent all his spare time chatting with her online. He also chatted with his family and college friends to get updated on their activities and news. Shortly afterward, Alfred realized that he was not really living in Paris, as he was more concerned about the way his girlfriend, other friends, and parents lived their lives back home, and he changed his behavior so that he was no longer "tied to the computer." Eventually Alfred ended his romantic relationship and acknowledged that he wanted to experience living in Paris "full-time."

In differentiating between diasporic and transnational communities, Levitt (2001:15) argues that "transnational communities are the building blocks of diasporas that may or may not take shape." Diasporas include the transnational communities that immigrants form around their sending and receiving countries. In addition to these transnational connections, diasporas form "out of the real or imagined connections among migrants from a particular homeland who are scattered throughout the world. If a fiction of congregation takes hold, then a diaspora emerges" (ibid.). The narratives of Lebanese immigrants offer many examples to support the idea that the Lebanese diaspora is more than "a fiction of congregation." Relatives that live in Paris, London, Dubai, and Los Angeles; spouses who live in Copenhagen or Berlin; friends in Vancouver and Minneapolis; and children who went back to Beirut or moved to Toronto all form ties that extend beyond transnational networks and shape the diasporic reality of the lives of the many members of the Lebanese immigrant communities.

The diasporic community of many respondents not only includes other Lebanese family, friends, or co-nationals who have an important role to play in affecting change in Lebanon. Rather, many Lebanese immigrants realize that they belong to a larger Arab diaspora that shares a similar culture and history. For example, many Lebanese immigrants in the three cities examined here took part in Arab ethnic organizations (such as the Canadian Arab Federation, the Arab American Anti-Discrimination Committee, and the *Institut du Monde Arabe*), and most participated in Arab activities (such as lectures, exhibitions, and festivals). In most cases, these organizations and activities did not foster their ethnic attachments per se but signaled their belonging to a community with extended national boundaries and regional territories. As globalization "reduces the impact of nationalist discourse on the routine of daily life" (Trouillot 2003:93), Lebanese immigrants render linguistic, religious, or political identities more inclusive and meaningful to their experiences. An Arab immigrant community, being a "segmented diaspora" (Werbner 2000), allows many Lebanese immigrants to construct attachments with other immigrants from the Arab world who share similar cultures of consumption (food, arts, or dress, for example) to create "communal enjoyment that cut[s] across the national origins or religious beliefs" (ibid.:13). More important, participation in Arab activities and organizations allows Lebanese immigrants to organize around political issues that are specific to their position in their host societies.[5]

Membership in the diaspora, however, was somewhat ambiguous to many immigrants I interviewed. In a study of Arab American diasporic aesthetics, Sally Howell (2000) contends that membership in an Arab diaspora is only tentative. She believes that, despite the construction of a pan-Arab, pro-Palestinian political lobby, the specific "sentimental geographies of Lebanon, Egypt, or Palestine" continue to persist. Similarly many respondents found that the "sentimental geography" that is sustained by being Lebanese only adds to their sense of ambiguity and transience. Ethnic attachments notwithstanding, the triadic relationship, which includes Lebanon, the host society, and the diaspora (Lebanese or Arab), is characterized by conflict as each member has his or her own interests (Davies 2000). Lebanese political activists in the diaspora described various areas of conflict between themselves, Lebanese politicians, and other members of the diaspora with political views that differed from their own. More important, many Lebanese immigrants had a vision of the diaspora not as a unified entity but rather as one that is divided along economic, religious, and political lines. As such, unifying the diaspora, as expressed in Chady's assertion that "we need to agree on our identity," is an important goal for some political activists but not necessarily for other members of the diaspora. Accounting for the tensions within Lebanese diasporic communities, Humphrey (2004) warns against the homogenizing tendency when analyzing a "diaspora" and contends that diverse processes shape the reality of Lebanese immigrants. In his analysis, Humphrey focuses on the differences in experience among Lebanese immigrants based on generation and country of settlement, and stresses the relevance of sectarian affiliations in shaping the integration of Lebanese immigrants in their new settings. Yet Humphrey affirms that the Lebanese diasporic experience is constituted through "national disintegration and the destruction of the social world" (ibid.:32), which allows for an understanding of collective realities shared by Lebanese immigrants. In my own analysis, I believe it is important to highlight the sites of contention within the diasporic community in order to better comprehend the shared experiences of its members.

Exclusionary identities seemed to be an important site of contention. Specifically, many Lebanese immigrants found that when diasporic communities attempt to reify ethnic boundaries and traditions, they end up feeling excluded. Abeer explained that she was a member of a Lebanese professional group that was oriented toward addressing the Lebanese diaspora in general. Abeer, however, quickly became alienated from the group:

I didn't like their politics, and I felt that I'm dealing with a male-dominated society where women really have no voice, and there was a lot of totalitarian politicians that have the mentality that Lebanon is their possession, and I don't want to deal with this. I left Lebanon for this whole patriarchal mentality, and I'm not ready to embrace it back here again.

In Abeer's example, belonging to a Lebanese diasporic community is not necessarily empowering, as it maintained gender discriminations.[6] The replication of Lebanese social and political problems in the diaspora led Abeer and many others to avoid any formal organization that aimed at unifying Lebanese immigrants. Sometimes an individual would attempt to start his or her own organization, as Michel did when he first moved to New York; in most cases, however, the interviewees explained that they prefer focusing on the specific issues that concern them instead of becoming involved in organizational politics and struggles. Such interests lead many members of the Lebanese diaspora to move away from specific national issues and become involved with cosmopolitan concerns and global communities.

From a Diaspora to a Global Society

Although Lebanese immigrants seem to emphasize a sense of unity and shared identity, as members of diasporic communities they also realize that "they are not and will never be unified in the old sense, because they are irrevocably the product of several interlocking histories and cultures, belong[ing] to one and at the same time to several homes" (Hall 1995:206). Most respondents said that ethnicity no longer forms a singular basis for their sense of connection with friends and larger networks. Rather, similar opinions, dispositions, and community lifestyles takes precedence (Bellah et al. 1985). In this sense, most respondents' participation in political or social activities was not tied to nationality or ethnicity per se but more to their concern about specific issues such as justice and freedom.

Because most immigrants do not return home permanently, connections with the larger diaspora compel immigrants to exist in multiple social, economic, and cultural worlds and cross-national boundaries in their daily experiences (Lavie and Swedenburg 1996). With their multiple loyalties, members of a diaspora see themselves as belonging to a larger diaspora that includes a number of nation-states, their current host community, and their homeland, the latter through their memories and ties with those left behind. This three-way relationship informs Vertovec and Cohen's (1999) understanding of a diaspora as a social form. In maintaining this three-way relationship, members of diasporic communities construct forms of solidarity that transcend physical boundaries and make manifest important features favorable for the organization of a global society.[7] Diasporas are often assumed to rely on a single homeland (see, e.g., Tölölyan 1996), but this assumption has been challenged by a number of studies (e.g., Hall 1990). In the next sections I argue that, in place of a nationalist project, some members of the Lebanese diaspora are engaged in global communities and are active participants in cosmopolitan social movements.

Communities of Lifestyles

Although Lebanese immigrants generally emphasized their sense of unity and shared identity, they also contested assumptions that national origin or ethnicity is the basis for sharing a similar outlook with others. Consider the experiences of Sherif, for example, a thirty-one-year-old engineer in Montreal who emigrated from Lebanon to Canada via France and does not share a sense of belonging with other Lebanese individuals in Lebanon, France, or Canada. Sharing a birthplace, for Sherif, does not signal a common belief system or worldview, as he sees individuals as products of their various experiences and cultures. He believes that lacking a sense of belonging to the homeland or an ethnic community does not necessarily lead one to feel that one belongs to the host society. Instead, Sherif questions traditional forms of belonging and contends that similar experiences and dispositions are more significant in forging friendships and social connections. Most respondents agree with Sherif, preferring to be part of a community of people with similar lifestyles (Bellah et al. 1985) or shared interests and tastes (Hall 1997) than with people who simply have common national origins. In contrast to Sherif's lack of belonging, Pierre, a thirty-one-year-old banker in New York believes that he is fully integrated in U.S. society and that he could be a part of Lebanese or Armenian ethnic communities if he chose to. He, too, however, did not believe that ethnicity is the basis for the kinds of relationships he prefers:

> I think it just has to do with what I like to do. So I like going to restaurants, I don't like bars. I used to enjoy clubs, I don't anymore. The kind of people I hang out with or I socialize with are not the average typical Americans who go to bars. Back in business school I used to like throwing parties at home. People would come around and they were very different, Americans don't usually do this. At present, my friends are mostly European, Arabs,

and to a certain extent Americans, but it is not where they come from that matters, it is what they like to do.

Khaled presented a similar view when he pointed out that his social network in New York City is largely Francophone:

So, I really think of it more in terms of class and culture, the culture—what you learned as a kid, what you learned to like. And these are the people I have things in common with. Very few are Americans, so it happens, and most of them are either French or Arab Francophones, that's the majority of my friends.

These kinds of social relations are often intermittent but remain meaningful for the individuals who invest in them. Hisham, a twenty-one-year-old graduate student in Paris told me, for example, that he does not communicate with his friends regularly:

I contact some every week, some once a year, but I don't think there is a difference because when I go to them once a year; it seems as if I spoke to them yesterday. We are used to having these periods of no communication. This is how you realize that the relationship is really valuable. It doesn't matter if you see them every day or every year, because they will still understand you and want to be with you.

For Hisham, meaningful relations do not necessitate frequent communication or continuous activity. Importantly, these "stretched out social relations" (Allen and Hamnett 1995) allow Hisham and many other immigrants to see themselves as belonging to a global community based on their shared interests and lifestyles.

In the experiences of my respondents, class, shared interests and lifestyles, tastes, and occupational and educational backgrounds were more important than ethnicity in defining the communities they belonged to. These shared systems of meaning can develop between people living in different places—a process strengthened by increasing globalization and immigration (Hall 1997). Although national identities were created around shared affinities and coincided with shared geographical territory (Anderson 1991), global cultural, economic, and political processes produce similar affinities in disparate regions and bring people together so they can share their dispositions and form communities based on them. In this regard, globalization and immigration shift people's emphasis on traditional territorial boundaries to qualitative differences of gender, race, class, sexuality, and age (Scholte 1996). Although non-territorial group boundaries may lead to forms of social exclusions, many Lebanese immigrants I interviewed claimed that focusing on social issues and targeting social change are more meaningful ways to forge solidarities and affinities with others.

Global Solidarity

For Lebanese immigrants, as noted, the diasporic community they choose extends beyond different nation-states to include co-ethnics in other parts of the world. Indeed, the diaspora is "a space where nation and citizenship come to be intertwined with . . . global dramas" (Werbner 1998:18). Despite the various forms of public involvement in which Lebanese immigrants engaged, they all wanted to be active participants in social change. The various examples sited above suggest that they seek to be effective in Lebanon as well as in their new settings. Their awareness that they exist between the two societies also allows them to challenge given traditions and constraints. Combating sectarianism, political corruption, and violations of personal freedoms are important aspects of their involvement in the homeland. Demanding full participation in the host society allows them to gauge a basis for inclusion and participation. These concerns, while motivating participation in their homeland and host societies, also triggered a universal sense of belonging and more global forms of involvement. Recall Alain, the restaurant owner and journalist in Paris, who expressed a strong sense of ethnic identity. Despite his ethnic identification resulting from his refugee (and thus temporary) status and his overriding interest in Lebanese politics, he spoke of his desire to move beyond traditional attachments to achieve a different sense of belonging and acting in the world and stated that his approach to participating in Lebanese issues was affected by universal ideals and global awareness:

We wanted it to address what people are really worried about. We have a political standpoint and a vision for the future. We need to move beyond the traditional way of doing politics, of being affiliated to particular parties, ethnic groups, or certain individuals. There are larger issues in life and more important concerns. We need to worry about basic freedoms, the freedom to exist as who you are and voice your opinion. We need to be recognized and granted our rights regardless of what is your family background, the way you dress, or the accent in your speech.

Alain's account points to the need to form an identity that is not rooted in traditional narratives of ethnicity, national origin, or religion. Instead, he stresses the need to define his identity through his engagement with universal concerns.

In a globalized world, expansive social relationships are meaningful vehicles for migrants to pursue their interests in social change. In this sense, most respondents point out that their participation in political or social activities is not tied to nationality or ethnicity per se, but more to their sense of concern about specific issues such as justice and freedom which shape their understanding of their global realities. Referring to a recent antiwar protest in New York City, Carol, a thirty-two-year-old lawyer, observed the following:

> One would expect many Arabs to be at the protest, since it is an Arab country that is being attacked. But no, this was not the case, and it definitely was not my reason to be at the rally. True, there were groups of people who took this as an opportunity to advocate for the Palestinian cause and a sense of Arabness. This is not how I saw the rally, however. For me it was an opportunity to make a statement that we need global solidarity. We need to realize that we are all in the same boat, and that we should stick on the side of justice no matter who is targeted by the violence.

Similar to other respondents, Carol is critical of the attitudes of other Lebanese and Arab immigrants in New York and Lebanese society more generally. She also realizes that given her experience with migration, she sees the world differently than do many Americans around her. Instead of focusing on her differences, Carol knows that shared dispositions are important sources of identifying with others and forging a sense of belonging to diverse groups. The search for a shared community based on specific interests and values allows immigrants like Carol to forge universal alliances and participate in global action and discourses.

Many respondents stressed that their experience with migration allows them to become aware of the universal nature of many issues they are concerned with. For example, Alfred explained that while living in Lebanon he was immersed in Lebanese social and political issues relating to the civil war. Then, upon moving to Paris, he became totally immersed in French political and European concerns such as the rights of undocumented migrants. While Alfred recognized that different societies have different concerns and different strategies to address them, his experience was most beneficial in that it made him aware of the more global issues such as liberation, ecology, and nation building. He concluded, simply, by saying: "We do not have these debates in Lebanon."

As my fieldwork suggests, the multiple worlds in which members of the diaspora live are not confined to co-nationals and co-ethnics but expand to include others who share a similar sense of belonging and acting in the world at large. Lebanese immigrants illustrate forms of actions, networks, and formal organizations that include particular concerns based on their membership in the homeland, host society, and the larger Lebanese diaspora. While immigrants' interest in Lebanese political and social spheres continues to be an important source of public engagement in the homeland and host societies, such engagement is shaped by a belief in universal equality, emancipation, social justice, and individual rights. As expressed by Roy, a graduate student in Montreal who moved from Beirut to New York City to Montreal:

The fundamental thing in Lebanon is a moral problem. It's a problem of ethics. You have to abandon the ethics of power, and shame, and patronage, and vandalism for a more universal approach.

Roy's remark refers specifically to his experience in engaging with issues in Lebanon after he left Beirut and migrated to North America. Despite his focus on Lebanese-related issues of corruption, abuse of power, and moral decay, Roy advocates a universal approach that allows him to deal with these issues while in Canada and as they apply to Canadian society. In his view, once his interest is focused on specific issues, seeing them within a universal approach allows him to confront them in various locations around the world as the problem itself is generally universal. All these illustrations show that participation in the homeland and the host societies are grounded in the immigrants' interest in effecting social change and transforming both societies in becoming more democratic. Given their experience with migration, many respondents realize that their goals are not specific to either society but are emphatically global, and so they seek forms of global membership and universal attachments. Alfred, for example, explained that Lebanon was not the only concern in the activities of his group:

I do enough for Lebanon. I spend summers there, and I do not just go on vacation. I participate in projects. For example, during my last visit, I helped in fund-raising money for our magazine . . . Still there are larger issues that one has to think about. The world is more complicated and what is going on in Lebanon is not the worst part.

Alfred's experience with immigration made him realize that his public involvement should be focused on broader issues rather than a specific society or country:

> I know I can still get involved in Lebanese issues while here in France, and that's why I am still involved in various activities that focus on Lebanon. I also realize that my world is not only Lebanon anymore . . . Having experienced life in a different country, now I can put Lebanon in a larger context and I also realize that there are larger issues that we should be concerned about . . . like human rights, the environment, and inequality.

Similar to Alfred, many respondents referred to their experience of migration as allowing them to see things more globally. A large number of Lebanese immigrants believe that they belong to a larger group of world immigrants who, though their origins may be diverse, share a common predicament of navigating two or more societies and trying to belong to multiple communities. Speaking for immigrants in general, Alfred exclaimed:

> We are all in a common destiny, and we must share the experience. We must give the best of ourselves to succeed in this violent and uncertain environment. So maybe that would be the basis to get together and share what we have in common.

In "The 'Diaspora's Diaspora,'" Rogers Brubaker (2005) warns against assuming that a diaspora is an entity to which all immigrants from a particular territory belong. Instead of analyzing diaspora as a bounded entity, Brubaker suggests that we think of diaspora as

> an idiom, a stance, a claim . . . As a category of practice, "diaspora" is used to make claims, to articulate projects, to formulate expectations, to mobilize energies, to appeal to loyalties. It is often a category with a strong normative charge. It does not so much *describe* the world as seek to *remake* it.

Many of the immigrants I interviewed provided narratives that support Brubaker's claim. Most Lebanese immigrants in Montreal, New York, and Paris, because of their experience with migration, believe that they are more capable than previously of bridging interests that are based on national or ethnic attachments and the universal ones that are not tied to a territory or a nation-state. Simply put, as immigrants consciously discard traditional forms of attachments to the homeland, they are impelled to advocate for universal causes and cosmopolitan ties. In Carol's words:

> I have lots of opinions about what is going on in Lebanon, and I am very vocal about them . . . I also get involved in other issues that allow me to see myself as a global citizen and not as someone who has a very narrow understanding of the world . . . I volunteer a lot with other lawyers who work on immigrant issues in New York . . . not just Arab immigrants but all sorts of immigrants, especially ones from African countries.

Many immigrants attributed their sensitivity to issues of justice and freedom to memories of war, whether evoked by their own experiences or those of their parents. Fareed explained his concerns about social justice in general: "I think what bothers me more [than the situation in Lebanon] is just seeing a lot of social injustice out there, and I guess growing up in Beirut and growing up in a very political environment, you tend to be a bit more aware of these things."

The global attachments in which members of the Lebanese diaspora engage are not always opposed to their traditional national or ethnic attachments. In *Culture, Power, Place*, Gupta and Ferguson (1997) warn against the opposition of "the local," understood as original, centered, natural, and authentic, to "the global," understood as new, external, artificially imposed, and inauthentic (see also Dirlik 1997). In the lives of Lebanese immigrants, global experiences are quite real and are shaped by migration and living in a diaspora, and they give coherence to immigrants' daily social experiences. It is important to note as well that such global experiences do not mean that their local attachments to their host city or homeland disappear. Indeed, the understanding that their social worlds are composed of multiple localities is at the center of their awareness of their global presence and reality or, as Dirlik (1997) describes it, their "simultaneous cosmopolitanism and localism."

Literature on transnational immigrant communities tends to emphasize exclusion, segregation, or subjugation as shaping immigrants' networks and identities. For example, Catherine Wihtol de Wenden (1998) describes the experiences of North African immigrants in France as having been shaped by push factors from their countries of origin (the result of political instability and civil strife) as well as exclusionary rightist forces in France. The author argues that both these forces lead many Franco-Maghrebians to organize in "the center around French nationality, European identity, while defining a citizenship dissociated from nationality and elaborating a Franco-Maghrebian network and culture" (ibid.:278). Analyses of transnational migration and postcolonialism alike contend that immigrants' sense of fragmentation, exclusion, or segregation fosters the construction of nontraditional forms of solidarity and consciousness, and drive immigrants to seek global forms of attachments (see, e.g., Vertovec and Cohen 1999).

However, the kind of universal solidarity that is sought by members of the Lebanese diaspora whom I interviewed is not a result of a sense of exclusion by the societies to which they belong. Although many of these immigrants have experienced discrimination and exclusion, they emphasize that these experiences are not a central aspect of their goal to forge nontraditional forms of solidarity. Instead, in their view, it is their experience with migration that has made them more capable of bridging national or ethnic attachments and universal ones not tied to a territory or nation-state.

Sociologist Jan Nederveen Pieterse (1994) argues that globalization increases individuals' ability to simultaneously avail themselves of several organizational options. In this regard, globalization provides a framework for the diversification and amplification of "sources of the self," or the routes through which an identity can be understood and negotiated. To illustrate a diasporic sense of identity, Soysal (2000) draws on the experiences of immigrant groups in Europe and contends that some mobilize around claims for particularistic provisions to strengthen their group identities. Their claims, however, are not simply grounded in the particularities of religious or ethnic narratives, which is the perspective of Vertovec and Cohen (1999). In her rejection of the popular understanding of diaspora, Soysal (2000) highlights the paradox entailed as these immigrants draw on notions of universal rights and participate in diverse public spheres.[8] As such, their mobilization is not simply a reinvention of ethnic or religious particularisms but rather is a process of forging an identity within the complexities of globalization and immigration:

> In this new topography of membership, what constitutes the grounds for civic projects is no longer the "horizontal connectedness" among members of an ethnic community (that is, mutual trust and solidarity on the basis of ethnic belonging). Here, the "ties that bind" manifest themselves through participation in and by "vertical connection" to common, universalistic discourses that transcend the very ethnic idiom of community. (Soysal 2000:11)

The vertical connections in Soysal's analysis and the range of diasporic organizational options operating simultaneously enable members of diasporic communities to forge a sense of belonging and an understanding of themselves that moves beyond traditional processes of group membership and identification. Many Lebanese immigrants explain that their desire to address universal concerns and global inequalities derives from their cosmopolitan identity. For example, May, a thirty-one-year-old lawyer in New York City, said that her membership in multiple publics corresponded to her various forms of identification:

> I write letters to the City Council and the mayor, and I also write letters to the president of the U.S. and the secretary general of the UN. This is because I am a New Yorker, an American, and a citizen of the world. It becomes meaningless after a while, when identity becomes a hat that you put on depending on the circumstance or the cause you happen to be interested in. Still, it is not all that meaningless. I cannot sit there and do nothing, I have to get involved and my involvement takes different forms from day to day and from one issue to the next.

Although many immigrants do not express their "vertical connections" in ways that are similar to May's, many utilize a number of communal attachments that operate simultaneously and allow them to forge a sense of belonging that moves beyond traditional forms of group membership and identification.

Diasporic processes of identification may also reconcile an apparent contradiction described by Charles Taylor (1992) between the politics of universalism and the politics of difference, which he argues is the result of increasing cultural diversity and the emergence of multiculturalism. The many narratives provided by members of the Lebanese diaspora illustrate attempts to reconcile these potentially contradictory discourses. For example, Ziade explained his interest in bringing diverse people together as a way to realize their similarities. As an example, he spoke of the activities he organizes for his literary group:

> First of all, I started because I really found in New York that every community tried to separate itself, alone, tried to vote alone, have its own newspaper, the Latinos, the blacks, the Jews, and at one point I said, I want to do something for everybody. And at our readings and events, we have the blacks, the Latinos, the Asian, the Arab, the Muslim, the Christians, the Jews, the gays, the lesbians, everybody was at our readings. Everybody. And we had great fun.

Many immigrants I interviewed emphasize that their interests and sources of identification go beyond the homeland and host society. Instead, they see their public engagement as addressing universal issues of equality and freedom. The constant pursuit for belonging allows members of the diaspora to escape the "thin" form of cosmopolitan identity that is based on rationality and legality. Arguing against the Habermasian conception of "thin" cosmopolitanism, Calhoun (2002) stresses that the public sphere offers more than reaching consensus on legal and political issues. Rather, a cosmopolitan public offers "new ways of imagining identity, interests, and solidarity" (ibid.:171). As a realm of mutual engagement, public action, when undertaken at a global level, supports universal solidarity and forms of belonging. Josiane describes her sense of mutual engagement in the form of a duty toward other human beings around the world:

What we need more now, in our period that we live, is the sense of duty. The duty is not an obligation, the duty is a pleasure. I feel this way when you do something [for] your country, when you do something [for] the people around you, when you do something for the whole world, when you extract discipline to yourself, you help somewhere, you present to the society a good world citizen . . . Your duty is everywhere.

In stressing a sense of duty and engagement with global issues, many Lebanese immigrants challenge traditional forms of belonging but not forms of solidarity altogether. Rather, they maintain a strong sense of membership through their involvement in the various societies they belong to as well as a global society that they envision. This kind of membership is formed by their awareness of their diasporic disposition and is organized around universal causes and concerns. Through their various activities, members of the Lebanese diaspora participate in new social movements, use the globe as the reference point for political activity, and act on the basis of a global consciousness (see, e.g., Axtmann 1997; and Lipschutz 1992), all important conditions for the rise of a global solidarity.

Conclusion

Invoking Marx's statement that "men [and women] make their own history, but they do not make it just as they please, they do not make it under circumstances chosen by themselves, but under circumstances directly encountered, given and transmitted from the past" (Marx 1967:15), postcolonial analyst Arif Dirlik (1997) argues that the social construction of in-betweenness and cosmopolitan history are strategic mechanisms to cope with conditions of displacement and diaspora. As a product of specific historical experiences, diasporic communities construct forms of solidarity that are shaped by past experiences of displacement, present problems of inequality and exclusion, and future interests in solidarity and freedom. In the process, they challenge traditional forms of attachments that are based on nationality, ethnicity, or religion. The context of globalization facilitates the construction of social relations that transcend national boundaries. Global cultures, political interdependence, and economic encounters, in addition to providing the structure for global solidarity, make global solidarity necessary at least in the experience of immigrants who wish to challenge the traditions of both their homeland and host societies.

So why did my respondents deny their participation in Lebanese immigrant communities in the cities where they lived, despite their engagement with diasporic networks and activities? To many respondents, especially those in New York and Montreal, a Lebanese community was regarded as the old, third-plus generation of Americans and Canadians of Lebanese origin that was often found in religious or political organizations. Members of these organizations have no experience with migration and little firsthand experience with life in Lebanon. My respondents, being first-generation immigrants, saw these communities as ethnic ones that emerged within specific national contexts of ethnic relations in the United States or Canada. As a result, they did not wish to be associated with members of these communities and so did not participate in them. Although they participated in consuming the products and activities put together by earlier cohorts or non-immigrant generations, they did not have a sense of ownership over these activities since they did not identify in strictly ethnic terms.

As important actors giving rise to a "universalistic solidarity" (Alexander 1991), diasporic communities are creating global attachments instead of emphatically ethno-national ones. These attachments include ties with the homeland and an interest in Lebanese issues. Transnational solidarities are also an important component as immigrants participate in various communities and groups in their host societies. Membership in a larger diaspora that includes other Lebanese immigrants in different countries is another source of solidarity. Importantly, members of the Lebanese diaspora see themselves as active participants in a global society that transcends borders and ethnicities, and is centered around common interests and visions for an equal, just world. Thus, as a diaspora, Lebanese immigrants forge "new postessential, postterritorial, and postnational realignments that sometimes crack open the fault lines of ethnic, religious, class, and gender differences repressed by ideologies of sacrosanct national unity" (Sullivan 2001:1).

As members of the Lebanese diaspora illustrate, immigration processes are not adequately captured by underscoring transnationalism. Intensified global processes are bringing traditional understandings of community and belonging into further question. Analyses of transnational communities connected to immigrant groups have focused on links across nation-states that are constructed primarily around specific ethnic or national loyalties, affiliations, and concerns. This chapter presented a case where immigrants' concerns, interests, and claims can lead them to construct attachments and participate in communities based on their interest in becoming global citizens and participating in global spheres. As the previous chapter argued, the desire to maintain or return to the homeland is not shared by all Lebanese immigrants. This chapter illustrated that a shared desire to bring about social changes in Lebanese society provides a stronger source of attachment to the homeland as well as others in the diaspora who may share similar visions. Continued contacts and social networks that extend between immigrants and those who are still in the homeland create a transnational public sphere that encompasses both countries (Mahler 1998). Using the framework of diaspora problematizes immigrants' relationships to their homeland and their identification with their host societies. Opening up these relationships that are often taken for granted when understanding transnational practices allows us to investigate more creative ways of forging solidarities and communities that are not tied to ethnicity and nationality. Understanding their experiences with migration, settlement, and exclusion, as affected by global dynamics of war, inequality, and politics, Lebanese immigrants end up participating in global public spheres and wanting to become active in shaping these global dynamics instead of accepting them passively.

Cultures of Expression

Translation, Remembrance, and Global Burden

I filmed myself walking in an in-between space.
Unlike usually, the more I came closer to the camera,
the smaller my image became till I disappeared.
— Mounira Al Solh

The previous chapters analyze forms of identification and social solidarity created by members of the Lebanese diaspora. On the one hand, Lebanese immigrants are in a constant process of identifying with their homeland and host societies. Additionally, they identify with other members of the larger diaspora, which leads to their engagement in global communities. This chapter addresses the topic of diasporic cultural expression to illustrate ways in which the Lebanese diaspora engages in global and local cultural practices that parallel their multilayered forms of identification and community involvement. The definition of culture that I use encompasses culture as a way of life as well as processes of representation. British sociologist Anthony King (1997:2) advocates that "culture in its sense of art, literature, film, practices of representation of all kinds, both draws from and participates in the construction of culture as a way of life, as a system of values and beliefs which, in turn, affects culture as a creative, representational practice, [and thus] we can bridge what is often a gap between these different meanings." Given that many of my respondents were keen on attending cultural events such as public lectures, music and cultural festivals, and museum exhibitions that relate to Lebanon and the Arab world, the significance of studying these events and the individuals who put them together emerged while designing the present project and were strengthened over the course of data collection. Cultural constructions are avenues for understanding how a group understands itself and wishes to present itself to others. At times when Lebanese and Arabs are considered by mainstream media representations and political discourses in their host societies as terrorists, conflict-ridden, and religious fanatics, these cultural representations gain consequence in understanding the ways in which members of the diaspora engage with these negative constructions and wish to alter them for more positive portrayals in their host societies. In light of King's suggestion, this chapter focuses on the relationship between Lebanese diasporic cultural workers (visual artists, musicians, curators, and writers) and the dynamics of diasporic identities and communities. Specifically I focus on these cultural workers' participation in different public spheres as an avenue for understanding their expressions of diasporic experiences and identities. These forms of cultural expression are taken to illustrate key examples of Lebanese immigrants' cosmopolitan identities and attachments.

My last stay in Paris was in 2007 when I was engaged in a research project that focuses on the second-generation North Africans in the city. I had already decided that I was not going to seek more data collection from Lebanese immigrants, as I was already in the final stages of writing this book. I was forced to reverse that decision at the very end of my stay as I was finishing up my research and getting ready to return to the United States. In July the Paris film festival started, and Lebanon was the festival's guest of honor for the annual event. Lebanese movies, many of which were produced and directed by Lebanese immigrants, were featured during the two-week festival, and the people who put these movies together were available for interviews and press conferences. During the festival, I had a chance to reconnect with some of the cultural workers I had already interviewed during my first visit in 2002. After a five-year absence, I was updated on their new activities and changing views on the postwar reconstruction efforts in Lebanon. I was also able to follow the progress in these artists' careers, as many were becoming more famous than when they first agreed to participate in my study. Through the festival's events, I was also introduced to a handful of cultural workers whom I had not met before and who agreed to participate in my research. Through the second encounters with some of these artists, their increased pessimism about the future of Lebanon was made more explicit. Because the festival took place a year after the Israeli attacks on Beirut, many of the short films especially dealt with the physical devastation caused by these attacks as well as the social fragmentation that was further produced. For immigrant artists, these films expressed their ambivalence toward Lebanese society. At the same time their films accentuated their interest in expressing cosmopolitan attachments and participating in global cultural activities as opposed to national and ethnic ones. Once I returned to the United States, I sought out the other artists I had interviewed in New York and Montreal and was able to detect similar patterns among them. Many of them had gained international fame and recognition in the years following my meetings with them. They, too, had become more pessimistic about the situation in Lebanon and looked at their work that deals with the situation as representative of a specific moment in Lebanese social history. Like their counterparts in Paris, Lebanese immigrant artists in New York and Montreal grew more interested in producing works that were detached from national and ethnic roots.

This chapter shows that Lebanese immigrant artists emphasize feelings of nostalgia and displacement as the condition of living in multiple societies. The diaspora artists are in a constant process of identifying with their homeland's culture and traditions. As members of the Lebanese diaspora, their interest in participating in their homeland is based on the desire to challenge assumptions of Lebanese history and culture, pushing for the development of more collective forms of solidarity to overcome sectarian divisions. Such strategies of "picking a quarrel" with their homeland were explained in the previous chapter. In addition to these strategies, Lebanese immigrant artists have an overwhelming desire to confront the Lebanese civil war as a result of their interest in promoting collective healing and communal solidarity through their work. Engagement with the homeland notwithstanding, Lebanese artists are also involved in the host society and its cultural life. Combating negative stereotypes of Arabs and Arab immigrants by presenting Lebanese/Arabic art reflects their desire to inspire their host societies to be more multicultural and inclusive. Additionally, expressing their experiences with war and sectarian divisions to members of their host societies allows Lebanese artists to engage in global forms of expression and collectivity while highlighting local and national conflicts. These immigrants' ability to bridge the gap between the two cultures leads them to participate in different public spheres and produce innovative forms of diasporic identities and cultures. Moreover, diasporic artists also express their belonging to a global community and emphasize their cosmopolitan duty. Lebanese immigrants' desire to address their universal ideals artistically and within multiple contexts provides an avenue for investigating the relationship between global and local processes empirically as well as a way to understanding the gaps between abstract ideals and particular interests dynamically.

Portraying the Homeland: The Burden of Global Art

The local retains the concrete associations of the local community—but more as reference than as a specific description (or prescription). (Dirlik 1997:85)

Analyses of transnational communities illustrate the ways that immigrants' lives are shaped by their political, economic, and social interests in the homeland (see, e.g., Jones-Correa 1998; Levitt 2001; and Vertovec and Cohen 1999). Transnational cultural practices also illustrate the ways in which cultural events such as religious festivals, national holidays, and traditional celebrations are transported and re-presented to the host society. These events serve as important vehicles through which communal solidarity and consciousness are maintained. Examples of such forms of maintaining cultural traditions abound in the life of the Lebanese diaspora in Montreal, New York, and Paris. For example, many respondents are keen on their annual participation in religious festivals and gatherings organized by Lebanese and Arab organizations. Similarly, many participate in Lebanese film festivals, artistic exhibitions, and national celebrations. These activities are considered important sources of identifying with and attachment to their homeland. In many ways, the respondents also use these activities to maintain their ethnic and national pride either by affirming their Lebanese heritage or stressing successful integration and recognition in their host societies.

In terms of cultural representations, the artists, musicians, and writers I interviewed expressed their interest in maintaining their attachment to Lebanon and expressing it in their works. In fact, cultural portrayals of Lebanon were central to almost all the artists as they realized their advantage as "representatives" of their homeland and produced works that focused on presenting particular visions of Lebanon to their host societies. For example, Josiane, a painter who divided her time between Paris and Beirut, emphasized that her paintings point to her Lebanese roots, even when she drew outside Lebanon.

The presence of the arch is kind of symbolic, because the arch captures the architecture of Lebanon. Now I express myself in a very personal way, starting from a concrete idea, but drawing my arch according to my mood, in a very gentle way, in color and in shape, so the painting has something to do with the country, but it has nothing to do with [a] specific geographic state, a specific place or time. It has to do with a period, an ambiance, so it has something to do with the Mediterranean. And I think it also expresses the spirit of what we are going through ourselves. I deeply believe that an

artist, a painter, a novelist, or a musician could express more, whenever [s]
he is outside his [or her] country, the soul of his [or her] country which
allows him [or her] to go back home to his [or her] roots.

While meeting with Josiane in her loft in Paris where she showed me a
number of her paintings that were still in progress, she explained the various
meanings behind her paintings. Josiane's paintings included variations on
the theme of the arch in an assortment of color schemes and angles that, in
her views, were chosen to portray a peaceful and inviting condition. According to Josiane, her paintings were clearly those of a Lebanese artist given her
choice of design (the arch), color (Mediterranean), and urban layout (Middle
Eastern). She maintained that, although she did not paint during the time
she spent in Lebanon, she believed that she still presented a specific Lebanese
style in her drawings that was not affected by her presence in Paris or the fact
that she was a famous artist in France.

Josiane first arrived in Paris in 1976—a year after the war started—as a
young student, and she regularly returned to Beirut every six months to visit
her family. She explained that throughout her stay in Paris, even when there
were no means of flying to Beirut, she still flew through Damascus and went
to Beirut by road, as she was keen on spending time with her family. For the
first two years of her stay in Paris, Josiane thought of her presence there as
temporary. In 1978, however, during one of her visits to Beirut, her family
house was destroyed in the war, and "the shock of coming out of the ruins
alive" made her realize the extent of the destruction surrounding her. Josiane's family is prominent in Lebanese politics, and many of her family members were actively engaged with the war. Given her young age at the time,
Josiane could not initially understand the stakes involved, but knew that she
could not interfere. Despite the fact that Josiane was critical of her family's
actions in the war at that time, and despite her desire to express her concern
for her country and people, Josiane made the decision to stay in Paris. In her
words, that decision was "almost an involuntary reflex, one without much
reflection and analysis, yet it lasted till today."

More than twenty years later, Josiane reconsidered her decision to remain
in Pairs permanently. In 2001 she decided that it was time to go back to Lebanon, and she started dividing her time between Beirut and Paris.

So I started sharing my time between here and there, which means that I
have my *atelier* here, I have my status here as an artist, as a citizen. As an
artist, I belong here, to France. In the meantime, I am also from Lebanon, I

have a presence there, I have activities there, not only as an artist, but I also support my family, which is an important activity, in politics.

The kind of support that Josiane offers her family is a political one. Following the end of the war, her family continues to be engaged in politics and her presence in Lebanon as a French renowned artist is an important resource that the family draws on.

Given her political involvement—although indirectly—in postwar Lebanese politics, Josiane's emphasis on portraying Lebanon by using urban Mediterranean symbols should be understood in the context of Lebanese postwar reconstruction politics. The Mediterranean ambiance in Josiane's paintings parallels the postwar reconstruction efforts in Beirut that are put together by the Lebanese state. These efforts consciously aim at re-creating the city in generic Arab Mediterranean form to erase the effects of the war (Cooke 2002). The absence of any reference to the civil war or its remnants was a deliberate effort on Josiane's part as well. While reconstruction efforts in Beirut aimed at "a return, a reversion to a pre-war past . . . that flattened, homogenized, and aestheticized the traces of war" in Lebanese public culture (Cooke 2002:409), Josiane's purpose was to flatten the memory of war in the French psyche. She believes that her paintings are an important representation of "true" Lebanese culture, especially during times of crisis in the homeland:

> Presenting myself as a Lebanese painter here [in Paris] during the war, showing a cultural part of Lebanese society while people were watching TV and hearing about the war and guns and everything, it was my contribution to give a different image of my country.

In this respect, Josiane shares the views illustrated by other immigrants who believe in their task as presenting positive role models of Lebanese people to their host societies so that they counteract the negative stereotypes and assumptions about the Lebanese (and sometimes Arabs). For these immigrants, cultural activity is an important mechanism in achieving that goal. Thus Josiane's emphasis on the role she played in educating French society reflects the views that are held by Lebanese immigrants in general. Nonetheless, Josiane's choice in defining the elements of what is to be considered "Lebanese" is shaped by her own personal history and experiences. As we know, she comes from a prominent political family which, similar to other political actors in Lebanon, has committed its share of misfortune during the civil war. Since Josiane's family is involved in the rebuilding of Lebanon, her choice of representation parallels projected official visions that emphasize a distant past and impel it onto the future in the hope of obliterating the memory of the civil war and the atrocities that were committed by all the political actors involved.

Other Lebanese immigrant cultural workers expressed similar sentiments and beliefs that their work is strongly shaped by their interest in the homeland. Similar to Josiane, their interest was exhibited mostly through works that illustrate Lebanese society and culture, mainly to a non-Lebanese audience so as to inform members of the host societies of Lebanese issues. However, their choices of defining Lebanese culture varied with their context of reception as well as their personal experiences. For example, Michel started an Arabic Music Radio show that used to broadcast in New York once a week. The main purpose of the show was to introduce New Yorkers, Americans, or others who can listen to the show on the Internet to Arabic music and culture. Michel's motivation is "to let people know that Arabic culture is more sophisticated than people may think." Aware of the tendency of mainstream Americans to believe in simplistic understandings of the Arab world, Michel wanted listeners "to know that Lebanon is not just war, corruption, and destruction. We belong to an old civilization that had many contributions and achievements for many, many years."

The selection of music Michel chose come from different parts of the Arab world, and his interests were not always specific to Lebanon. Unlike Josiane's choice of placing Lebanon within a Mediterranean context, Michel focused on an Arab context to narrate Lebanese culture. The different choice of context that Josiane and Michel selected was clearly affected by immigration politics in their host societies. In France, "Arab" refers mostly to the marginalized immigrants from North Africa, and Lebanese immigrants tend to occupy a favorable position in French society, which explains why Josiane's paintings were devoid of any Arab references as she emphasized a Mediterranean ambiance instead. The Mediterranean context would also bring Lebanon closer to Southern European countries and thus frame its culture in ways that are favorable to the French. Michel, on the other hand, who lived in New York City, embraced Arab culture and, at the same time, consciously demonstrated the diversity within it. Unlike Paris, where the French public differentiates Lebanese from other Arabs, in New York a pan Arab categorization provides the main path for participating in the city's ethnic politics. Despite the larger Arab context that Michel chose, he was still interested in introducing his listeners to the culture of his origins. Believing that "ethnic cultural spectacles are opportunities for a given group to choose how they wish to be understood by nonmembers" (Bramdat 2001), Josiane's work reflected the tendency to exclude "Arab" from the Lebanese immigrant narrative in France and to differentiate Lebanese from North Africans. While Josiane herself was critical of Lebanese traditional politics, her family had been historically involved in Maronite political activism, which likely influenced her decision to distance herself from Arab culture. Michel, on the other hand, and despite his Maronite background, took issue with sectarian politics in Lebanese society and, in terms of cultural activity, he wished to contribute to an existing stream of Arab cultural production in the United States that both affirmed his Lebanese identity and differentiated him from the mainstream American society. Both Josiane and Michel demonstrate that their homeland was "a space of cultural distinctiveness rather than a geographic entity" (Kennedy and Roudometof 2002:35). Their artistic expressions were chosen to assert their uniqueness in their host societies while at the same time seeking empathy to establish an identity in their adopted countries (see, e.g., Fernandez Kelly 2006).

The interest in presenting the homeland and its culture and engaging in a cross-cultural dialogue between Lebanon (or the Arab World) and the countries of settlement is considered an important vehicle for granting immigrants a positive image and welcomed presence in their host societies. Although host societies are often assumed by diasporic Lebanese artists to be lacking in their understanding of Lebanese and Arab culture, members of the diaspora themselves and sometimes cultural workers in the homeland are considered to be at fault for that deficiency. For example, Gilbert, a professor of English at a Canadian University, expressed the reason behind his interest in translating Arabic literature into English:

> There is a great need for us to be known as we are: naked. Through our publications and our literature, especially our art, the West will be able to have a clearer glimpse of who we are. Unfortunately, there hasn't been much. We are not known as artists, writers and singers. We are known as terrorists, fighters, and warmongers. That loud voice is much, much stronger than the quiet voice. I try to engage in activities that tell the West that we do have culture, that we know beauty. We know humanity. We know what is peaceful . . . Hopefully, my writings and my translations would contribute to a little understanding of this part of the world or of the people who wrote it.

In a number of interviews I came across Gilbert's assertion that Arabs are not known for their arts and literature in Western countries. First waves of Arab immigrants were largely poor and uneducated, and thus unable to promote their culture in the New World. More recent waves, those arriving in the 1960s and 1970s, were comprised of highly educated professionals. With a few exceptions, immigrants of these waves considered success in politics and the professions as the main path to socioeconomic mobility in their new settings, and art and literature were considered distractions to achieving success.[1] Having established himself within Canadian academia, Gilbert believes that he can cross cultural boundaries with relative ease, since he is as proficient in both Canadian and Arab cultures. His interest in translating Arabic works for the Canadian public was based on his interest in making Canadian society more just and multicultural by providing a "naked" portrayal of Arabic culture and, as a result, benefiting both Canadians and Arabs alike. More important, his goal in translating Arabic literature into English was aimed to fill a gap in Arabic literature in Montreal. Writing in English, Gilbert attempted to avoid the double exclusion of being an immigrant writer in Québec. According to Gilbert, writing in French to address Québécois society would only signify his double exclusion in Canada. As an immigrant, his writings are already tagged as ethnic literature even if he provided more than translations of Arabic texts and wrote as a "Canadian literary critic." The French language would only further isolate his works given the estrangement between Québec and the rest of Canada (see Dahab 1999).

Although they spoke with authority about their desire to represent Lebanese and Arab culture to their host societies, Josiane, Michel, and Gilbert define the ways that culture can be portrayed based on their own choices and contexts. In many ways, their attempts to represent Lebanese culture to their host societies end up replicating the modes of representation that they wish to dispute, namely, the tendency to homogenize Arab, Middle Eastern, and, by association, Lebanese societies and cultures, as well as the diaspora itself. Because their representations are context-specific, however, their constructions of Lebanese culture escapes monolithic assertions of a stagnant Lebanese identity and culture. Despite the tendency to reproduce what they attempt to challenge, the works of Lebanese diasporic artists provide avenues for challenging dominant modes of representation, both in their homeland and host societies. In his analysis of Black British art in the 1980s and early 1990s, Kobena Mercer (1994:235) maintains that, when artists are positioned on the margins of the institutional spaces of cultural production, they are burdened with the impossible task of speaking as "representatives," in that they are widely expected to "speak for" the marginalized communities from which they come.

Although most of the Lebanese diasporic artists I encountered were not on the margins of the mainstream cultural institutions in their host society, they relied on their ability to "authentically" represent their culture as a source of their privileged position in their new setting relative to those who are still in Lebanon. Speaking for Lebanon, the Arab World, and the Lebanese diaspora in their host societies, my respondents elected to represent what they saw as an authentic Lebanese or Arab culture, or both. Josiane's emphasis on the Mediterranean nature of Lebanese culture sought affinity in a French European context, where her audience knew and appreciated Mediterranean cultural forms. Michel's choice of classical Arabic music aimed at highlighting the contributions of the Arabs to world music in composition and instruments in a context where world music was popularized and understood. Gilbert's expertise in literature and poetry brought in underrepresented elements of Arab culture in a context where ethnic literature contributed to Canada's multicultural society. As these cultural workers represented what they consider the quintessential aspects of Lebanese/Arab culture and saw themselves as ambassadors of the Lebanese/Arab diaspora, they ultimately essentialized the culture they wished to represent.[2]

In explaining the phenomenon of global art, art historian John Peffer (2003) contends that it is produced by writers and visual artists who were born and raised in postcolonial societies but have studied, lived, traveled, and, more important, have achieved mainstream prominence in Europe and North America. "The Burden of Global Art," as the title of Peffer's essay suggests, is that these artists are taken as "representatives" of their homelands as well as their diasporic communities. Their presumed mastery of the two cultural milieus may lead many to engage in acts of translating their non-Western origins to a Western audience. Such was the case of some of the Lebanese immigrant cultural workers I interviewed. They were considered by their host societies as representatives of Lebanon and the Arab world. At the same time they found that form of representations to be meaningful in their choice of artistic expressions. For cultural anthropologist John Hutnyk (2005:87), translation is a popular task among individuals who traverse two cultural worlds and have the ability to "enforce their way" and define the culture they wish to translate. As a result, the outcome of such process of translation becomes an "appropriation of (cultural) ownership and even of creativity without attention to contexts." Hutnyk employs Spivak's *Critique of Postcolonial Reason* (1999:169), where she criticizes diasporic migrants who take on the authority of representing the culture that they claim is their origin and opt to stand for "the native informant." Hutnyk refers to this as a practice of "going native" that reflects the opportunism of diasporic migrants who are "seduced by complicity and advantage" and exploit their favorable position in their host society for personal gains and Western recognition. At first glance Josiane, Michel, and Gilbert may be considered as examples of such opportunistic artists who wish to gain recognition in their host societies by "going native" and enforcing their own definition of Lebanese/Arab culture. Their interest, however, in combating negative images of Lebanon and the Arab world provides cultural critiques more than an appropriation of cultural ownership. Moreover, their awareness of the ethnic structures in their host societies and their ability to construct images of Lebanese culture and society that specifically address the way Lebanon is placed within these structures affirms their understanding of their object as malleable and non-monolithic. While not undermining the critiques of migrant cultural production offered by Spivak and Hutnyk, Peffer (2003) argues that a number of diasporic artists are influenced by countercultural critiques of the 1960s art in the West that intends to disrupt mainstream modes of representation. Peffer concludes that, "the result, and sometimes the intent, has been to infect the master discourse so that its own codes become disrupted and other sites of enunciation might emerge" (337).

Having to represent Lebanese/Arab culture in a singular form may be an unconscious strategy to provide coherence and significance to their original culture that is often misrepresented and undermined in their host societies. More important, however, these diasporic artists also participate in challenging dominant modes of representation and crafting a culture of displacement and ambivalence. In addition to speaking on behalf of their marginalized communities, Mercer (1994:266) stresses that diasporic artists also adopt a "critical 'voice' that promotes consciousness of the collision of cultures and histories to constitute our very conditions of existence." Mercer suggests that we approach diasporic artistic expressions as political representations that question nostalgic stereotypes and undifferentiated identities that may exist in the diaspora. In some ways Josiane, Michel, and Gilbert can be seen as offering representations that question stereotypes of Lebanese and Arabs, Lebanese nostalgic desires of a return to the past as they draw attention to the present and the future instead, and highlight the diversity within the

Lebanese and Arab diasporic communities. The problem remains that these diasporic artists find themselves in a double-bind where they have to speak for their homeland and its culture while criticizing it at the same time. Still, these artists build on their privileged positions in Western societies to challenge power relations that inform the negative constructions of their homeland. Such a double-bind is explained by Peffer (2003:338):

> The burden of representation for the new global art is to elucidate the condition of the self in novel ways precisely by remaining critical of the ways that the commodity of the "other" can offer a temporarily privileged platform for speaking in the mainstream.

In the next section I illustrate ways in which Lebanese diasporic artists intervene in the construction of collective memory in Lebanon and homogenous identities in the diaspora as well as challenge mainstream discourses in their host society which demonstrate the double-double bind in which they find themselves. The third section deals with representations of belonging and displacement to show the ways that they challenge conceptions of home and otherness.

Interrupting Memory and Recognition

> It seems proper that those who create art in a civilization of quasi-barbarism, which has made so many homeless, should themselves be poets unbound and wanderers across language. Eccentric, aloof, nostalgic, deliberately untimely.
>
> —Said 1990: 363

Interest in portraying the homeland through various works reflects a level of nostalgia to the past which many of the immigrants left behind. Nonetheless, the artistic productions of Lebanese immigrants reflect a strong interest in addressing the present more than the past. Many of the individuals with whom I spoke emphasized the long history of Lebanese civilization and contributions to various cultures around the world. (I was constantly reminded by my interviewees that their Phoenician ancestors had introduced the alphabet to the rest of the world.) Many also expressed their memories of prewar Lebanon as a thriving, lively young state that rivaled its Middle Eastern counterparts. This nostalgia for the "Jewel of the Mediterranean"—as Lebanon was coined— parallels the culture of amnesia that describes Lebanese society itself. In his essay, "Public and Private Memory of the Lebanese Civil War," Sune Haugbolle (2005:194) asserts that such nostalgia for the past that proliferates in the Lebanese public sphere "can be seen as an attempt to overcome creeping feelings of meaninglessness and discontinuity" caused by the civil war. This form of nostalgia contributes to the public impulse to look to the future instead of trying to scrutinize the past and thus "provide personal and national history with a linkage that it seems to be missing" (ibid.). Notwithstanding the strong pride in their ancestral heritage, the forms of cultural expressions in which many Lebanese diasporic artists engaged in the diaspora did not always focus on a distant past. Rather, narrating the recent history and experiences of Lebanese people provided an important theme in the works of many Lebanese immigrant cultural workers. Specifically, representing personal experiences was intended to challenge existing cultural environments in both Lebanon and their host societies. More important, these works aimed at "the politicization of memory that distinguishes nostalgia, that longing for something to be as once it was, a kind of useless act, from that of remembering that serves to illuminate and transform the present" (hooks 1991:147). As I illustrate in this section, the kinds of transformations that Lebanese immigrant artists sought were targeted toward both homeland and host societies.

Remembering the Civil War

Narrating their personal experiences was a popular strategy among Lebanese immigrant artists. This strategy is considered a way of breaking with the public culture of amnesia in Lebanon—a culture based on conveying an illusory form of stability and coherence. Remembering the war is a theme that figured regularly in the narratives and works of the Lebanese diasporic artists whom I interviewed. In the process of remembering, these artists contest popular social practices in Lebanon that interpret the war within the basic binary of "friends" and "enemies." Such a simple interpretation is seen by cultural workers and analysts as detrimental to the future of the Lebanese as it "feed[s] into simplified antagonistic discourses of 'the other,' exacerbating the division between the Lebanese along sectarian lines" (Haugbolle 2005:192). Making scapegoats of the other factions and holding them responsible for the war helps warlords and politicians maintain their positions of power that they gained during the very war itself. Since those politicians were key players in the atrocities of the war and ended up as major actors in the rebuilding of Lebanon, they continue to maintain their powers by relinquishing and erasing any memory of the war. The Lebanese public sphere has also shown strong resistance to public memory, which led to "a culture of amnesia" mostly because of legal structures that indirectly censors the topic in the official media. Because members of the Lebanese society lived through the war, however, many find themselves "victims of a lacuna between personal memory and collective amnesia" (ibid.).[3] In summarizing the ways in which the Lebanese state has dealt with the memory of war, Cooke (2002:422) claims that because of the government's inability to eradicate the power of warlords, it becomes easier to eliminate memories of the war and perpetuate collective amnesia: "The State must destroy the conditions of possibility for the reappearance of the war machine. If that is not possible . . . then it must erase the memory of the process which was the war itself."

These efforts of the Lebanese state were relatively successful. Film production was one indicator of that success, with the first Lebanese film appearing in 1998, nine years after the signing of the National Reconciliation Accords. Ziad Dooueiry's *West Beirut* was the first film to address the conflict by tackling the war from the perspective of a civilian family.[4] The film marked the opening of the debate on the war in Lebanon, specifically the debate surrounding the purpose of remembering (Haugbolle 2005).[5]

The culture of amnesia that surrounds the civil war was an issue taken up by many cultural workers in the diaspora. Lebanese diasporic artists especially opposed the general affinity of the Lebanese state and society to submerge any memory of the civil war. For example, the Internet group 111101, which mostly includes diasporic artists and intellectuals, aims to "regroup Lebanese artists and writers, of all disciplines, living in Lebanon and abroad, who work on memory, through its different aspects: a space to search for traces of memory, a medium for archiving, and search for the structure of memory."[6]

Similarly the Lebanese diasporic cultural workers in my study expressed their interest in contributing to that search for the structure of memory. In their views, the state's emphasis on ancient Lebanese history alongside visions for a cosmopolitan future while erasing any memory of the war leads to a situation where it is no longer relevant to address individual responsibility or recognize the stakes of replicating the conflict in the near future. Challenging the public culture of amnesia in diasporic artistic expression takes many forms, but narrating personal experiences seems to be a dominant strategy of individuals whose work attempts to give meaning to their own experiences. The main goal for restructuring the memory of the civil war is to encourage Lebanese society to draw lessons from the conflict in order to avoid repeating it in the future.

Alfred and Simon, both graduate students who decided to live in Paris given the lack of economic opportunities in Lebanon, emphasized the importance of expressing their personal experiences of growing up in a wartime environment. Although they acknowledge their privileged class position in Lebanese society, Alfred and Simon both contend that there is a gap in understanding the war from the perspective of the young generation. One of the many artistic activities that the two men engaged in was the production of a documentary on the civil war in Lebanon. They emphasized that their motivation was not only to inform the French about the war, as they found the French public to be well informed about the subject, but rather, as Alfred described it, they wanted to present a version of the story that was left untold:

> So I decided to make this film, and it was really a challenge because I am not objective. I have some ideas, I cannot say I am really neutral, and I don't mind. So the challenge was to be honest with myself and to try to make something objective. And we made it.

In the process of putting the film together, both Alfred and Simon wanted to come to terms with their experiences of growing up during the civil war and trying to see events from different angels besides their own. Their film then had an element of catharsis—both personal and collective. Choosing to tell a personal story and stressing the importance of being honest to themselves in representing their own experiences replaces neutral narrations of the war. Since Alfred grew up as a Greek Orthodox and Simon was a Shiite Muslim, they believed that blending their perspectives provided a voice different from the dominant view; their religious difference would also enable them to represent the war and their experiences without sectarian victimization or blame. They also realized, however, that they could not be objective in their analysis, and so they had no desire to provide a comprehensive analysis of "what really happened" to all members of Lebanese society.

Using a semi-documentary style, Alfred and Simon chose to present an incoherent narrative, as they "were not trying to make sense of the war." Their aim, instead, was to express their own ambivalence and criticism regarding the war. Narrating contradictory memories of the war in a manner that makes no mention of heroes—in their words, "nobody wins" —Alfred and Simon transgress hegemonic constructions of Lebanese national harmony and shed light on contradictory understandings of history, which, in their opinion, need to be addressed to avoid the further disintegration of Lebanese society.

Alfred and Simon's efforts resemble those of other more famous diasporic Lebanese artists whose tales of the war "resist the exigencies of a coherent narrative" (Cooke 2002:401). In describing the ways that the Lebanese war has been portrayed artistically in Lebanese public cultural life, Miriam Cooke (2002) emphasizes the importance of constructing a moral memory that was integral in making sense of the chaos of war. Such moral memory, Cooke explains, is important for providing closure, which is a dominant strategy in dealing with the Lebanese civil war. Again, unlike these public representations, diasporic artists avoided logical narratives that aimed to "make sense" of the war. The following films by Lebanese artists in the diaspora highlight the impossibility of coherence when addressing the war: New York–based Walid Raad's *Missing Lebanese Wars* (1996), Paris-based Jocelyn Saab's *Once Upon a Time in Beirut* (1994), and Vancouver-based Jayce Salloum's *This Is Not Beirut* (1994).

Furthermore, Alfred and Simon took issue with Lebanese postwar efforts for reconstruction, as these efforts work to erase war memories. Referring to the absence of a war memorial in Beirut, Simon stated that "negating the war does not negate the effects it had on people, and we need to account for that." Both men also took issue with social divisions in Lebanese society, and stressed that omitting the role these divisions played in the civil war weakens any potential for establishing nonsectarian solidarities in Lebanon. Their interest in contributing to the memory of war, and their film as one example, signal their belief in the value of cultural expressions in shaping the future. Their emphasis on the meaninglessness of the war reflects their own experiences as children growing up in an environment where it was hard to make sense of the violence and destruction around them.

The erasure of the memory of war in Lebanon is a contentious issue for most Lebanese diasporic artists. In 1999 Walid Raad, the New York–based Lebanese filmmaker cited above, put together the Atlas Group, which aims "to locate, preserve, study and produce audio, visual, literary, and other artifacts that bring to light the contemporary history of Lebanon."[7] By emphasizing contemporary history, Raad's work focuses on the Lebanese civil wars as well as the postwar reconstruction. Similar to other diasporic artists, Raad's work does not attempt to reconstruct or recollect what actually happened during the war—indeed, the archives are a fictional work of art. Instead, Raad's work attempts to examine the power of control or monopoly over memory. For example, in a video installation titled "The Dead Weight of a Quarrel Hangs," Raad (1999) investigates

> the possibilities and limits of writing a history of the Lebanese civil wars (1975–1991). The tapes offer accounts of the fantastic situations that beset a number of individuals, though they do not document what happened. Rather, the tapes explore what can be imagined, what can be said, what can be taken for granted, what can appear as rational, sayable, and thinkable about the wars.

Raad's position on representing the war without recounting actual events and portraying an image of truth is clearly a political position that intends to counter hegemonic approaches to the civil war in Lebanese society. Raad's work, as well as Alfred and Simon's film, is based on actual moments of Lebanese history. However, the choice of representing imaginary situations rather than real ones undermines historical objectivity and the possibility of putting forth a unified Lebanese experience.

In an attempt to explain the politics of remembering, Marita Sturken (1997) observes that the point of analyzing cultural memories is not to discern "what really happened," in any given past events, but to look into "what its telling reveals about how the past affects the present" (1997:2). Consequently "cultural memory" is different from "collective memory" because, as Sturken argues, it encompasses the self-conscious processes through which memories are constructed and attached to "objects of memory." Lebanese immigrant artists are well aware that their works provide important objects through which the cultural memory of Lebanon is intentionally constructed and directed toward opposing social orders. Their attempts to explore the memory of the civil war intend to counter efforts to erase that period from Lebanese national memory. For example, Alfred and Simon cited the "peace memorial" in a small town outside Beirut that was constructed to glorify "the renewal of national peace in Lebanon" instead of remembering the war itself. Based on their reflection on the peace memorial, it closely resembles what Barbie Zelizer terms a form of remembering in order to forget (2000). The peace memorial serves to steer people's attention away from the events and the losses of the civil war and toward an orderly "cosmopolitan" future. The problem, however, is that the war continues to shape political and social life in Lebanon, an issue that many of the Lebanese diasporic artists wanted to bring to the forefront of public debate in order to counter the possibility of another civil war.

Demanding Recognition

In addition to contesting illusory notions of national peace and cohesion in Lebanon, Lebanese diasporic cultural workers also contest portrayals of their immigrant community that are sometimes imposed by members of their host societies or members of the diaspora itself. Most of my respondents critiqued the Lebanese immigrant community that existed "out there" and emphasized that they did not belong to it. In most cases, such a community was "too ethnic" in the sense that it focused on specific Lebanese and Arab issues without any interest in participating in the mainstream societies in the new settings. Furthermore, such a community was also fraught with gender inequality, homophobia, and religious intolerance. In some cases, such criticisms led my respondents to stay away from ethnic organizations or only to participate in a few events. In the case of the cultural workers, however, they chose to challenge the monopoly of a small group over the power to define the character of the community.

Roy is one artist who was originally driven to participate in the Lebanese immigrant community in Montreal through organizing various cultural events. Roy explained that his initial reaction to living in a foreign environment was to adopt an ethnic Lebanese and Arab identity, which motivated him to organize ethnic cultural events. During the first two years of his stay in Montreal, Roy organized an Arabic movie festival, called *Images du Monde Arabe* (Images of the Arab World), as well as a number of exhibitions for Arab artists, concerts for various musicians, poetry readings, and conferences. Roy valued his activities because of their secular nature. In his view, cultural and political organizations in the Lebanese immigrant community in Montreal are the monopoly of religious institutions, and he resented these institutions' power in defining the character of the entire Lebanese immigrant community and the ways it is perceived by Canadian society. As Roy explained:

> This is very important—for a secular to organize an event here, as it goes against the grain of the community. The community here centers on religious institutions. If Hezbollah organizes an event, you have three thousand people who would come. If the Catholics—the Maronite Church organizes an event, you have thirty-five hundred people coming. If somebody is trying to do something secular, organizing an event, it's very very difficult. You are going against the brunt of the community.

Roy was aware that members of the community themselves are religious and prefer to participate in events organized by the religious institutions with which they are affiliated. Roy also pointed out, however, that many members of the Lebanese immigrant community, like himself and others in his inner circle, do not belong to particular religious institutions, and therefore their views and identities needed to be voiced. Roy also knew that cultural representation in Lebanon followed similar patterns, and this motivated him to provide a platform for artists from Lebanon and other Arab countries to exhibit their work in Canada. Ultimately Roy found himself in a double-double bind, where he was representing his culture and at the same time wishing to critique both his home country and the diaspora. That position was discouraging, as he was becoming more aware of the ways that the immigrant community had replicated the same problems that existed in Lebanon, to which he reacted by distancing himself from the Lebanese immigrant community in Montreal:

> I organized a few events: I organized festivals and exhibitions. I did that for a period of two years. And at the end I was simply tired of spending eighteen hours a day for a year, organizing an event to which three hundred people came. I simply quit. I no longer focus on the Lebanese community in my work, and I don't necessarily wish to follow the art world in Lebanon either.

Roy's efforts were not entirely successful in challenging the monopoly over organized cultural events in Montreal. However, other cultural workers based in the same city successfully challenged Canadian society's omission of Arab culture in the construction of its cultural memory. For example, Marcel, a Canadian university professor, noted the various political events that led to strengthening his identity as Lebanese-Canadian. Having moved to Canada as an infant, and though initially detached from a Lebanese ethnic community, the political crisis following the Israeli invasion of Beirut in 1982 caused Marcel to participate in various activities that were focused on Lebanon and other parts of the Arab world. Over the years, as he was still searching for his roots, he noticed the lack of a narrative describing the contributions of early Arab immigrants to the history and development of the city of Montreal:

> I looked around me, and there are all kinds of stories about the multicultural history of the city, but somehow, my narrative was missing from this history . . . I knew from my family's stories that such narrative needed to be told, so I decided to tell it.

Marcel's inspiration came from his grandmother's memorabilia, and he put together an exhibition, held at the Centre d'Histoire de Montréal, narrating the story of Arab immigrants, who are mostly of Lebanese-Syrian origin. "Min Zamaan" (Since Years Ago), the exhibition that Marcel put together, describes the experiences of the early Syrian-Lebanese immigrants in Montreal and in other parts of Québec. The exhibition covered a variety of themes ranging from the causes of departure, the challenges of living in a new society, efforts at adaptation, and subsequent achievements in Québec. Although the planning for "Min Zamman" was in process before the 9/11 terrorist attacks, the events only reinforced Marcel's devotion to execute the project. "After Sept. 11, there was an even greater need for all Montrealers to realize that the Arabs among them were co-citizens who have helped build this city" (Polak 2003).

Like Marcel, many Lebanese diasporic artists emphasize that they have an important role to play in shaping cultural life in the places where they currently live. Specifically diasporic artists engage with the host society's negative media representations of Arabs and Arab culture, and produce works that challenge such mainstream depictions. For example, in the documentary *Introduction to the End of an Argument* (1990), Lebanese-Canadian artist Jayce Salloum collaborated with Palestinian producer Elia Suleiman in mixing clips from American news and popular media representations of Arabs and the Arab world that challenge Western constructions of these subjects. The artists' work conveys that "representation itself [i]s a politicized practice" and wishes to deconstruct these modes of representation through overloading the viewer with pejorative images (Westmoreland 2009). Similarly a group of Arab Canadian artists used the controversy surrounding the exhibit "The Lands Within Me" to deconstruct Canada's discourse on multiculturalism by exposing its limitations. "The Lands Within Me" was put together at the Canadian Museum of Civilization in Ottawa, and the intention was to take it to other Canadian cities and eventually other countries in Europe and the Middle East (Farah 2003). The exhibition displays the work of twenty-six Canadian Artists of Arab origins that deal with experiences of migration, immigration, and multiple identities. The exhibition was scheduled to start in October 2001, one month after the 9/11 attacks. Shortly following the attacks, however, the museum director announced that the exhibition would be postponed. In response, the participating artists stormed the museum director's office with phone calls and letters, and rallied the support of public officials to intervene in defense of Canada's multicultural policies that promote ethnic tolerance and understanding. The exhibition finally opened, but a public controversy continued to surround the exhibition, and it was eventually terminated in March 2003. Consequently the group of disappointed artists participating in the exhibition joined forces to announce that the termination is a threat to Canada's multicultural mandate. In an open communication, the artists stated that,

Cultural events such as this have an important educational and humanitarian role, and that they are needed at times like this more than ever. We believe that the museum needs to stand up and show support for the Arab Canadian community and to exhibit exemplary art works made by Arab Canadian artists. This will help bridge the divide between Canadians and will assist in bringing about an understanding between the Arab Canadians and other communities. (Artists Against the Occupation 2003)

Dealing with the controversy surrounding "The Lands Within Me," the artists stressed the need to carve out a position for Arabs within Canadian society and their contributions over the years. They believed that they have an important role to play in shaping cultural life in Canada, and the exhibition was considered an important step in that direction. Unfortunately the efforts of such artists did not reverse the decision to terminate the exhibition, and it never traveled as was initially planned.[8]

In her analysis of Asian cultural productions, Chin (2000:275) contends that "whether or not people of Asian decent identify as Asian American, in order to fund [their] cultural productions they must inhabit the Asian American label." As the narratives of the Lebanese diasporic artists indicate, this form of ethnic identification and the interest of portraying the homeland are "at best metaphorical rather than a rigid translation (Papastergiodis 1997:183). Similar to the ethnic narratives discussed in chapter 2, these strategies may be utilized to provide a sense of continuity and meaning to combat fragmentation and discontinuity. However, strategically inhabiting an ethnic label to secure recognition does not preclude the critical voice that Mercer (1994) observes among diasporic artists. The concept of "interruption" is especially useful in understanding the kind of cultural representations in which Lebanese immigrants engage. Interruption "seeks not to impose a language of its own, but to enter critically into existing configuration [of discourse] to reopen the closed structures into which they have ossified" (Silverman and Torode 1980: 6). Josiane, Michel, and Gilbert's interest in translating Lebanese (or Arabic) culture and presenting positive images of Lebanon to counter the negative ones that exist in their host societies are attempts to challenge the existing discourses that present Lebanon in a negative light. Likewise, Alfred and Simon's film, while representing the civil war, also challenges the given assumptions about the causes and consequences of the war. Alfred and Simon's film, as well as the Arab artists' entry to the Canadian exhibition, illustrate ways through which immigrants do not simply take on the cultures of their homeland or host society. Instead, these artists actively enter into existing debates on the civil war in Lebanon and multiculturalism in Canada to both challenge and contribute to them. By engaging in these debates, the works of the Lebanese immigrant artists do not settle disagreements or present a narrative of "truth." Instead, the "critical voice" that these artists adopt emphasizes ambivalence, incoherence, and discomfort. Because these artists are not interested in replacing one hegemonic version of truth with another, their works are best understood as interrupting collective memory to question it and uncover its volatility.[9] Moreover, they also stress the need to challenge existing discourses on multiculturalism, identity, displacement, and belonging, which I discuss in the following section.

Displacement and the Search for Belonging

In the narratives of Lebanese immigrant cultural workers, interest in homeland culture and history does not take place for the sake of folkloric representation of traditional Lebanese culture but explicates the artists' ambivalence about their own positions. In *Displacements: Cultural Identities in Question*, Angelika Bammer (1994) contends that the separation of individuals and their native culture through experiences of migration or colonization is among the most significant experiences of the twentieth century. Such separation, Bammer argues, leads to a form of identity that is "both here and there and neither here nor there at one and the same time" (ibid.:xii). As with all forms of identity construction, diasporic identity relies on cultural performance. Klimt and Lubkemann (2002:151) argue that with regard to constructing diasporic identities, "convincing cultural performances are not just the result of a physical 'geography of belonging' but are the very processes through which histories of movement and a sense of connectedness are invoked, created, and rendered authentic." The constant passage between belonging and not belonging and the existence between home and host societies are understood as leading to a sense of homelessness and heightened awareness of a lack of belonging (see, e.g., Lavie and Swedenburg 1996). Lebanese immigrant artists illustrate their own passage between belonging and not belonging. For example, Bassam's description of his contribution to "The Lands Within Me" emphasizes that the sense of impermanence and the myth of return to the homeland are important themes in understanding immigrants' experiences:

> I had wanted to tell a story, almost a biography. . . . I think that all immigrants feel that sense of transience. Sometimes people don't accept the idea

of being here permanently; they deny it. Their denial is a form of hope, the hope of having the choice to return. (Canadian Museum of Civilization)

Bassam, who was thirty-nine years old when I met him through a New York respondent in 2002, is a photographer and writer living in Montreal. He left Lebanon twenty years earlier for Cyprus and then went to New York City. During his nine years in New York, he earned a diploma in photography but was never able to maintain legal status. In Montreal Bassam found a better environment to pursue his education as well as his artistic ambitions. In 2001 he participated in "The Lands Within Me" exhibition. His participation in that exhibition, as well as several others, was informed by his desire to weave the Arab/Lebanese experience into the Canadian general culture, to make it truly multicultural. Bassam's statement above, as well as the emphasis on incoherent representations of the homeland expressed by other artists, does not lead us to think that immigrants' awareness of existing in a transient state between two societies results in a fragmentation of identity or an inability to express coherent narratives of migration. Instead, and similar to the majority of Lebanese immigrants who stressed their belonging to multiple communities, belonging in-between two or more cultures is considered an important source for artistic imagination as it motivated the forms of expression in which Lebanese artists were engaged. A similar observation is made by Patricia Fernandez Kelly (2006) in her study of first-generation Cuban artists in exile, as she concludes that "aesthetic expressions concretize and diffuse existential uncertainties and anxieties common among those who cross real and imaginary borders."

In his essay "Reflections on Exile," Edward Said (1990) poses the question: "But if true exile is a condition of terminal loss, why has it been transformed so easily into a potent, even enriching, motif of modern culture?" Said goes on to remind us that "modern Western culture is in large part the work of exiles, émigrés, [and] refugees." Lebanese immigrant artists explained that their experiences with migration provide a creative source for their cultural expression, and they stressed their contributions to the cultures of their host (Western) societies. Bassam's earlier statement emphasizes hope and choice in experiencing and understanding displacement and fragmentation. "The Lands Within Me" is an example of Bassam's attempt to establish himself within the Canadian cultural milieu and forge new forms of belonging.

Contrary to the assumption of fragmentation and homelessness, Josiane's continual attachment to Lebanese culture is also coupled with her strong involvement in the French artistic scene. It is true, however, that her transnational existence causes her to question her identity and belonging in both societies:

Going back and forth, each time, I have to addresses the question of who am I. It is a very bad feeling actually, and I cannot get used to it. You know what I mean, each time, I feel myself very divided between the two places. I feel like a child who has been taken from his mother but who wants to hold on to her dearly.

Despite that she feels divided every time she travels between Paris and Beirut, Josiane's experience has allowed her to mature artistically and to find harmony in her ability to navigate two cultural worlds:

I came to the result that one can see a lot of harmony having two orientations and belonging to two cultures. It is not easy, because one could go through a lot of interrogation wondering where she is, what she is, to whom does she belong, to what does she belong . . . I came back to France, because France has brought me a lot, I belong to this country. I belong not because I can speak French, or that I have the French nationality, I belong in a cultural way, in the things I express. And I recognize that I did my full share in Paris, and my art is recognized. But I will always acknowledge that my experience helped me to come to a kind of harmony, and to develop my possibilities . . . It is wealth, a continual wealth that I did not know existed in me.

Emphasizing that it was her choice to travel between Beirut and Paris, Josiane believes that she belongs to both societies and that such dual belonging is an enriching state of being. While acknowledging the different modes of belonging that she has to both societies, Josiane realizes that the state of being in-between two cultures and modes of thinking contributes to her art in unique ways. As a result, she sees her work as a result of her commitment to both societies instead of her fragmentation and lack of belonging. One of Josiane's paintings was selected by the French postal service to celebrate an archeological arch in Paris. In her view, the experience she has with painting Lebanese Mediterranean arches contributed to the French postal service choosing her painting. As described earlier, Josiane believes that her initial interest in arches is influenced by her Lebanese origins and desire to represent Lebanese culture. Her sense of achievement following the selection was not only based on the recognition of the painting but, more important, on her ability to contribute to cultural life in Paris and participate in the memorial of an important part of the city's history.

For Lebanese immigrant artists, establishing themselves in their host societies' cultural setting cannot be fully understood as a choice to assimilate to new societies. Contrary to assimilation arguments, these artists are equally involved in Lebanese artistic life through their participation in a number of exhibitions in Lebanon. More than the transnational attachments, Lebanese immigrant artists are more interested in depicting a general state of displacement and multiple forms of belonging that extend beyond the homeland and host societies. In the words of Hamid Naficy: "*Home* is anyplace; it is temporary and it is moveable; it can be built, rebuilt, and carried in memory by acts of imagination" (1999:6). Lebanese diasporic artists illustrate Naficy's notion of temporary homelands and challenge traditional notions of belonging. For example, having lived in a number of societies and experienced multiple displacements, Bassam's work attempts to offer alternative visions to understanding displacements and belonging. Instead of unitary understandings of home as the ancestral land, Bassam's work demonstrates Naficy's notion of a moveable home and mobile memories. Specifically he wishes to express experiences of displacement beyond the popular binaries of home/host, failure/success, oppression/liberation, and so on, and, in so doing, illustrate the possibility of "settlement in motion." For example, Bassam describes a collection of photographs that he included as part of an online exhibition by artists of Lebanese origin:

> The images for the most parts are traces of passages through various locations, places, and countries that I have lived in. The photographs were never intended as public documents. It is the subjective and the personal that I have emphasized, shamelessly, the personal and private space of encounter that I have stressed. It is in the diffusion and the display of the work that I hoped to transform the personal into a part of the collective memory.

Bassam's collection narrates experiences of war, displacement, and a search for belonging—experiences that he believes are shared by many Lebanese immigrants of his generation, giving him reasons to express and document them. Having lived in Lebanon, Cyprus, the United States and Canada, Bassam sees his long search for belonging and settlement as being similar to that of many Lebanese and other individuals in various parts of the world. Such experiences are a more adequate reflection of the cultural memory that Bassam wishes to narrate than those from an ancestral distant past that do not reflect his life or those of others around him. Through depicting photographs of a hotel sign, a lonely bartender, or hazy Arabic inscriptions, Bassam describes his experience with displacement, isolation, and a search for meaning in a collection titled *Crime*, which refers to the civil war and the impact it had on his life. In a second collection, *Pinholes*, he includes photographs of his living and work spaces to convey the slender hope he has for his new setting. The last collection, *Monastery*, further alludes to the hazy comforts that may be found in religion or in any general form of traditional community. The three collections of photographs are part of an exhibition by Lebanese immigrant artists in various parts of the world, and they are intended to signify general experiences that are not specific to Lebanese immigrants but address general conditions of migration, displacement, and ambivalence. As a result, these artists end up expressing forms of art that describe the diaspora as an existential condition of ambivalence and displacement, which is very much the way they view the contemporary world.

Bassam is also a novelist and his writings express the same interests as his photography. He has published a number of short stories that deal with issues of displacement and belonging in general. When I met with him, he was hoping to publish his first novel whose protagonist is a teenager growing up during the civil war in Lebanon and manages to escape to Paris in search of a different life.[10] According to Bassam, the novel presents an alternative definition of the war as lived by the innocent members of society. Written in a semiautobiographical style, Bassam's novel is an attempt to express the way the civil war affected many individuals who had no stake in the actual fighting. The novel also recounts an important part of Lebanese social history which, according to Bassam, needs to be remembered and to be taken as a lesson. Furthermore, the novel points to an internal state of displacement that preceded the protagonist's migration from Lebanon which disputes the assumption that culture or society offers coherent entities for belonging. Through his writings, Bassam deals with diasporic issues of migration and settlement in unpredictable ways to challenge popular assumptions about return and nationalistic forms of attachment.

Experiences of migration and displacement are often understood within frameworks of exclusion and discrimination (see, e.g., Wihtol de Wenden 1998). Arab immigrant experiences have also been understood within similar frameworks. For example, Elizabeth Dahab (1999), in her overview of Arab Canadian literature, claims that what partially unites the Arab Canadian trilingual body of writing into one literary system are the recurring themes:

> often in binary oppositions, which permeates it: acculturation, duality, discrimination, unemployment, freedom, alienation between parents and children, memories of wars, the cold Canadian weather, poverty and prosperity.

However, a number of postcolonial analysts draw our attention to the need to understand new forms of belonging that many immigrants, and especially the cultural workers among them, engage in. For example, in *Imaginary Homelands*, literary critic Salman Rushdie (1991) maintains that Indian writers in England are negatively marked through their exclusion from both English and Indian culture. Instead of focusing on their double exclusion, this group of writers finds intersections, as opposed to roots, through "the culture and political history of the phenomenon of migration, displacement, life in a minority group" (124). Such emerging communities of displaced individuals, Rushdie adds, provide open possibilities for their members. In line with Rushdie's observation, many Lebanese immigrants challenged traditional forms of belonging that are based on collective memory, nationality, or ethnicity, and underscored similarities in lifestyles and dispositions instead. They also stressed the immigrant condition as more influential in their experiences. Analyzing the works of postcolonial women writers, Françoise Lionnet (1995: 5-6) observes that these writers "wish to speak to a community of readers whose diverse experiences they address, their purpose is one of inclusion rather than exclusion. Their works de-exoticize the non-West, indicating the centrality of their concerns to the self-understanding of people everywhere." Similarly Lebanese cultural workers define their belonging to a diasporic network of immigrant artists from various origins and present their issues to a generalized audience. Seeing themselves as products of transcultural processes that mark their unique position in the world, many of the Lebanese cultural workers stress the ways in which such processes impact their ability to bridge different cultures and address general audiences. For example, in narrating his personal experience, Bassam's intentions are to engage in debates around migration and belonging to a multicultural society from the perspective of the immigrant as opposed to the perspective of policy makers and politicians. Like other Lebanese immigrant artists, Bassam defines broader commonalities between him and members of the host society, and other immigrants in general, in an effort to present a general rather than a specific condition. The forms of broader commonalities that Bassam seeks are not grounded in traditional forms of belonging to a specific society or religion. He emphasizes, instead, a shared condition of displacement to which a general audience can relate.

Almost all the first-generation Lebanese artists I interviewed were eager to narrate their migration experience. In the process of telling a Lebanese story, these artists also participated in Lebanese cultural life through various activities and events in Lebanon. Their audiences, however, are mostly global. Middle Eastern historian Timothy Mitchell notes that, in the past, migrant artists were likely to have abandoned their homeland, "written imaginatively and heretically of the experience, and . . . been read only within the new

example, Hisham, a musician and art curator in Paris, explained the ways in which his malleable identity and lack of full belonging allowed him to produce artistic expressions that correspond to his vision of the world as an intermixture, a product of cultural fusion:

> Well, I am Lebanese-Palestinian, Arab, Muslim, French, all of these things. But I am not any of them really. I have other concerns and like to address very different issues . . . I play music, and it is a fusion of jazz, world music, pop, it's very experimental, and this is how I see the world, a fusion of different things that you mix together without really knowing the outcome until you see it for yourself.

Emphasizing that the goal of his art production is to bring about social change, Hisham spoke of the need to educate people about the various social problems that exist through artistic expression. Hisham's most recent activity, before our meeting through another respondent, was more oriented toward change at the grassroots as he, and other members of his student group, organized exhibitions and seminars in popular areas of Paris. Based on a text they wrote titled *The Fetish Features of Merchandise and Its Secrets*, Hisham and his friends collected images from popular culture and various media to illustrate commodity fetishism in modern capitalist society. The small exhibition was presented at people's homes and at coffee shops, and also included readings and presentations on the topic by various group members. According to Hisham, the event was aimed at changing consumerist culture that is ever intensifying in the global world. In response to my question about the political nature of his work, he said:

> Actually I think politicians are very scared to help those who work in the cultural world because they see it as very dangerous because culture helps you think. And, if you think you will realize that the country, that the whole world, is being ruled by fools and culture is always captured by politics.

Hisham's efforts start with an awareness of a global problem but move toward engaging with solutions at the local level. Similar to the forms of solidarity illustrated by Lebanese immigrants, the narratives related by the various artists indicate their choice to belong to both host society and homeland, and a desire to effect change in both societies. These choices are based on their interest in participating in global change and forging global solidarity and cosmopolitan ideals—which I turn to in the following section.

Searching for Global Harmony

Tracing the different forms of identification and community participation, this chapter highlights the ways in which Lebanese immigrant cultural workers maintain an attachment to and an engagement with their homelands and their host societies. Underscoring the transnational networks that Lebanese artists construct and maintain allows for an understanding of the ways they critique the societies and cultures in their homeland and host societies instead of merely adopting them passively. Given their interest in social critique, Lebanese immigrant artists often move beyond transnational networks and emphasize their participation in global communities that are shaped by their cosmopolitan identification and global attachments. Through this process, Lebanese diasporic artists participate in the construction of a global public sphere where "master discourses"—which are often national ones—are contested and reinterpreted. The diasporic global public sphere is "the space in which different transnational political imaginaries are interpreted and argued over, where fables are formulated and political mobilization generated in response to global social dramas" (Werbner 1998:12). More important, participants in the Lebanese diasporic public sphere regard their public engagement as an important source for their identity and their membership in the community.

Through their engagement with existing discourses on war and displacement, the artists I interviewed expressed their vision of culture "as collective voice rather than individual genius" (Chin, Feng, and Lee 2000:272). It is true that their expressions were informed by their personal experiences and particular understandings of political and social events. Their aim, however, was to present a more generalized narrative from which others can learn. Their cultural production was presented as drawing on and at the same time renovating "the social imaginary," which Paul Ricoeur (1986) defines as "a whole set of collective stories and histories which need not bear the signature of any individual author, and which exercise a formative influence on our modes of action and behavior in society."

Based on Ricoeur's definition of the social imaginary, the works of Lebanese immigrant artists should be analyzed based on their ability to effect social change. As illustrated in the previous sections, an interest in shaping cultural memory is important to the Lebanese immigrant artists, as it maintains the presence of certain events and histories of experience in their narratives of the diaspora. Equally important to them was creating, through their work, the kinds of societies to which they aspire. Similar to other migrants who wanted to act as models for the "good Lebanese" through their involvement in community organizations, Lebanese artists understood their role more as "cultural workers," based on "the idealized vision of the artist as serving the people" (Chin, Feng, and Lee 2000:272). The creations of these artists emphasized the rhetoric of liberation, recuperation, visibility, voice, and consciousness-raising (see Kondo 1997). Similar to the interest in combating racism, segregation, and exclusion expressed by North African cultural workers in France (see, e.g., Wihtol de Wenden 1998; and Ireland 1996), Lebanese immigrants participated in cultural activities that addressed various forms of inequality. Unlike the second-generational movement that is specific to the French context, the first-generation Lebanese immigrants expressed a strong desire to participate in processes of global change that begin with issues specific to the homeland and then move beyond it. These artists wish to challenge dominant aesthetic discourses and contest marginality and stereotypes (Hall 1997).

The forms of community participation that Lebanese immigrants provide demonstrate their wish to move beyond their particular Lebanese experiences to address global issues, and yet they address these issues at the local level. For example, Josiane, who divides her time between Paris and Beirut emphasized that she is not interested in particular Lebanese issues:

I have the right to say what I say because I am observing outside and from inside. So, the reality there is totally different from utopia that other people who are living outside want. It is very dangerous to claim things outside that could be utopic and not realistic according to the reality on the ground . . . When we look at all the troubles happening everywhere, and we look to Lebanon, we do not find it worse than somewhere else. Unfortunately, this is the reality.

Placing problems related to Lebanon and Lebanese immigrants in a larger context, Josiane emphasized that she prefers to express global concerns that are, to an extent, informed by the specific context but, at the same time, universal in nature. Referring to her recent work that deals with the U.S.-led wars in Afghanistan and Iraq, Josiane noted that:

[It is important] to express your opinion and to express your opposition . . . Human rights are very important to address. And the present attacks in one country, or another, on people's freedoms, it's an infringement on our basic rights as individuals, and I wanted to express it.

Many of the Lebanese artists emphasized that war is a principal issue in their works. In addition to focusing on their own experiences living in Lebanon during the civil war and narrating the ways these experiences affected their personal lives, many of the artists presented the ways in which their particular histories led them to engage in global messages dealing with the destructive nature of war in any society. Christine, a filmmaker in Paris, described some of her projects and reports:

> I started out by reporting on the war in Lebanon, since I am Lebanese and was familiar with the story. Given my experience I was able to move on to cover other forms of war, in the Gulf, in Central Africa, and I was able to communicate the same message to different groups of people: that war is destructive and that we should find an end to all wars . . . Now my work is changing a bit, but I still address the different forms of destruction that human beings introduce to their own people and their own societies.

By reporting to various news agencies and often putting together her own documentaries, Christine addressed the civil war in Lebanon as well as other civil wars in Asia and Africa. Having lived in Paris for more than twenty years, Christine's initial interest was to engage Western and global audiences. Her experience with the war in Lebanon led to an interest in war-related issues worldwide as well as to a concern for cosmopolitan issues rather than particular regional or national matters. The intention of many of the artists, in focusing on wars around the world in their works, was not merely to represent the human misery and destruction that results from war. They also wanted to contribute to putting an end to war altogether, stressing the role art can play in bringing about social harmony. Christine's new project focuses on collective memory in a postwar society. Her new film compares Lebanon to Vietnam and the way each society has managed to recover after war; both these nations also appeared in her earlier works. Christine believes that the comparison is important, as it addresses culturally specific ways of social healing. More important, by focusing on memory she wishes to prevent political actors from committing the mistakes of the past, the same mistakes that led to civil war in the first place. According to Christine, "people need to remember not only war but what happened before the war, because nothing has changed." In Lebanese society the focus is on the Lebanon of the future with almost no attention given to the past. For diasporic artists like Christine, however, the future is doomed to repeat the past if the past is not scrutinized and taken as a lesson. When I met with Christine, she was about to change her target audience by taking on issues specific to the Arab world. She knew that her work would be met with censorship and criticism, because she was planning to address issues of gender and sexuality and venture into feature films instead of documentaries. However, similar to the transnational community organizers, Christine was in a privileged position because of the recognition she received from the West, and this would allow her to endure the anticipated criticism. Her interest in working on Arab issues was still a result of her cosmopolitan status and her awareness that universal ideals had to be targeted in specific locales.

Sophie, a sculptor living in Paris, used to work for the United Nations and quit her job to dedicate her time to her art. Through her sculpture Sophie has the means to express her feelings about Lebanon, France, and humanity in general. More important, she believes that her work sends a clear message to people around the world and allows her to express her vision for the future.

The first part of my work emphasizes harmony, an image of comfort, of love and understanding. It's quiet, and it's passionate. It's because when I started, I wanted to express what I would like to see in Lebanon. For me, a couple is the two parts of Lebanon: one part Christian, one part Muslim. The couple is one and the other. It's the beginning of every social or political group. I expressed how I wanted to live in Lebanon, how I would like Lebanon to be: harmonious and equal.

Although the early stage of Sophie's work, as she described it, emphasized a search for communal harmony that erased the effects of the civil war from the collective memory, Sophie stressed the important message that her work represents in expressing future social change. She explained that her nostalgia for social harmony in Lebanon represented her desire to see peace throughout the world. Emphasizing that she had Lebanese society in mind, she also stated that she sees herself as a cosmopolitan artist, meaning that her sculpture belongs to a global society. Thus Sophie's sculpture does not represent a specific regional or national context but focuses on conveying the message that she wants to expand her horizons. Similar to Christine's interventionist strategy of representing wars in ways that critiques them, Sophie, as a sculptor, explained how the silent figures she puts together have a global political message. For instance, she told me that her latest figurine of a seated man, tied up and with a bandage on his mouth, was much appreciated in Lebanon where people felt that Sophie's sculpture was expressing feelings that they were unable to express themselves. The figurine tackles issues related to the lack of freedom of expression in Lebanese society, especially on topics such as corruption, sectarian conflict, gender inequality, and lack of individual sovereignty. When I inquired about the specific message the figurine is sending, her response was immediate: "Rebellion."

Both Christine and Sophie can be understood as taking part in a more recent debate within Lebanese society on the importance of remembering the war in order to understand the roots of the conflict and to avoid repeating it. Sune Haugbolle (2005) traces this public debate to the year 2000, when two important political events took place: the withdrawal of Israeli troupes from the south of Lebanon and, shortly afterward, the death of the Syrian president Hafez al-Asad. These events, Haugbolle explains, led to the creation of a freer public environment, one more conducive to debating about the current state of affairs in Lebanon, including the ways in which state and society have dealt with the memory of the war. "Although this might destabilize the present system, speaking the truth about the past is the only way to face up to the social and political problems in Lebanon" (196). All the Lebanese artists in the three cities examined here expressed their interest in engaging with public debates in Lebanon as well as portraying their homeland to the mainstream societies they currently live in. Like many respondents, they share a cosmopolitan identity that defines their work and personal experiences without negating their Lebanese origins. Instead, they form networks that benefit their homeland and their host societies, and move beyond them. For example, Christine's experience with the Lebanese civil war gave her the needed expertise to cover other wars around the world and an interest in speaking against future wars not only in Lebanon but in other regions with different political climates. Similarly, Sophie's sculpture is influenced by her concerns about Lebanese issues, but she also emphasizes the universal meanings that her work represents. Roy's work also moves from the local to the global with an interest in influencing both. He identified himself as an animation designer and lived in Montreal when we met in the spring of 2003. His opening statement in his personal homepage describes the aim of his designs as well as the various activities he engages in, and his belief in the role of his art in bringing about cosmopolitan social changes:

> Art is the bridge between my individuality—unconfined by symbolic communication—and the fact that I coexist with other similar individuals with whom I communicate. . . . Informed by the ethical dimension, my recent choice of subject matter is an examination of identities in their arbitrary differences and exclusion. This choice implies a political position. I am a believer

in a global democracy, one that will supersede national, tribal, and religious boundaries and control [humans'] inherent tendency towards tribalism.

Roy's interest in examining identity issues was a result of his participation at an event in Lebanon on issues of national identity. Having lived in the United States and Canada for many years before he had the chance to participate in a cultural gathering in Lebanon, he was disappointed by the traditional forms of attachment that participants at the meeting adhered to in their analyses. This experience led Roy to realize that identity is a central obstacle toward alleviating the various conflicts taking place all over the world and to utilize art to inform people of his vision of a society that is not tied to traditional forms of identification. The desire to contest traditional forms of identification was common among Lebanese immigrant artists whose works often represented the damaging impact of the postwar construction on the Lebanese nationalist identity. Following the sectarian strife, Lebanese nationalist discourse flattens any differences within Lebanese society for the sake of a manufactured national narrative of unity and patriotism. These artists' works emphasize social differences that constitute the fabric of Lebanese society, as in Sophie's nostalgic sculpture. The artists want to acknowledge and bridge these differences in order to create a more inclusive society.

While Roy's vision points to general processes of change in people's perceptions and understanding of their history, other Lebanese artists acknowledge the need to address global issues from a local perspective. Bassam provided a specific form of engagement in influencing world conflicts from a local perspective. Focusing on the Arab-Israeli conflict, Bassam was a co-curator for the Montreal exhibition "Artists Against the Occupation" that took place in September 2003. The exhibition's press release communicated Bassam's interest in ending the conflict and a desire to place artistic production at the center of resolving various political conflicts:

Artists Against the Occupation is a multimedia exhibition that addresses the conflict in the Middle East . . . Many national and international artists involved have a history of engaged art production and have variously dealt with issues of displacement, exile, postcolonialism, globalization, racism, feminism, the environment, and identity . . . Through the power of art, the curators wish to encourage a deeper understanding of the Israeli/Palestinian conflict amongst viewers, and of the urgent need for a peaceful solution. Art has the potential to move, persuade, inspire, and activate. It can resonate in ways that are universally relevant. (Artists Against the Occupation 2003)

Bassam's choice of topic is clearly governed by his personal interests and experience, and yet his particular interest is not local in its significance. As indicated in the press release, the universal relevance of the exhibition cannot be undermined as it relates to general conditions of conflict and occupation. In organizing the exhibition, Bassam was eager to bring together artists from diverse origins with multiple perspectives on the occupation in order to illustrate its universality. As the press release indicates, the purpose of the exhibition is clearly one of creating world peace, but the universal goal is to be achieved by targeting specific issues and dealing with concrete contexts.

Various examples provided by Lebanese immigrant artists point to the ways that immigrants negotiate their ascription to local and global narratives of belonging. As Bassam's activities indicate, immigrant artists engage with cosmopolitan issues, but at the same time they do not wish to participate in abstract universal discourses that may have little meaning to the particular groups to which they belong. Abstract universal discourses, such as world peace, equality, democracy, and so on, are valued to the extent that they are concretized in specific contexts and toward localized goals. Charles Taylor (1992) argues that increasing cultural diversity and the emergence of multiculturalism lead to potentially contradictory discourses: the politics of universalism and the politics of difference. Similar to the kinds of social attachments that Lebanese immigrants construct, the many accounts provided by Lebanese diasporic artists illustrate attempts to reconcile these potentially contradictory discourses by framing their particular experiences and concerns within global discourses and dialogues. At the same time the universal values that they preserve are expressed by their engagement with particular contexts. In some accounts, Lebanese artists have taken issue with the politics of difference in general and have advocated more general discourses that addresses humanity at large. For example, Ziade, a musician in New York City, initiated a cultural group that aims at "offering a platform for *all* human voices." Ziade explained to me that he and other group members "believe in using art as a means of portraying not only our diversity but our commonality as humans." Despite the abstract ideal of realizing the commonality between humans, Ziade's activities focus on the specific issue of the racial/ ethnic dialogue in New York City. In the process, Ziade's group aims to provide more than an expression of the human condition. While Ziade indicated his belief in the importance of providing a forum for different groups to communicate and to realize their similarities in place of difference, he also stressed the fruitful outcome that may come out of such gatherings. He explained that, for him, multiculturalism is more than the sum of the different groups participating equally in cultural and public life. The more important aspect of multiculturalism for Ziade comes from the innovations and unexpected creativity that unfolds.

Inspired by the musical innovations of Ziryab,[12] an Arab cultural historic figure after whom the cultural group is named, Ziade also started a music quintet in New York. The process by which the quintet came about illustrates the creative aspect of true multiculturalism as Ziade described it. The group started out as a four-hand piano jam and then evolved into a two-piano project with a French musician:

> The special timbre of two pianos and the combination of their very different musical personalities opened up a vast new horizon of discoveries. To their own amazement, they found themselves intuitively complementing one another, using their classical backgrounds and their keen interest in American jazz improvisation while finding inspiration in the musical traditions of their respective countries, Lebanon and France. (Ritter 2001)

The duet soon became a quintet by first adding a nay (a Middle Eastern flute) and then a cello and percussion. The mixing of Middle Eastern and classical Western instruments was not intended to bring about a fusion of Western and Eastern music. Instead, the outcome was not predetermined, and the results were unusual. A reviewer of the band's first album emphasized the novelty of the group's music:

> Two pianos are plenty rare in an acoustic rhythm-and-roots group, world music band, avant-garde jazz combo, or "new music" improvisational ensemble. In an Arabic improvisational outfit this arrangement is heretofore unheard of. (Ritter 2001)

The diversity Ziade brought to his band successfully produced new sounds that express forms of experience not tied to any particular region or culture. Similarly, other artists' emphasis on expressing a transient experience speaks to a more general human condition than one that is attached to traditional forms of belonging. In the process, these artists not only express values and traditions that are common to human beings in general, but, more important, they advocate a form of multiculturalism that aims to bring about global harmony and social justice.

Conclusion

By his hand she took him,
through her story
showing him the bridges of sound
Telling him tales
A mixture of genes and Round Midnights
Explaining the constellations and what they sound like
How to travel between them the heart on the hand

By her hand he took her
On a camel ride between the deserts of loneliness
and the one of freedom

Over the quarter tones and the broken beats
Drinking from the Milky Way
Eating from the one and one thousand nights
—Moufarej n.d.

Frequently immigrant artists in Europe and North America are understood as representing their homeland to a Western audience. Given their competence in the two cultural milieus, the works of such artists are often categorized as hybrid cultural productions. When understood within the framework of hybridity, Lebanese immigrant cultural production can only be understood as creative productions that blend two distinct cultures. Processes of translation, ethnic representation, and "going native" are definitely important aspects of the cultural expressions observed among Lebanese diasporic artists. However, assuming the singularity of both cultural elements to be mixed and hybridized precludes an understanding of the importance of individual choices and specific contexts of reception in determining the basis of mixture (for an elaborate critique of hybridity (see, e.g., Karla, Kaur, and Hutnyk 2005). As Lebanese diasporic artists set out to represent and translate the culture of their homeland, their individual histories and desired positions in the new settings influence the forms of expression they produce. Thus the concept of hybridity does not account for the multiple ways that diasporic artists express their wish to "go native." Speaking for Lebanon, the Arab World, and the Lebanese diaspora in their host societies, my respondents elected to represent what they took to be the quintessential aspects of Lebanese/Arab culture and to become the ambassadors of the Lebanese/

Arab diaspora in their host society. As the narratives of the Lebanese diasporic artists indicate, this form of ethnic identification and portrayal of the homeland are more metaphorical than factual. These strategies may be utilized to provide a sense of continuity and meaning to combat fragmentation and discontinuity. The artists I interviewed also adopt strategies that question notions of belonging and national harmony in important ways.

Diasporic cultural expression is taken to fashion "a zone of intense, cutting edge creativity, born out of the existential angst of the immigrant who is neither here nor there" (Karim 1998:4). As cultural workers in the Lebanese diaspora forge attachments to multiple societies and seek identification with several spheres of interaction, their work reflects their search for settlement as well as their discontinuous realities. The ways that Lebanese immigrants understand who they are as well as the conditions that shape their identification process emphatically shape their participation in various social institutions as well as their cultural expression in the arts, music, the media, and so on. Their attachments to the homeland, while sometimes privileging them in their new settings, often reflect their interest in challenging official constructions of Lebanese history. Although Lebanese history and culture are important themes in their work, the artists do not offer nostalgic representations. Svetlana Boym (2001:xviii) differentiates two kinds of nostalgia: "restorative nostalgia" attempts to reinstate a homeland in singular transhistorical ways, and "reflective nostalgia" accepts "the ambivalence of human longing and belonging" and challenges national narratives of cohesion and stability. Lebanese artists' representations of their homeland may be understood as a form of reflective nostalgia that uses personal narratives to oppose rigid constructions of history and identity (ibid.:49). More than providing critical reflections, however, Lebanese diasporic art is better understood in terms of intervention.

The history of the civil war is a major issue that Lebanese diasporic artists engage with as a result of their personal experiences and their interest in becoming active in shaping Lebanon's postwar future. Similarly their attachments to their host societies and their desire to contribute to the respective cultural lives are shaped by their desire for acknowledgment and recognition. However, their involvement in the cultural life of their host societies by engaging with and challenging dominant discourses also demonstrates their interest in contributing to the cultural life of their new settings. The multiple dimensions of their cultural interventions reflect their desire to contribute to the cultural memories in both societies instead of merely adapting to them. As the narratives of Lebanese immigrant artists convey, diasporic forms of expression are not the simple appropriation of different cultural symbols. Rather, being part of a different culture drives the diasporic critic to subject both "cultures to analytic scrutiny rather than combining them" (JanMohammed 1992:97). As migration gives rise to new subjects, new ethnicities, and new communities, it provides diasporas with "the means to speak for themselves" and express their displaced reality (Hall 1997). My respondents shared the view that cultural activities are important vehicles for such forms of expression. These artists offer critiques both of their homeland and of their host societies' representations of it. Both forms of criticism are informed by their positions as insiders to the two societies. As forms of interventionist art, diasporic cultural expression among Lebanese artists negotiates new modes of belonging that extends their traditional attachments and nostalgic understandings of their experiences.

Placing their experiences with migration and the quest for belonging at the center of their work, Lebanese artists in the diaspora see themselves as agents of social change. These processes represent contradictory sentiments and affiliations, and challenge traditional notions of belonging and membership. In many ways, the desire to fully participate in the host society's cultural life is considered an important means for success. Existence between home and host societies is understood by some authors as leading to a sense of homelessness and heightened awareness of a lack of belonging (see, e.g., Lavie and Swedenburg 1996). While most analyses of diasporic communities emphasize the importance of fragmentation and lack of belonging in understanding the immigrant experience, my analysis illustrates ways through which members of diasporic communities achieve stability and creativity in mobility and transition. As members of a diaspora, Lebanese émigré artists understand their work as more than mere products of their experiences of exclusion and alienation. Instead, they emphasize their active contributions to the artistic spheres in their host societies and underscore their cosmopolitan status. At the same time their continual interest in the homeland affirms that their work is not simply a development of transience or marginality. As such, diasporic artistic representations reflect the tensions between exile and alienation, on the one hand, and cosmopolitanism, on the other. Such tension calls for an understanding of exile as an enriching state and important source of creativity. Following this line of analysis allows for a conception of cosmopolitan attachments that are rooted in specific locales and experiences. Finally, through their engagement with discourses on displacement and membership, Lebanese immigrant artists also give rise to new ways to express universal experiences that are communicated through particular narratives of belonging, displacement, solidarity, and harmony. As a result, they participate in creating global forms of expression that address universal concerns and sentiments. All these cultural workers believe that their art is an important tool for bringing about global solidarity and cosmopolitan ideals. More important, the analysis of narratives obtained from Lebanese cultural workers highlight the point that global art is not only a novel way of expressing contemporary experiences but also a vehicle for creating more inclusive societies where multiculturalism and diversity are truly transformative and democratic.

immigrants were also at the gathering, and so I decided to focus on establishing my contacts in Montreal.

At that gathering I was introduced to three individuals who agreed to participate in my research. Along with Tony, they were all very helpful in introducing me to others whom I later interviewed. However, I did not realize the added value of the interactions I had at that gathering until I was deep into the analysis of my data two years later. In addition to the Lebanese in the crowd, almost all the others present were first-generation immigrants who had arrived in Canada within the preceding ten years. They had come from Algeria, Morocco, Ukraine, Portugal, Turkey, Senegal, India, Mexico, and the United States. There were a few Canadians (that is, they had been born in Canada and their parents were probably also Canadian born) who had lived in other countries. Looking back, it seems obvious that all those in attendance shared an experience with migration and living in more than one society. The discussions I engaged in that night mostly dealt with issues relating to migration experiences and navigating multiple cultural worlds. I did not view the gathering as unusual; it was no different from other social gatherings I had attended in New York City. In fact, it was precisely what one would expect in a worldly city such as Montreal, New York, or Paris.

To most of my respondents, belonging to a large group of immigrants of diverse origins who, like them, navigate two or more social worlds is more important than belonging to a particular ethnicity, nationality, or religious group. Besides the common predicament of crossing multiple societies and cultures, immigrants share experiences of simultaneous inclusion and exclusion vis-à-vis their national, ethnic, diasporic, and host communities. As a result, these diverse immigrants endure similar encounters in their daily lives that make their ethnic or national differences less significant in their experiences. Once understood as general experiences that are not specific to Lebanese immigrants, their perceptions of migration, displacement, and ambivalence take on global meanings and attributes. In this book I attempted to highlight Lebanese immigrants' understandings of their global positions that are marked by their awareness of difference as well as their desire to belong. As the analysis shows, such contradictory experiences are the basis for creative mixture of cultures, nontraditional communal attachments, and an interest in global social change. In this final chapter, I highlight some of these contradictory experiences and positions, and relate them to the immigrants' cosmopolitan outlook and global setting. Looking at immigrant experiences through the lens of the diaspora allows us to perceive simultaneous experiences of inclusion and exclusion to both homeland and host society, and highlights creative forms of belonging that are informed by the immigrants' awareness of their global position.

All Diasporas Are Ethnic

The majority of first-generation Lebanese immigrants left Lebanon because of the civil war and its aftermath. My respondents' war experiences shape their narratives and influence their political commitment and cultural production. The injustice of war is central to the ways in which Lebanese immigrants construct their diasporic awareness that shapes their identities and social affinities. Although I am not suggesting that traumatic experiences that lead to a mass exodus is a defining feature of diasporic communities, such experiences are relevant to the Lebanese immigrants' awareness of their membership in a diaspora that is spread throughout the world. The impact of the war also affects the ability of these immigrant to relate to their homeland and shapes their desire to engage with social issues in their host societies. For many scholars, "a rhetoric of restoration and return" that relates to the homeland (Tölölyan 2007) provides an important feature of diaspora communities. Lebanese immigrants sustain their social and political engagement with the homeland and maintain relations with family and friends in Lebanon. The desire to return was rarely mentioned, however, as political and social conditions in Lebanon continue to be unfavorable. In a global world the myth of return is no longer meaningful, even as a rhetorical device, since moving back and forth is relatively easy. As a result, maintaining transnational attachments is a preferred mode of keeping the homeland alive in the daily experiences of members of the Lebanese diaspora.

Despite the absence of the myth of return, first-generation Lebanese immigrants preserve elements of their culture of origin in order to sustain a sense of continuity and coherence in their new environment. Religious, social, and cultural practices allow them to continue identifying with the homeland. Cultural activities (such as exhibitions, lectures, seminars, and festivals) are popular strategies for maintaining a connection to the homeland. The immigrants' philanthropic activities are also aimed at increasing public awareness of Lebanese issues as well as providing material assistance to certain groups in Lebanon that are in need. Interest in the homeland has distinct meanings for the different immigrants. In some instances, maintaining continuous communication with family and friends still in Lebanon or staying informed about political, social, or cultural events in Lebanon are common strategies that shape transnational attachments. For many immigrants, however, interest in the homeland motivates their involvement in public activities that are related to Lebanon or the Middle East in the cities where they live. Transnational cultural practices also illustrate ways that events such as religious festivals, national holidays and traditional celebrations are transported to the host society. These events serve as important vehicles through which communal solidarity and consciousness are maintained.

Furthermore, ethnic identities are employed to connect their past experiences in Lebanon to present social, cultural, and economic conditions in their new environment. In my analysis, ethnicity does not mean a reinvention of ethnic, national, or religious particularities but instead indicates a process of forging an identity that connects the past to the present within complexities of migration and multiculturalism.[1] In the different urban contexts of Montreal, New York, and Paris, ethnic identification brings about specific social, political, and cultural consequences that are sought after by the immigrants. Unitary ethnic identification was only observed in Montreal and Paris, as all the immigrants interviewed in New York narrated their identities along multiple lines. In New York ethnic affinities are expressed alongside others such as Arab, white, or Catholic. Because Lebanese immigrants are generally stigmatized and homogenized as undesirable others, many react by affirming their identities and the multiple cultural sources that inform them. State policies following 9/11 have led to the strengthening of Arab ethnic identities, and the Lebanese immigrants are growing increasingly aware of this. In Montreal ethnic identities are meaningful reactions to Canadian multicultural policies that emphasize ethnic difference and support ethnic organizations. In Paris, however, ethnic identification is based on the support granted to the Lebanese by the French government and the general perception of the Lebanese as non-challenging to the French Republic and its values.

The strength of attachments to unitary ethnic identities is shaped by gender and class. In Montreal the focus on patriarchal family relations as a defining feature of ethnicity allows men to delay the weakening of their position as patriarchy itself becomes weakened in the new environment. For women, family relations remind them of the sacrifices they made by leaving their extended families for the sake of attaining a better future for their children. For both men and women, ethnicity is a vehicle that keeps the homeland alive in their new realities and provides an avenue for making sense of their position in a multicultural society like Canada. Generally women had only a faint desire to return to the homeland, for they were fully aware of the unbalanced gender positions in Lebanon and of the economic downturn they would likely experience were they to return. Ethnic identities are also shaped by the respondents' class position. In Montreal ethnic narratives are associated with a working-class background.[2] The awareness that their class background will likely prevent them from enjoying the same standard of living in Lebanon as they have in Montreal reinforces the realization among members of this group that their nostalgia for Lebanon will never actually cause them to return. The deteriorating economic and social conditions in Lebanon and, in some cases, the presence of children heighten their realization that Lebanon will not offer the kind of future that they want for themselves and their children. Although these immigrants have accepted the fact that they are not likely to return to Lebanon, they are also unable to accept full membership in Canadian society given the constant reminder of their difference. Ethnic identification thus provides a mechanism whereby they can negotiate their belonging to Canadian society based on their perceived difference. Despite their participation in mainstream Canadian institutions and the awareness that their children are likely to grow up as Canadians more than Lebanese, immigrants in this group hold on to their ethnic identities to preserve their space within Canadian society.

Unlike the Canadian context, ethnicity in Paris was associated with a business-class background whereby owners of restaurants and other small businesses and financiers displayed strong attachments to their Lebanese or Arab identities. In Paris, moreover, political orientations (based on privileged economic positions) activate the articulation of ethnic identities as they reflect desired political positions and changes. A few Maronite immigrants claim to have a Lebanese identity devoid of Arab identification, which reflects their desire to construct Lebanon as a non-Arab and non-Muslim country. For members of other religious groups, the Maronite project is not attractive, and they seek identification as both Lebanese and Arab. In any case, ethnic identification provides a mark of distinction when individuals do not wish to become full members of their host societies.

When immigrants are constantly reminded of their difference, as some respondents experienced in New York and Montreal, ethnic identification provides a sense of coherence to the immigrant's position in society. Paradoxically, when immigrants wish to preserve the favorable acceptance they receive from members of the host society, as in the narratives based in Paris, ethnic identification is also strengthened. Whether perceived as an undesirable alien in New York, a welcome stranger in Montreal, or an honorable other in Paris, the attitudes of the host society toward Lebanese immigrants shape their ethnic attachments. The impossibility of returning to Lebanon still provides a common theme in their narratives and thus marks the immigrants' diasporic sentiments. The ethnic narratives provided are negotiated along diasporic lines whereby issues of belonging, return, and homelessness are dealt with and articulated. Ethnic identification is more than a direct result of processes of differentiation in host societies. These immigrants' various narratives illustrate a form of diasporic identity that centers on temporality and the desire to return: they continually point out that they "are not here to stay," but at the same time they "cannot and will probably not go back."

Analyses of diasporic communities often fail to take into account class and gender differences (see Anthias 1998). In my respondents' narratives, these differences affect how they relate to the diasporic community at large, a topic I discuss in greater detail in the next few sections. These differences also affect how they uphold their desire to return to Lebanon. This desire to return is central to the various identity narratives and illustrates different views based on gender and class background. All those who construct their identities through an ethnic narrative hold on to their desire to go back to Lebanon permanently but are aware of the impossibility of their return. For those who identified ethnically in Montreal, awareness of the limitations imposed by their disadvantaged class background is the basis for their perception that they cannot go back to Lebanon. Among those in Paris, differences in political orientations and family ties in France prevented them from returning. Having a privileged class position in Paris also allows many immigrants to travel regularly to Lebanon, and so the issue of return is less meaningful in the daily reality of their lives. The different narratives also revealed that women feel less strongly than men about returning to Lebanon permanently, despite women's continual involvement in homeland and ethnic issues. Given the impossibility of return, however, ethnicity provides a second-best source of coherence. As the narratives illustrate, Lebanese immigrants define their ethnicity as that aspect of their social practices that they are not willing to change. Rendering these practices ethnic preserves their sense of uniqueness when they have given up on returning to Lebanon.

For the Lebanese immigrants I interviewed, their relationship to the homeland and their membership in an ethnic diasporic community are fraught with conflict and a sense of exclusion. Objecting to sectarian divisions, class inequalities, bigotry, corruption, and a lack of democracy, many of my respondents underline the different perspective they have gained after moving out of Lebanon. These respondents also express critical views of Lebanese society and point out their greater ability to participate effectively in processes of change while in the diaspora. As these respondents "pick quarrels" with their homeland, they also become more active in their host societies and diasporic communities. Focusing on social change also allows them to understand Lebanese social problems within a global context and seek global solutions. Similar to their criticism of Lebanese society, many members of the Lebanese diaspora also find that the diaspora itself is a site where many of the homeland's problems are reproduced. The sense of exclusion from the diaspora weakens my respondents' identification with their co-ethnics, which leads them to question the logic of privileging national and ethnic identities. The affinities they share with other immigrants from various backgrounds foster further detachment from ethnicity and nationality as sources for communal belonging and identification.

Being a Good Lebanese

Although immigrants' initial public involvement is mostly based on homeland issues, an interest in their host society soon follows, marking these immigrants' incorporation into the social, cultural and political realms of their ethnic communities. Public involvement takes place through civic organizations and initially has two related goals: to effect changes in Lebanon and to change the host society's perception of the Middle East. While host societies are often assumed by diasporic Lebanese immigrants to lack an understanding of the Lebanese and Arab culture, members of the diaspora themselves are sometimes considered to be at fault for that deficiency. As a result, many respondents wish to present a positive role model (which possibly informed their participation in my project in the first place). Their interest in presenting a positive image of the homeland and its culture, and their wish to engage in a cross-cultural dialogue between Lebanon (or the Arab World) and the host society, are important vehicles for granting immigrants a positive image and welcomed presence in their host societies. In many ways, their attempts to represent Lebanese culture to their host societies only replicates the modes of representation that they wish to dispute, namely, the tendency to homogenize Arab, Middle Eastern, and, by association, Lebanese societies and cultures, as well as the diaspora itself. However, because their representations are context-specific, their construction of Lebanese culture escapes monolithic assertions of a stagnant Lebanese identity and culture. Given the different political contexts in the three cities examined here, articulating the positions of Lebanese immigrants within the larger society takes different forms and results in different constructions of social positions.

In New York Lebanese immigrants focus on combating their stigmatization as Arabs and Arab Americans following 9/11. They realize that their goals are better achieved by working with other organizations that adopt a general Arab identity. For most of the respondents, however, working within ethnic or religious institutions does not provide an avenue that truly reflects their identities and interests. These organizations are believed to focus on ethnic politics that do not always reflect the respondents' understanding of their position in American society. Lebanese immigrants have historically understood that in the U.S. racial system they are categorized as white (see Gualtieri 2009; and Khater 2005), and they have not questioned the exclusionary and racist system of categorization itself. Arab ethnic organizations currently emphasize the nonwhite position of Arabs in the United States and accentuate their opposition to American foreign policy in the Arab world and the domestic treatment of Arab Americans (see Cainkar 2009). For Lebanese immigrants in New York, these ethnic organizations and especially their ethnic identity politics could symbolically entail the relinquishing of white privilege to which some Lebanese respondents have grown accustomed. Although some respondents have questioned their identification as white ethnics as a result of the post–9/11 policies that targeted Arab Americans, contesting whiteness was a more central narrative to Muslim immigrants in New York. While most respondents claimed not to believe in or practice religion, religious background is relevant in understanding their racialization in American society. To an extent, Christian Lebanese can more easily integrate into the white middle-class mainstream relying on similar religious practices and beliefs. For Muslim Lebanese, regardless of the level of their beliefs, their inability to participate in these religious performances leads to their unmistakable differences from other whites. For many of these secular Muslims, their fragile religiosity is a marker of difference in the more traditional and religious Lebanese society as well as the somewhat secular American society. As a result, they draw on their secular backgrounds to dispute the stereotype of Arabs and Muslims as religious fanatics. For Muslims and non-Muslims alike, questioning a white identity also involves a growing hesitation to take on an unhyphenated American identity and is a further symbol of their difference within American society.

Unlike Lebanese immigrants in New York, those in Montreal are not inclined to view Canadian identification as strictly white or Christian, or both. Instead, Canada's explicit multicultural policies and its state identification of Lebanese immigrants as members of visible minorities allow my respondents to take on a Canadian identity with more ease than can those in New York. At the same time the majority of Lebanese respondents in Montreal believe that integration into Canadian society is not simply granted based on the multicultural polices. Many of the Lebanese-Canadian respondents are aware of the need to demand inclusion in Canadian society, and these policies provide important avenues for such demands. The exhibition at the Canadian Museum of Civilization is an important illustration of the possibility of drawing on Canada's multicultural discourse to demand a space in its cultural life. The museum is financed by the federal government with the purpose of constructing "a vision of the nation" (Abu-Laban 2002). When the museum's director had initially decided to postpone the opening of the exhibition by Canadian artists of Arab origin, the issue was raised in Canada's House of Commons and the prime minister criticized the museum directors for "making the wrong decision" (Conlogue 2001; cited in Abu-Laban 2002). Following the debates and mobilization of the Arab Canadian community, the "Lands Within Me" opened according to plan in October 2001. Public support notwithstanding, the exhibition was abruptly terminated in March 2003, and, for some, Canada's multicultural policies and the artists' efforts to challenge the termination can both be seen as failures. The artists' ability to draw on Canada's multicultural discourse, however, should not be overlooked. The subsequent debate lasted for years, and the potential for Canada's multiculturalism has not been exhausted. In terms of identity constructions, in order to successfully make claims for inclusion, immigrants had to perceive of themselves as members of the host society and supporters of its culture. In the process, they saw themselves as pioneering the integration of Arabs in Canada in the post–9/11 international climate that stigmatizes immigrants from Arab and Muslim countries.

Similar to New York and Montreal, constructing a Lebanese immigrant identity in Paris is a political position. The postcolonial ties between Lebanon and France grant Lebanese immigrants in Paris a favorable position, as they are perceived as highly educated, Catholic, hardworking and French-speaking who fell victim to foreign intervention and regional political conflicts (and, to an extent, multiculturalism). For many Lebanese immigrants in Paris, this perception is contrasted to the image of the Maghrébins (French North Africans) whose religion (Islam) poses a threat to French core secular values and beliefs (see, e.g., Miles and Singer-Kérel 1991; and Wihtol de Wenden 1991). Because the French government has sided with the Maronites during the civil war, Maronite respondents see themselves as "honorary French," draw on their favorable position in French society, and emphasize that there is no real distinction between being "French" and "Lebanese." As a result, their integration into French society is taken for granted, and many of them find Paris a logical place to pursue their Maronite political interests. Sunni respondents, who are aware of their group's privileged position in Lebanon, stress their Frenchness that follows from their Lebanese identification and the privileged class and political positions that stem from it. Members of other religious groups, however, are more likely to contest the meaning of being Lebanese or French in their immigration narratives. For these respondents, being Arab is an important attribute that marks their difference in French society and their disagreement with French politics in Lebanon. Either as a unitary ethnic form of identity or one among multiple sources of identification, this latter group draws on their Arab identity and underlines it as a secular, modern, and socialist ideal that is inclusive of various religious and cultural differences. As Alfred, a Greek Orthodox respondent, clarified, being Arab entails the recognition of one's history and culture, which includes the French influence on Lebanon and, consequently, his French identification. Identifying as French, on the other hand, would entail a negation of Alfred's Lebanese and Arab identity, and he stressed that he was not willing to negate that part. Alfred and other members of various religious groups in Paris utilize their honorary position in French society to oppose the popular stigma attached to Arab culture and identity.

The various narratives provided by the Lebanese immigrants demonstrate that difference is marked more by political and historical positions than by racial or cultural attributes. Regardless of the specific contexts and articulations of identities and belonging, most respondents reject belonging to an ethnic community that is not integrated into the mainstream society. Although they refuse to exclude themselves from the general culture of their host societies, their narratives also delineate the experiences which they don't share with many people around them. For Lebanese immigrants, the differences in culture, history, and positions of power are integral in shaping their migration and settlement experiences. Such differences motivate some immigrants to engage in activities to educate others about Lebanon and Lebanese culture and history in the hope that they might persuade their host society to appreciate and value Lebanese immigrants. Nonetheless, many immigrants realize that education is a two-way process and that their acceptance in their new environment is also based on their ability to let go of their difference. As a result, choosing to live in a new society requires that one is aware of one's difference and has to learn new norms and values so that one can achieve a sense of belonging that makes life in a new environment agreeable. In the process, the respondents regard themselves as pioneers in navigating their sense of belonging, cultural competence, and public participation in multiple societies. Similar to their pioneering roles in representing their society and culture, Lebanese immigrants' cross-cultural competence is also accentuated as an important performance of their cosmopolitan outlook and global citizenship.

A Diaspora's Diaspora

Transnationalism has recently emerged as a popular framework for analyzing immigrant identities and practices. It indicates incomplete assimilation and relative exclusion from the host society's mainstream institutions. Transnational analyses tend to take homeland attachments for granted and the framework does not allow for nontraditional solidarities that are not based on ethnic or national backgrounds. Analyses of diaspora communities allow us to probe into the construction of multiple forms of belonging and identification by immigrants in various settings.[3] At the same time diasporic communities establish themselves by underscoring their difference. Members of the Lebanese diaspora are aware of their difference from those who never left Lebanon; their migration experience allows them to place Lebanese social, economic, and political issues within a larger context. Their global awareness, gained in part by migration, leads them to realize that Lebanese issues "are not the worst in the world," as Josiane has concluded. For some, rejection and exclusion faced in the host society strengthens such awareness of difference. Sometimes the immigrants themselves seek differentiation as a reaction to such exclusion or to assert their unwillingness to assimilate to their host society. Rather than assuming the quintessential difference between Lebanon and their new societies, Lebanese immigrants construct their difference contextually as they respond to specific societal and state regulations.[4] Furthermore, the respondents also highlight their difference from other members of the Lebanese diaspora.

For many respondents, maintaining solidarities that extend beyond transnational ties that include Lebanese immigrants in various regions of the world is a daily reality that strengthens their awareness of belonging to a diaspora. Participation in the larger diaspora community, independent of contacts with the homeland, is granted political, economic, and social importance in the lives of the individual immigrants I interviewed. Although the Lebanese civil war, which started in 1975, is the main reason why most respondents have left Lebanon, the Lebanese diaspora precedes the war. Khater (2005) illustrates that Lebanese immigrants of the first waves (mostly arriving in the mid-1800s and early 1900s) were aware of their diasporic condition as they created cultural spaces that retained their ties to the homeland, integrated them into their host societies, and forged ties with other Lebanese immigrants as they "journeyed up and down North and South America" (317). Analyses of diasporic communities emphasize that group members continue to relate to their co-nationals in the homeland and elsewhere in the diaspora and that their collective consciousness is significantly defined by these relationships (see, e.g., Safran 1991). The reality of belonging to the diaspora is experienced by many respondents on regular basis, as they support networks of extended family and friends in different parts of the world. Focusing on diaspora is important as it highlights global awareness and transient positions. Unlike ethnics, members of a diaspora "are not here to stay." Unlike transnationals, members of a diaspora may have problematic connections to their homeland, and their daily realities are likely to be informed by experiences of other Lebanese (or Arab or Muslim) immigrants around the world. Their view that the diaspora is its own entity influences their integration in the host society as well as their understanding of their histories and individual positions. However, assuming the existence of a diasporic community to which all immigrants may belong is problematic. The experience of the Lebanese immigrants I interviewed indicates that the triadic relationship, which includes Lebanon, the host society, and the diaspora (Lebanese or Arab), is characterized by conflict as each member may have her or his own interests. The narratives that many Lebanese immigrants provide do not point to a vision of the diaspora as a unified entity but rather one that is divided along various economic, cultural, and political lines.

Unifying the diaspora, as expressed in Chady's assertion that "we need to agree on our identity," is an important goal for some political activists, but not necessarily other members of the diaspora. Chady further explained the position of political activists:

> To secure a better future for Lebanon, we need to move beyond our tribal identities and start questioning the basis of such identifications. We need to find what unifies us as Lebanese, but that is not enough. We also need to have one voice so that we can be heard in the international order. We will not be taken seriously by the rest of the world if we keep insisting on archaic forms of belonging.

Chady's assertion seems desirable, as it reflects the wish to bring together the Lebanese and possibly restore national unity in a post–civil war environment. However, the unified identity to which he aspires is based on a particular understanding of Lebanese social and cultural identity that other immigrants find exclusionary. Exclusionary identities are an important site of contention. Specifically many Lebanese immigrants find that when diasporic communities attempt to reify ethnic boundaries and traditions, they end up feeling excluded. In the Maronite project that Chady supports, being Lebanese excludes the possibility of being Arab or Muslim, which re-creates political conflicts that exist in Lebanon. The Lebanese professional association that Abeer once joined in New York reproduced gendered hierarchies and marginalized her as a woman. Roy found that Arab organizations in Montreal have no room for secular individuals like him. The replication of Lebanese (and Arab) social and political problems in the diaspora leads many respondents to stay away from any sort of formal organization that aims to unify Lebanese or Arab immigrants. Outside of formal organizations, many respondents still find other Lebanese and Arab immigrants eager to uphold traditional religious or cultural practices and ideas. Understanding this tendency as mostly a product of a different class background (mostly lower than theirs), a parochial upbringing and outlook, or a different immigrant generation, most respondents move away from specific national and ethnic issues toward involvement with cosmopolitan concerns and participation in global communities. For example, Roy rejected the form of social coherence offered by traditional identities. In his explanation, Roy believed that all identities were problematic:

> I have an issue with identity right now. I tend to consider it more and more as a very bad idea; as something that's always causing trouble and without any validity. So, what constitutes my identity? [pause] I tend to abandon the idea of identity as such. I don't like it anymore, I don't enjoy it. It doesn't give me the same glow it used to.

In Roy's account, the rejection of all forms of identity was an active choice that some immigrants make in response to the conditions of their migration and displacement. As expressed by Roy, a sense of not belonging added to his feeling of ambivalence; this "liminality," however, could also be a comfortable position when there are common issues that might temporarily unite people. For Roy, participating in antiwar campaigns and labor-related activities allowed him to forge a feeling of commonality with others that he did not feel through traditional forms of identification. Arab immigrants are usually studied where they congregate and, as a result, ethnic identities tend to be exaggerated. What happens when we look for Arab immigrants elsewhere? Although I recruited many respondents through ethnic networks, I did not solely focus on ethnic organizations as sites for finding respondents. As a result, many respondents expressed contested notions of ethnic communities and identities, and emphasized their membership in multiple social spheres.

Rogers Brubaker (2005) emphasizes the study of diaspora as a process, something that people claim and practice, which is the approach my respondents share regarding their membership in the Lebanese diaspora. Despite the various forms of public involvement that Lebanese immigrants engage in, they mostly share a desire to be active participants in bringing about social change. The various examples suggest that they seek to be effective in Lebanon as well as in their new settings. Their awareness that they exist between the two societies also allows them to challenge given traditions and constraints. Combating sectarianism, political corruption, and violations of personal freedom are important aspects of their involvement in the homeland. Demanding full participation in the host society allows them to gauge a basis for inclusion and participation. These concerns, while motivating participation in the host society, also trigger a cosmopolitan sense of belonging and more global forms of involvement. Instead of seeking coherence of their experiences and positions, many Lebanese immigrants focus on bringing about specific social changes in their host societies, exploiting their unique social positions at the crossroads of multiple cultures and societies. Exploring the diaspora as a way of investigating immigrant communities leads us to examine the claims its members make about who they are or how they wish to be portrayed by others. It also allows us to look into their political, social, and economic practices within transnational and global perspectives. Understanding diaspora as a process of seeking coherence within conditions of fragmentation, as stability coupled with a heightened awareness of transience and mobility, diaspora underscores the immigrant condition that is global, that is integrated to multiple societies and yet questions and challenges traditional norms for understanding identity, ethnicity, and integration.

Locating Cosmopolitanism

Key to my respondents' ability to contest flat, unitary identities is their ability to engage in practices of social change that occur at the global level. The ways Lebanese immigrants challenge rigid forms of ethnic and national identification illustrate their cosmopolitan positioning in the world. Facing exclusion in the United States, Canada, France, or Lebanon, they are motivated to improve the various societies of which they are members. Recognizing the broad forms of inequality and exclusion that they face, the form of social change most important to them is global in nature. Because global problems call for global efforts, Lebanese immigrants understand their position as cosmopolitan citizens who are interested in global social change. These changes, however, can only be realized in specific societies and at the local level. Lebanese immigrants' attachment to their homeland and host societies is expressed in their interest in challenging social norms and engaging in activities that aim at social change in both contexts. Issues of sectarian divisions, class inequality, gay visibility, corruption, and illiberal ideas (economic and political) are among the topics in which Lebanese immigrants engage in their homeland. In their host societies, they take on similar concerns for equality, desegregation, and multiculturalism. Such interests are global in nature, and many Lebanese immigrants emphasize their experience with migration as informing their understanding of the world as interconnected. The cosmopolitan attachments that are sought by Lebanese immigrants through their engagement with universal causes are usually framed within their experiences with migration that allow them to understand their personal experiences within global narratives. Emphasizing the globe as a single place, Lebanese immigrants understand experiences of fragmentation, homelessness, injustice, and displacement as universal conditions that only strengthen their ability to avail themselves of several identities, as well as social and political causes.

As illustrated by the analysis of the Lebanese immigrant experience, diasporic communities exemplify a form of global attachments that move beyond cross-national boundaries and extend to unbounded spheres of interaction such as extended family networks or engagement with global political issues. The global society that Lebanese immigrants portray centers on a rising global consciousness that influences their actions and understanding of their position in the world. Roudometof (2005) differentiates the various meanings of cosmopolitanism and transnational attachments. According to him, being transnational does not necessitate being cosmopolitan, as transnationalism only entails local attachments to a number of places and participating in transnational social spaces. In the accounts of Lebanese immigrants, their transnational attachments lead them to participate in both their homeland and host societies. Their narratives also illustrate that their transnational practices inform engagement with global concerns that characterize their cosmopolitan outlook. As such, focusing on transnational practices overlooks the global positions that most members of the Lebanese diaspora perceive. As the experiences of my respondents indicate, engaging in transnational practices may not always be desirable and even when present does not preclude feelings of detachment and fragmentation. Inquiring about diasporic identities and attachments enables us to understand the ways in which Lebanese immigrants deal with such feelings. Diasporic attachments and sentiments move beyond transnational ones as they underscore global cosmopolitan identities and nontraditional forms of attachment.

In this regard, the Lebanese immigrant experience demonstrates that immigration, transnationalism, diaspora, and the multiple forms of membership that they imply have "diluted the nationalist core of conventional citizenship" (Zolberg 2000). Although the nation-state remains the source of formal citizenship and a site for influencing action, Lebanese immigrants possess a concurrent awareness of their global citizenship and the desire to engage in universal causes. As discussed in the previous chapters, when immigrants discard traditional forms of attachment to their homeland and host societies, they are motivated to support universal civil causes. My fieldwork suggests that immigrants' interest in the Lebanese political and social spheres persists and continues to be an important source of public engagement in the homeland. Such engagement, however, is shaped by their belief in universal equality, emancipation, social justice, and individual rights. Interest in such global ideals is informed by the immigrants' realization of their global position and the multiple forms of belonging that they forge given their experiences with migration and exclusion.

Similar to the concept of diaspora, cosmopolitanism has recently become a popular term whose meaning has been reinterpreted in order to grasp contemporary global processes. One of the most influential contributions to the understanding and rethinking of cosmopolitanism is offered by Cheah and Robbins (1998). In his contribution to the volume, Bruce Robbins differentiates "old" and "new" forms of cosmopolitanism. According to Robbins, the old form is based on Western liberal notions of universalism which assumes that individual differences can subside in face of a common good for all humanity. The new form, however, is based on "transnational attachments and experiences" that emerge in diverse situations and contexts. Robbins includes global diasporas of ethnic or cultural groups (such as Chinese) among these new cosmopolitans. The distinction between the two ways of understanding cosmopolitanism has been carried over in the literature, and the two variants have been termed "thin" and "rooted" forms of cosmopolitan attachments. Thin cosmopolitan dispositions are those that are devoid of social or cultural attachments, in contrast to rooted cosmopolitanism which implies strong attachments to a national community as well as openness toward difference and otherness (see, e.g., Calhoun 2002; and Roudometof 2005). The two types of cosmopolitanism are also assumed to operate at two distinct levels: the thin variant emerges at the global level, and the rooted form is local, emerging within countries and regions. Roudometof (2005: 126) elaborates the distinction: "Irrespective of national variation . . . locals should value cultural membership to the nation— and cosmopolitans oppose it—since, by definition, such membership excludes people on the basis of ascribed criteria."

The narratives provided by Lebanese immigrants and their emphasis on cosmopolitanism complicate the binary oppositions given in such analyses of cosmopolitan outlooks and forms of belonging. On the one hand, Lebanese immigrants engage in forms of thick cosmopolitanism as they assert the multicultural aspects of Lebanon—and especially Beirut—that produced their worldly outlook before their migration. In fact, for many, it was precisely this worldly outlook that instigated their desire to leave Lebanon and facilitated their ability to establish a life in their new settings. Their attitudes about Lebanon reflect their cosmopolitan nationalism, which is a source of national pride for both the Lebanese in Lebanon and those in the diaspora. Based on an ethnographic study of Beirut, Seidman (2011) argues that the Lebanese rhetoric of cosmopolitan nationalism is based on an appreciation of Western culture and religious diversity. Seidman detects that such rhetoric is contradicted by the realities of inequality and injustice faced by gays, gender dissidents, migrant workers, and Palestinians. These realities of injustice and discrimination are the specific issues that my respondents confront in Lebanese society and choose to engage with while in the diaspora. Their diasporic experiences allow them to contest cultural traditions and national narratives of identity in their homeland. A transnational analysis illustrates the ways in which these immigrants participate in and reconstruct their homeland through their participation in homeland politics, remittances, or family obligations. The framework of diaspora allows us to look at how immigrants challenge homeland traditions and contest its norms through engaging with them. As members of the diaspora who also possess an understanding of their position as global immigrants, the Lebanese immigrants also move beyond nationally rooted cosmopolitanism to engage with these issues universally. For most, a cosmopolitan engagement with the world is a primary source of their self-identification. For example, Carol asserts that "I get involved in issues that allow me to see myself as a global citizen and not as someone who has a very narrow understanding of the world." Her statement is a claim to an identity that is constructed through difference with others who may have a "narrow understanding of the world." Stressing difference is an important strategy for identity claims in general but more so for members of a diaspora who share a heightened awareness of their ambivalent position. Their efforts to engage with global causes are rooted in their desire to establish cultural attachments to specific locales while maintaining their differences within these specific societies. Cosmopolitan identities give the immigrants a basis for engaging with their multiple societies instead of withdrawing from them.

The cosmopolitan attachments that Lebanese immigrants portray are a result of specific historical and geographical contexts. The understanding of Lebanese identity in cosmopolitan terms emerged in opposition to the non-cosmopolitan and traditional Arab world. The memory of the Lebanese civil war and the inability of Lebanese society to overcome the inequalities and sectarian divisions that led to that war deem nationalistic attachments to Lebanon less desirable to the immigrants in my analysis. Since cosmopolitanism itself is "a reality of (re)attachment, multiple attachment, or attachment at a distance" (Robbins 1998:3), the cosmopolitan identification of Lebanese immigrants is based on their ability to belong to multiple societies, navigate diverse cultures, and participate in varied public spheres. In this understanding of cosmopolitanism, we can account for the way the myth of return to a homeland and traditional attachments to an ancestral origin are contested by members of diasporic communities without being replaced with notions of "thin cosmopolitanism." The cosmopolitan realities described by members of the Lebanese diaspora are grounded in their personal histories and memories. For example, Amaney, who moved to Paris in her early twenties and married a Frenchman shortly afterward, explains the reasons for her cosmopolitan attachments:

> So every time I told them [people in Lebanon], I explain to them that they are more happy than we [members of the diaspora] are, because we are broken. We are nothing on the inside. I tried during all my life here in Paris. I tried to be somebody. That's why I participate in associations. That's why I took a bank which was almost bankrupt and I got it out of trouble. I was a president of a bank when I was never interested in a high position before I left Lebanon. I tried to save this bank, you know, because I wanted to be somebody. I was looking to be somebody because in my country I was somebody.

Amaney remarkably became the president of a bank in her mid-thirties, a year before she met with me in her office in Paris. Her family disapproves of her marriage because her husband does not share her religious background, and, because of these severed family ties, she has given up on the idea of returning to Lebanon. Her "broken" state of mind motivated her to seek confidence and self-worth in her associational work and professional career. The real success she has achieved, however, is her ability to work to benefit all human beings regardless of their nationality and ethnic background. Speaking of her desire to be involved in a diverse work environment as well as different voluntary organizations, Amaney stated:

> I try to always bring in a progressive aspect and ask people to move away from what divides us and focus on larger concerns that we all have . . . We need to think of ourselves as sharing a basic humanity together.

Amaney's narrative illustrates a common element in the experiences of Lebanese immigrants, namely, the wish to overcome displacement and alienation. Despite personal experiences with exclusion and ambivalent social positions, Lebanese immigrants emphasize a new form of belonging, one that seeks to find a stable home in their new settings and moves beyond ethnic and national affinities to construct nontraditional communities of belonging. The homeland, though still present in their narratives, does not necessitate a temporary settlement in the diaspora but serves as a starting point for creating (new) homes. Stressing the sense of duty and engagement with global issues, many Lebanese immigrants challenge traditional forms of belonging but not all forms of solidarity altogether. Instead, they maintain a strong sense of membership through their involvement in the various societies to which they belong as well as a global society that they envision. This type of belonging is formed by their awareness of their diasporic disposition and is organized around universal causes and concerns. Through their various activities, members of the Lebanese diaspora participate in new social movements, use the globe as the reference point for political activity, and act on the basis of a global consciousness (see, e.g., Axtmann 1997; and Lipschutz 1992), all vital conditions for global solidarity.

As the previous chapters illustrate, Lebanese immigrants' awareness of their precarious situation motivates most of them to challenge traditional forms of belonging and coherent identities. Key to contesting coherence and stability is their ability to engage in processes of social change that takes place at the global level. While not glorifying their positions as "world immigrants," their narratives emphasize their desire to reshape the world instead of passively accepting traditional forms of being and belonging. According to Beck (2002:18):

The cosmopolitan perspective is an alternative imagination, an imagination of alternative ways of life and rationalities, which include the otherness of the other. It puts the contradictory cultural experiences into the centre of activities: in the political, the economic, the scientific and the social.

Whereas Beck goes on to argue that a cosmopolitan global consciousness does not necessarily incorporate specific actions, the experiences of Lebanese immigrants demonstrate that cosmopolitanism is a type of global consciousness that precisely manifests itself in specific actions in particular locales. Thus the alternative imagination that Lebanese immigrants have of the world and their belonging in it can only be understood through their "localized cosmopolitanism" which entails active participation in various societies and a desire to make these societies more inclusive and more accepting of difference. Recognizing this is useful for understanding identities in the twenty-first century (immigrant and nonimmigrant alike), as it is applicable to all those whose lives and dispositions are impacted by intensified processes of globalization in the form of media, communication, travel, political activism, and a culture of consumption. The notion of "localized cosmopolitanism" provides an entry to understanding how people can continue to be rooted in their societies, cities, or neighborhoods and at the same time understand their identities and positions as global in nature.

The Lebanese diaspora illustrate ways in which the interaction between the global and the local can be understood and applied. Specifically, the multiple positions and processes of identification and belonging that Lebanese immigrants forge offer important opportunities for analyzing multiple cosmopolitanisms that operate at diverse levels of interaction and take on various contexts as arenas for social change. As a product of specific historical experiences, diasporic communities construct forms of solidarity that are shaped by past experiences of displacement, present problems of inequality and exclusion, and future interests in solidarity and freedom. For example, Josiane shared her approach to dealing with her own sense of displacement (she divides her time between Beirut and Paris) and her outlook on cosmopolitan citizenship. For Josiane, cosmopolitan citizenship means a commitment to the whole world that starts with immediate surroundings but does not stop there. Josiane sees a need for global involvement based on one's duty toward others. Fulfilling this duty provides her with a sense of comfort and harmony in the midst of her constant movement and dual displacement. Global duty, in Josiane's opinion, is not specific to her involvement in the homeland but is "everywhere." Like Josiane, who believes that an individual's social responsibility to alleviate the pain of others is a global duty, many respondents challenge traditional forms of attachments that are based on nationality, ethnicity, or religion. The context of globalization facilitates the construction of social relations that transcend national boundaries. More than providing the structure for global solidarity, global cultures, political interdependence, and economic encounters make global solidarity necessary at least in the experience of immigrants who wish to challenge the traditions of both their homeland and host societies. In the experiences of Lebanese immigrants, the global is a real experience that is shaped by migration and living in a diasporic community, which gives coherence to immigrants' daily social experiences. More important, such global experiences do not preclude the disappearance of their local attachments in the places they dwell or in the homeland. Instead, the understanding that their social worlds are composed of multiple localities is at the center of their awareness of their global presence and reality, or, as Dirlik (1997) describes, "simultaneous cosmopolitanism and localism."

Diaspora in the Global World

In their critical assessment of the concepts of diaspora and hybridity, Virinder S. Karla and associates (2005) point to a theoretical divide that separates descriptive analyses of diasporic communities (see, e.g., Safran 1991; and Cohen 1997) from processual approaches that emphasize cultural and textual analysis (see, e.g., Gilroy 1991; and Clifford 1994). The authors acknowledge the heuristic divide between the approaches but also believe that diaspora is "a way of looking at the world," a process that "denote[s] ideas about belonging, about place and about the way in which people live their lives" (Karla, Kaur, and Hutnyk 2005:28–29). The process emphatically takes place in host societies that shape immigrants' understanding of belonging (see Clifford 1997; and Gilroy 1994). However, the understanding among Lebanese immigrants that they are members of a global diaspora, a position they share with immigrants worldwide, also influences their processes of identification and belonging. The narratives of Lebanese immigrants demonstrate that just as immigrant lives are shaped through the interaction of global and national contexts of reception, their own understanding of their position is informed by their ability to interact with their surroundings and change their worlds. Thus their positioning as global citizens who wish to participate in universal processes of action is integral to their narrative of migration and the displacement it produces.

The meaning and utility of the concept of diaspora has been subject to a number of analyses and debates among scholars. In differentiating diasporic communities from transnational ones, Gabriel Sheffer (2006) stresses that the defining feature of ethno-national diasporic communities is their organizational capacity as they create institutions that represent their cultural and political interests. These institutions help construct the diaspora as an imagined community and, as a result, help maintain it over time. In his differentiation, Sheffer stresses the "ethno-national" nature of diasporas and their institutions, as "they clearly demonstrate greater cohesion and solidarity than the transnational communities" (129). Evidence from the Lebanese diaspora, however, challenges some of Sheffer's assertions, as these immigrants' forms of identification and community involvement move beyond ethno-national attachments and extend to global solidarity. The forms of social cohesion sought after by many members of the Lebanese diaspora in Montreal, New York, and Paris are themselves transient as they do not seek but rather challenge ethnic solidarities and national identities. Drawing on multiple identities and their competence in various cultural repertoires, members of the Lebanese diaspora convey that diasporic conditions blur boundaries between groups instead of strengthening them. Their experiences point to the significance of diasporic identities and attachments in understanding immigrant experiences in the contemporary era.

The durability of diaspora over time is one of its important features. The ideology of return to the homeland, a myth never really pursued in its own right, facilitates the maintenance of diaspora over time and across generations (see, e.g., Tölölyan 2007). It is hard to extract evidence on durability over time from the experiences of first-generation Lebanese immigrants, especially given the diminished significance of the ideology of return in their narratives. However, given their understanding of their position in global terms and their interest in challenging traditional forms of identity and solidarity, their diasporic consciousness is likely to persist over time as global processes impact people around the world irrespective of experiences of migration or displacement. The experience of the Lebanese diaspora does not contest assumptions about durability over time but puts into question assumptions about ties to the homeland and ethnic attachments that are often taken for granted in defining diasporic communities. In place of traditional ethno-national attachments, the experience of the Lebanese immigrants highlights awareness of fragmentation, displacement, temporality, difference, and ambivalence that can be generalized to all immigrants in the contemporary world. At the same time the awareness of their precarious position in their host societies and their homeland marks the diasporic condition and separates it from other immigrant realities. As immigrants who are not fully accepted in their host societies (owing to their homeland interests, ethnic background, or desire to mark their difference) and who are stigmatized in most immigrant-receiving countries around the world (as Arabs in the post–9/11 political environment), the Lebanese are aware of their conditional belonging to the societies they have chosen as their new homes. At the same time political instability, economic stagnation, and social inequalities deem their belonging to the homeland equally uncertain. This sense of transnational fragmentation marks their diasporic condition and is an integral element in the diaspora's durability over time and across generations.

Conditions of displacement and difference cause immigrants to see the various countries they traverse with "the same combination of intimacy and distance" (Said 1978:259). The exilic writer Edward Said describes such contradictory attachments by referring to the words of Hugo of St. Victor, a twelfth-century monk from Saxony who never left his homeland:

> It is therefore, a source of great virtue for the practiced mind to learn, bit by bit, first to change about in visible and transitory things, so that afterwards it may be able to leave them behind altogether. The person who finds his homeland sweet is a tender beginner; he to whom every soil is as his native one is already strong; but he is perfect to whom the entire world is as a foreign place. The tender soul has fixed his love on one spot in the world; the strong person has extended his love to all places; the perfect man has extinguished his.

Members of a diaspora can be understood as tender beginners when they identify with their homeland uncritically and unconditionally. They can be seen as strong when they extend their attachments to their host society or other areas of the world and wish to identify as global citizens. However,

Appendix

Profile of Respondents

TABLE 1. *Respondents by City and Gender*

Gender	New York	Montreal	Paris	Total
Female	14	12	16	42 (48%)
Male	13	14	18	45 (52%)
Total	27	26	34	87

TABLE 2. *Respondents by City and Religion*

Religion	New York	Montreal	Paris	Total
Sunni	10	2	10	22 (25%)
Shiite	4	2	3	9 (10%)
Maronite	9	12	11	32 (37%)
Greek Orthodox	1	2	4	7 (8%)
Other Catholics	3	7	5	15 (17%)
Other (Druze or Jewish)		1	1	2 (2%)

TABLE 3. *Respondents by City and Age*

Age Range	New York	Montreal	Paris	Total
20–25			2	2 (2%)
25–30	3	1	6	10 (11%)
30–35	14	10	7	31 (36%)
35–40	4	8	3	15 (17%)
40–50	5	6	9	20 (23%)
50+	1	1	7	9 (10%)

Notes

CHAPTER 1. GLOBAL IMMIGRANTS

1. Mount Lebanon was subject to the Ottoman Empire and was part of the province of Greater Syria. As a result, immigrants from that region referred to themselves as Syrians until the end of the Ottoman Empire in 1917. In the 1920s the term "Lebanese" as a national label or identity was given political legitimacy and was adopted by most immigrants originating in Mount Lebanon.

2. The opening of the Suez Canal and the diversion of trade routes from Syria to Egypt, the inability of the Lebanese silk industry to compete with declining prices of Japanese silk, and rapid population growth that was unmatched by agricultural and industrial productivity are among the major economic factors behind Syro-Lebanese emigration (Suleiman 1999). The beginning of the disintegration of feudalism also brought about social and political instability to the region in the form of communal clashes (which started in the 1840s and 1850s) and triggered large-scale migration from Lebanon. Specifically, the granting of special administrative status to Mount Lebanon in 1861, which meant relative autonomy from the Ottoman Empire, increased political and social instability and led to the mountain's isolation from the more prosperous regions as well as more freedom for individuals to migrate (Karpat 1985).

3. The sectarian conflicts started on April 13, 1975, when gunmen killed four members of the popular rightist Maronite Phalange Party during an attempt on the party leader Pierre Jumayyil's life. Believing the assassins to have been Palestinian, the Phalangists retaliated later that day by attacking a bus carrying Palestinian passengers across a Christian neighborhood, killing about twenty-six of the occupants. The next day intense fighting erupted, with Phalangists pitted against Palestinian militiamen. The confessional layout of Beirut's various quarters facilitated random killing. The government was unable to control the killing, and the prime minister resigned in May 1975. Soon afterward, more factions joined in the killing and took different sides in the conflict. Syria attempted to negotiate a halt to the conflict but ended up participating in the battleground.

4. Religious diversity is an important feature of Lebanese society and politics. The political system is based on confessionalism, whereby the highest political offices are held by representatives from the major religious groups. According to the last Lebanese census that took place in 1932, the Lebanese population is comprised of individuals identified as Sunnis, Shiites, Druze, Maronites, Greek Catholics, Greek Orthodox, Protestants, Armenian Orthodox, Armenian Catholics, Syriac Orthodox, Syriac Catholic, Chaldean Orthodox, and Chaldean Catholics.

5. Soysal (2000) differentiates the normative and analytical aspects of diaspora. Normatively diaspora is the classical model used for describing Jewish (and sometimes Greek and Armenian) history and experience, "lived in a state of 'worldlessness.'" According to Hall (1992), however, this notion of diaspora "is the old, the imperializing, the hegemonizing form of 'ethnicity,'" which involves the oppression of other peoples. The analytical utility of the concept recently progressed in immigration literature describing various processes of population dispersion. Unlike the normative conception, more recent understandings of diaspora emphasize the contested nature of diaspora identity and communities that has historically characterized migratory processes. For example, Clifford (1994:306) asserts that "we should be able to recognize the strong entailment of Jewish history on the language of diaspora without making that history a definitive model. Jewish (and Greek, Armenian, and Palestinian) diaspora(s) can be taken as non-normative starting points for a discourse that is traveling or hybridizing in new global conditions."

6. Concepts such as "homeland" and "host society" are not assumed to refer to homogeneous entities, and indeed the immigrants themselves have troubled relationships with both entities. For the sake of simplicity, however, I use these social constructs with the aim of highlighting the diverse approaches that my respondents have toward them.

7. Cohen (1997), for example, elaborates this point by comparing the number of Nobel Prize Laureates among Jews in the diaspora to those in the State of Israel.

8. Studies of international migration hardly explore the experiences of one national group in multiple contexts. The frameworks of understanding immigrant experiences are always national, even if comparative analysis is sought.

9. New York has the fourth largest number of Lebanese Americans following Michigan, California, and Florida.

10. In analyzing the role New York plays in shaping ethnic relations in the United States, Nancy Foner (2005) emphasizes that New York (and Los Angeles) are media centers that shape the national understanding of ethnic hierarchies. Thus she argues that ethnic relations in New York are not separate from those elsewhere in the country. Unlike other urban centers, however, New York is not an ethnic city in the same sense that cities like Los Angeles, Houston and Miami are.

11. Arab immigration to the United States started in 1870. According to Arab American historian Alixa Naff (1992), the first waves of Arab immigrants to the United States were Syrian Lebanese Christians, farmers or artisans, relatively poor, and poorly educated. Mount Lebanon was subject to the Ottoman Empire and was part of the province of Greater Syria. As a result, immigrants from that region identified with local towns and villages, and occasionally referred to themselves as Syrians, until the end of the Ottoman Empire in 1917. In the 1920s the term "Lebanese" as a national label or identity was given political legitimacy and was more commonly adopted by many immigrants originating in Mount Lebanon. However, since the majority of earlier waves of Lebanese immigrants to the United States were of the Eastern Christian sects, their religious identification continued to be stronger than their national one.

12. Also, according to the same 2000 U.S. Census report, 1.2 million people report an Arab ancestry, which makes the Arab American population similar in size to the Greek and Portuguese. This number does not include people from Mauritania, Somalia, Djibouti, or Sudan—countries that are members of the Arab League. This number also includes people who originate from Arab-speaking countries but do not necessarily iden-

tify themselves as Arabs, such as Berbers and Kurds. More than one-third of this ancestry group reported Lebanese origins, which is followed by a general Arab/Middle Eastern/ North African categorization (about 20%). Syrian and Egyptian followed Lebanese as the largest specific origin categories. Arab religious affiliations that are nationally based, such as Coptic or Maronite, were classified as "Other" and thus are not included in this estimate. The highest proportion of the state population that was Arab was in Michigan (1.2%), and Dearborn's population is 30% Arab. The largest number of Arabs, however, lived in New York City, where seventy thousand people of Arab ancestry lived. Almost one-third of the people with Arab ancestry reported an additional non-Arab ancestry, mostly Irish, Italian, and German.

13. Naber (2000) argues that Arab Americans become racially marked based on the assumption that all Arabs are Muslim and that Islam is a backward and uncivilized religion. Although most Arabs in the United States are non-Muslim, Arab Americans are racialized primarily through assumptions about their religion rather than by phenotype.

14. In one incident a supporter of McCain in Lakeville, Minnesota, proclaimed that Obama is an Arab, which McCain quickly negated by saying, "No ma'am, he is a decent family man." Notably the media praised McCain for defending Obama from what is taken to be a vile accusation.

15. People who are generally categorized as Arabs include Sunnis, Shias, Ismailis, Druze, Greek Orthodox, Greek Catholic, Roman Orthodox, Roman Catholics, Copts, Kurds, Alawis, Assyrians, Armenians, Berbers, Beduins, and Jews. Twenty-two countries are members of the League of Arab nations, and some declare Arabic as the only official language while others declare Arabic as one of many official languages.

16. Of course, forms of Arab American exclusion preceded the events of 9/11. For example, Arab American political analyst James Zogby (1998) describes the situation:

Sometimes, Arab Americans found that their mere existence had become a campaign issue. A few weeks before the 1985 mayoral elections in Dearborn, Michigan, every household received a campaign mailer from one candidate announcing in thick, one-inch black lettering his solution to the "Arab problem," xenophobic concerns about the increase of Arab immigration into the city. Dearborn happens to be the city with the highest proportion of Arab Americans in its population—over 20 percent.

Furthermore, in the few incidents when Arab Americans managed to form a quasi-interest group, there groups were not well accepted, as evidenced by the rejection of campaign contributions from Arab Americans to Walter Mondale, Michael Dukakis, and, more recently, Hillary Clinton, all because of the politicians' fear of being connected to a "fringe" group. This fear was perpetuated by the mainstream's view of Arab Americans, namely, condemnation. Numerous accounts point to the ways in which the media and mainstream institutions stigmatize Arabs which results in their exclusion from these institutions (see, e.g., Shaheen 2001).

17. For a historical account of the racial identification of Arabs in the United States, see Gualtieri 2009.

18. Special registration is shorthand for the National Security Entry-Exit Registration System (NSEER) which was announced in June 2002 and implemented the following September. Although the requirements may be applied to individual immigrants from any country, they have primarily been applied to men between the ages of sixteen and forty-five from the following countries: Afghanistan, Algeria, Bahrain, Bangladesh, Egypt,

Eritrea, Indonesia, Iran, Iraq, Jordan, Kuwait, Libya, Lebanon, Morocco, North Korea, Oman, Pakistan, Qatar, Somalia, Saudi Arabia, Sudan, Syria, Tunisia, United Arab Emirates, and Yemen. NSEER requires non-citizens to register at the port-of-entry and upon departure from the United States. Non-citizens already in the country at the initiation of the system were required to report to the Citizenship and Immigration Services for an interview about their stay in the United States. Non-citizens subject to NSEER are required to report to the immigration office at the anniversary of their arrival and whenever they change their place of residence. For a review of the impact of special registration and other policies on Arabs and Muslims in the United States, see Cainkar 2009.

19. In the mid-1960s Canada adopted a formally nondiscriminatory immigration policy and implemented a "points" system for the selection of immigrants. Under this system, immigration applicants earn points on the basis of education, occupational qualifications, knowledge of English or French, and assessment of the "occupational demand" factor in Canada. Although family re-union and humanitarian considerations have also been taken into account, the dominant criterion has been economic factors (Abu-Laban 1998; Richmond 1988; Simmons 1999). The change in policies of the 1960s opened the door for non-Europeans and changed the ethnic structure in Canada. Given the selective nature of immigration policy, it is evident that immigrants to Canada (excluding those from Southern Europe) are, on average, better educated, have higher occupational status, and earn larger incomes than those who are Canadian-born (Richmond 1988).

20. Specifically, the government started implementing the Act for the Preservation and Enhancement of Multiculturalism in Canada, whose purpose is to "promote the understanding and creativity that arises from the interaction between individuals and communities of different origins" (Canadian Multiculturalism Act, 3.1.g). The act allocated massive federal funding and the creation of a ministry dedicated to recognizing and promoting "policies, programs and practices that enhance the understanding of and respect for the diversity of the members of Canadian society" (ibid.:3.2.c).

21. For a discussion of Canada's multicultural ideals, see Kymlicka 1995.

22. According to the Employment Equity Act, "visible minorities are defined as persons, other than Aboriginal persons, who are non-Caucasian in race or non-white in colour." Chinese, South Asians, blacks, Arabs, West Asians, Filipinos, Southeast Asians, Latin Americans, Japanese, Koreans, and Pacific Islanders are among the groups identified as such (Statistics Canada 2008).

23. A meager 5.6% identified with their religion, and only 1.3% among them identified with their sect.

24. Because the survey was conducted almost immediately after 9/11, the respondents report a heightened awareness of prejudice and discrimination. The respondents almost unanimously agreed that Canadians know little about Arab culture and are influenced in their views of it by the negative stereotypes in the media. Among the survey respondents, 33.2% believe that Canadians do not like Arabs and 41.3% hold that Canadians do not like Muslims. The media was given the biggest share of propagating negative attitudes towards Arabs. The survey asked respondents to report on specific incidents of discrimination, and 24.8% of respondents stated that they, or someone in their immediate family, have experienced racism, mostly during the last two years (there is no information in the report of specific occurrences post–9/11). Acts of racism were encountered at workplaces and schools, as well as by the Canadian government in general.

25. For an analysis of the effects of Canada's multicultural discourse, see Dupont and Lemarchand 2001.

26. Until independence in 1962, Algeria was considered an integral part of French territory and all its inhabitants had the status of French nationals. Understandably, of the foreign population in France, Algerians comprise the largest group (805,000 in 1982) (Hargreaves 1995).

27. The claim that the Lebanese are mostly Catholic cannot be confirmed given the lack of the country's recent demographics. The last Lebanese census was conducted in 1932.

28. At times the Lebanese are seen as victims of multiculturalism, and the Lebanese civil war is used as a model of what multiculturalism may bring to France. French social historian Alain Torraine critiqued multiculturalism in France by signifying that it would lead to the "Lebanonization of France" (cited in DeGroat 2001).

29. The private/public dichotomy, at the heart of French multiculturalism, is central to the concept of *laïcité*, or secularism, which demands that religion be left at the door of public schools. In 1989 the French authorities ruled in favor of Muslim girls wearing headscarves to school despite the contradiction to the Republican tradition. The ruling, later referred to as the "Foulards Affair," as well as the "Rushdie Affair," resulted in making Islamic identity into a political problem (Castles and Miller 1993). While the French state has been flexible and pragmatic in the past, the recent ban on religious or political insignia in schools proves that it no longer is. The recent debate has centered around issues of national identity and ethnic pluralism, summed up by Pierre Tournemire, deputy general secretary of the Education League: "The French state is secular, but the French nation is pluralist" (Tager 2004).

30. In describing the place occupied by immigrants in French politics and public policy, Patrick Simon (2003) describes the French model of integration as one where ethnic differences are viewed in the same way as sex is viewed in Puritan societies, "as something to be neutralized, dissolved, and made invisible, all the while serving as an object of obsession."

31. I conducted more than one meeting with some respondents, especially whenever there were significant changes in their situation. For example, I started collecting data in New York City during the summer of 2001. Following the attacks of 9/11, which resulted in well-known disturbances within the Arab American community, I interviewed some of the same individuals to uncover how the current crisis within the Arab American community had affected their ways of understanding their experiences in the United States. Because I tried to maintain frequent contact with my informants after the interview, I sometimes learned that they had moved to another city; I then sought repeated interviews following their move. For example, after I had interviewed two respondents in New York, both moved to Paris, and so I met with them again while conducting my fieldwork in Paris. Repeated interviews with key informants allowed me to account for the possible ways that diaspora experiences are transformed within various socio-historical contexts.

32. Interviews lasted between forty-five and ninety minutes. Most were recorded and transcribed verbatim, but in the few instances when respondents refused to be taped I took extensive notes.

33. I supplemented the data collected through in-depth interviews and observations with text analysis. A number of individuals I interviewed provided me with books, newspaper articles, and references to websites that were very useful for my analysis. These

secondary sources allowed me to contextualize individual orientations and gain valuable information on some of the people I interviewed. However, throughout the analysis, I have omitted references to personal websites to maintain the respondents' anonymity.

CHAPTER 2. NARRATIVES OF IDENTIFICATION

1. Maktabi (1999) illustrates that at the 1932 census 85 percent of the emigrant citizenry (who were counted in the census for political reasons) were Christians.

2. For an analysis of Lebanese heritage activities, see Rowe 2010.

3. Although I assume that the former members of the Phalange Party saw me as an Arab, other respondents held a different viewpoint. Similar to the way some Lebanese view Lebanon, some Egyptians (both Muslims and Christians) do not see Egypt as an Arab country, and a few respondents were aware of the contested nature of Egypt's Arabness and its narratives.

4. Vertovec and Cohen (1999) argue that diasporic identity can be mandatory when constituted negatively by experiences of discrimination and exclusion. My respondents' narratives, however, highlight that while experiences of discrimination and exclusion often lead to a sense of exclusion from the host society, they do not prompt a construction of fixed ethnic identities.

5. The Phoenicians lived in the coastal parts of present-day Lebanon, Syria, and Israel. Many Lebanese, mostly Maronites, claim direct ancestry from Phoenicians to negate the Arabness of Lebanon and the Lebanese people.

6. For the disappearance of sectarian divisions in the Lebanese community in Montreal, see Lebnan 2002.

7. For the relationship between ethnicity and sociopolitical interests, see Glazer and Moynihan 1970.

8. I am only aware of one immigrant, Alain, who did return to Lebanon. In 2007, when I went back to Paris for another research project, I sought out some of my Lebanese respondents and was told that Alain had returned home after being rehired by a famous Lebanese newspaper. Alain's narrative is discussed in subsequent sections, but it is important to note here that he is the only political refugee I interviewed.

9. Historically, Lebanon has occupied a favorable position within the French Empire as a center for modernism and Catholicism amid a traditional Muslim Middle East. Despite Lebanon's independence from France, the French were active participants in designing the confessional power-sharing structure in Lebanon that leaves the presidency in the hands of the Maronites, who had welcomed the French presence in Lebanon. France continues to maintain special ties with Lebanon. One illustration is the frequency of bilateral visits: during the first eighteen months of French President Sarkozy's office (which started in May 2007), the minister of foreign affairs visited Lebanon ten times, the prime minister twice, and the president himself once. President Sarkozy was the first non-Arab head of state to visit newly elected President Sleiman on June 7. Although this period was also one of intense political unrest in Lebanon and a time when the French had hoped to play an important political role, the French Ministry of Foreign Affairs describes the relationship with Lebanon as "a comprehensive commitment that is not limited to political support, but is also expressed in the economic, cultural and cooperation fields" (France Diplomatie 2008).

10. Whereas eight out of twenty-two Lebanese immigrants in Montreal adopted an ethnic identity, nine out of thirty-eight in Paris described their ethnic identification as Lebanese based on their interest in political and social life in Lebanon. Of the nine Paris-based immigrants, five stressed their rejection of an Arab identity. Although I do not consider this small group of respondents representative of Lebanese immigrants in general or those in Paris in particular, I believe that their views reflect those belonging to the group of Lebanese immigrants who refused to be interviewed once they realized that I am of Muslim origin. All five are Maronite Catholics, and their rejection of an Arab identity is based on their perception that being "Arab" means being "Muslim." Of the remaining four, two are Shiite Muslims, one is Greek Orthodox, and one is Jewish. Among these nine immigrants, only one works in an entry-level service job as a waiter in a Lebanese restaurant, and the remaining eight hold various positions that reflect their middle- or upper-middle-class status. Of the nine respondents in this group, only two were French nationals, a sharp contrast to the eight respondents in Montreal who all had a Canadian nationality.

11. Michel Aoun returned to Lebanon in May 2005, following the withdrawal of Syrian troops. Many of his followers, like Georges, are believed to have returned to Lebanon as well.

12. Although these few immigrants possess an exaggerated sense of self-victimization, I highlight their cases to provide an understanding of ethnicity among members of the Lebanese diaspora.

13. Ali and Fares specifically referred to Hezbollah which was once an unpopular militia but grew to become a popular political party that is part of the Lebanese confessional political system. While supported by Iran, the party was also gaining popularity among Arabs in general for being a strong opponent to the State of Israel.

14. Samir may be expressing views that are exceptional among Greek Orthodox members of the Lebanese diaspora. In observing the 2006 Southern Federation of Syrian Lebanese American Clubs in San Antonio, Texas, Sarah Gualtieri (2009) notes that Catholics and Orthodox members of the Lebanese American community tend to identify as non-Arabs since the category is linked to Islam in the United States.

15. The Israeli attacks on Lebanon in the summer of 2006 confirmed to many respondents with whom I continued to communicate that their desire to return to Lebanon is truly a myth that will never be realized.

16. Gender differences are associated with the possibility of return. Men were more optimistic about their ability to save enough money in Canada that would eventually allow them to return to Lebanon while still be able to support their families. Women, on the other hand, despite their desire to return to Lebanon, were well aware of the practical impossibility of matching their living standards in Montreal.

17. The political structure in Lebanon stipulates that different religious communities are represented in the government by a Maronite Christian president, a Sunni Muslim prime minister, and a Shiite Muslim national assembly speaker. In the views of the Maronite political activists in Paris, power sharing between the three religious groups undermines the political power of Maronites since they do not control all three offices. Notably, however, it is the Maronite religious leadership that has traditionally refused to eliminate sectarian confessionalism. Earlier in 2010 the Maronite Patriarch Nasrallah Boutros Sfeir insisted that confessionalism is a fundamental feature of Lebanese society (Muhana 2010).

18. For a similar observation in Detroit, see Ajrouch and Jamal 2007.

19. Following the Israeli attacks on Lebanon in 2006 in retaliation for Hezbollah's hostilities, a few respondents I met in Paris a year later reiterated the same feelings of dissociation from Lebanese political instability and social unrest.

20. These terms mean, respectively, "that's it," "okay," "let's," and never mind.

21. For an elaboration on this point, see Cuccioletta 2002.

CHAPTER 3. THE POWER OF COMMUNITY

1. The Egyptian president Anwar Sadat's visit to Israel in 1977 and the signing of the Peace Treaty with Israel in 1979 led to much controversy over and criticism of Egypt's recognition of Israel. Egypt's resulting unpopularity among the Arab countries resulted in strengthening a reactionary identity among many Egyptians that emphasized their Pharonic origins as opposed to their Arab origins (see, e.g., Lorenz 1990).

2. For a review of ethnic organizations among Arab Americans, see Naff 1992.

3. A Lebanese Ministry of Emigrants was founded in 1993 and serves to maintain relations with Lebanese emigrants who are estimated to be 12 million worldwide. The Ministry organizes conferences for entrepreneurs to attract them to invest in Lebanon and summer camps for young people of Lebanese origin living abroad (Fargues 2004).

4. Following the assassination of former Lebanese prime minister Rafiq Hariri in February 2005, Lebanese people of all religious backgrounds united in what came to be described as the Cedar Revolution. The revolution focused on the withdrawal of Syrian troops from Lebanese territories and replacement of the government that was strongly influenced by Syria and its political interests (Daou 2010).

5. In an analysis of the political attitudes of Arab immigrants, Suleiman (1994) observes that younger Arab Americans more strongly identify as Arabs (as opposed to identifying as American only or choosing an identity based on their religion or national origin) but that such identification is mostly political, since younger Arabs are not necessarily devoted to cultural traditions and ethnic practices.

6. Gender bias in many of the Lebanese diasporic organizations can be observed in the male-dominated lists of these organizations' board of directors—especially the ones that are political in nature.

7. Basch, Glick Schiller, and Szanton Blanc (1994:7) have reported that immigrants "take actions, make decisions, and develop subjectivities and identities embedded in networks of relationships that connect them simultaneously to two or more nations." It must be emphasized, however, that diaspora transcends the dual allegiance that characterizes transnational communities that are caught between a place of origin and a place of current residence. Rather, diaspora is taken to embrace "a wider spread of allegiances" (Van Hear 1998:249).

8. In fact, Soysal primarily holds that diaspora is insufficient in the understanding of immigrants' global outlook or universal activities. She emphasizes global citizenship as a more comprehensive framework. I argue, however, that the given understandings of diaspora do not preclude the incorporation of such a dimension.

CHAPTER 4. CULTURES EXPRESSION

1. In an interview for the *New York Times*, Elie Chalala, editor of *al Jadid* magazine of Arab culture, explained that even prominent Arab and Arab American writers such as Edward Said focused on politics (Smith 2003).

2. Not all diasporic artists wish to represent their host societies or the diaspora itself. In one example, Rabih Alameddine, the Lebanese-born author of *I, the Divine: A Novel in First Chapters*, resisted pressure by his editor to speak for the Arab American community after 9/11. In fact, he prefers not to be identified as Arab American. "I am an Arab. I am an American. I don't do hyphens very well." Dissimilar to some diasporic artists who wish to be seen as representatives of their communities, Alameddine insisted that he was uncomfortable being "the voice of anything" (Shalal-Esa 2009).

3. The war is believed to have taken more than one hundred thousand lives as well as resulting in seventeen thousand unsolved disappearances (Hoang 2004; Hockstader 1999).

4. The movie was an immediate success and won an award at the Cannes Film Festival, a reflection of the French public interest in Lebanese social and political issues.

5. Movies dealing with the civil war continue to be subjected to much censorship in Lebanon. For example, an internationally acclaimed movie, *Civilized People*, which was honored by UNESCO and Human Rights Watch, was cut by fifty minutes, which amounts to half the original movie, before it was allowed to screen in Lebanon (Hoang 2004).

6. http://www.111101.com.

7. Atlas Group Archives. http://www.theatlasgroup.org.

8. In fact, the whole program that supported the exhibition was terminated.

9. Walid Raad's documentary *Hostage: The Bachar Tapes* (2000) is a clear attempt to uncover the volatility of notions such as memory and truth. In the documentary, a fictive Kuwaiti character is held captive with the American hostages during the systematic kidnapping of foreign diplomats that took place in Beirut in the 1980s. The Kuwaiti character, Soheil Bachar, was inspired by a real-life Lebanese, Soha Bachara, who spent ten years in solitary confinement after a failed attempt on the life of the leader of the Israeli proxy militia that was policing southern Lebanon. In his film Raad puts together seemingly opposing narratives of the occupation of the south of Lebanon and the hostage crisis, and instead of offering a narrative and a counter-narrative, the film challenges the integrity of dominant understandings of history and its representation (see Westmoreland 2009).

10. In the few years following our first meeting, Bassam published the novel and gained international recognition as a Lebanese diasporic writer.

11. Sometimes they were only able to attend the opening of their exhibitions in Lebanon "virtually" through the use of electronic means of communications.

12. As described in the group's communiqué, "Ziryab is an Arab who lived in Al Andalus, now Spain, in the 9th century AD. Ziryab was, by most accounts, one of the more fascinating figures of history, an unparalleled creator, inventor and arbiter of style and taste, who dictated fashions and arts. Ziryab designed new musical modes and methods, reworked scales, and constructed a harmonic theory which linked music and healing. He also is known for his influence on hairstyles, clothes (including which colors should be worn in what seasons), menus, tableware and etiquette, perfumes, cosmetics, toothpaste, philosophy, astrology and medicine. He was nominated as Man of the Millennium along with Albert Einstein."

1. Some members of the Lebanese diaspora undoubtedly maintain a relationship with the homeland that centers on nationalist and extremist politics. Only a small number of respondents provided such narratives, but others who share similar views have either refused or never volunteered to participate in my research. Those who share nationalist views provide the most institutional approach to the diaspora, whereby Maronite Lebanese immigrants around the world are being mobilized to join organizations at local, national, and global levels to affect politics in Lebanon. A handful of Maronite immigrants I interviewed see Lebanon as a Maronite nation, and their ethnic identification gives them a favorable position in Catholic French society.

2. I do not suggest that ethnic identities are in opposition to cosmopolitan ones and therefore do not hold that ethnic narratives are shaped by working-class experiences whereas cosmopolitan experiences are informed by elite or professional status. It is important to note that the ethnic narratives discussed in my analysis are emphatically diasporic, and therefore diasporic identities and solidarities are not specific to members of social elites.

3. Whether the diaspora is a framework that could apply to the study of multiple generations of immigrants is questionable. For an elaboration on this point, see Tölölyan 2007.

4. Waldinger and Fitzgerald (2004) argue that transnational networks take a toll on immigrants' lives as they are subjected to increased state and societal controls.

References

Abdelhady, Dalia. 2006. Beyond Home/Host Networks: Forms of Solidarity among Lebanese Immigrants in a Global Era. *Identities: Global Studies in Culture and Power*, 13:427–453.

———. 2008. Representing the Homeland: Lebanese Diasporic Notions of Home and Return in a Global Context. *Cultural Dynamics*, 20 (1), 53–72.

Abdul-Karim, Amir. 1992. Lebanese Business in France. In Albert Hourani and Nadim Shehadi, eds., *The Lebanese in the World: A Century of Emigration* (pp. 698–714). London: Centre for Lebanese Studies.

Aboud, Brian. 2000. Re-reading Arab World–New World Immigration History: Beyond the Prewar/Postwar Divide. *Journal of Ethnic and Migration Studies*, 26 (4), 653–673.

Abu-Laban, Baha. 1992. The Lebanese in Montreal. In Albert Hourani and Nadim Shehadi, eds., *The Lebanese in the World* (pp. 227–242). London: Centre for Lebanese Studies.

Abu-Laban, Yasmeen. 1998. Welcome/STAY OUT: The Contribution of Canadian Integration and Immigration Policies at the Millennium. *Canadian Ethnic Studies/Etudes Ethniques au Canada*, 30 (3), 190–211.

———. 2002. Liberalism, Multiculturalism, and the Problem of Essentialism. *Citizenship Studies*, 6 (4), 459–482.

Ajrouch, Kristine, and Amaney Jamal. 2007. Assimilating to a White Identity: The Case of Arab Americans. *International Migration Review*, 41 (4), 860–879.

Alba, Richard. 2005. Bright vs. Blurred Boundaries: Second-Generation Assimilation and Exclusion in France, Germany, and the United States. *Ethnic and Racial Studies*, 28 (January 2005), 20–49.

Albrow, Martin. 1997. *The Global Age: State and Society beyond Modernity*. Stanford, Calif.: Stanford University Press.

Alexander, Jeffrey. 1991. Bringing Democracy Back In: Universalistic Solidarity and the Civil Sphere. In Charles Lemert, ed., *Intellectuals and Politics: Social Theory in a Changing World* (pp. 157–176). Newbury, Calif.: Sage.

Allen, John, and Chris Hamnett, eds. 1995. *A Shrinking World? Global Unevenness and Inequality*. Oxford: University Press/Open University Press.

Al Solh, Mounira. n.d. http://www.xanaduart.com/mounira.html (accessed March 26, 2010).

Anderson, Benedict. 1991. *Imagined Community: Reflections on the Origin and Spread of Nationalism*. New York: Verso.

———. 1998. *The Spectre of Comparisons: Nationalism, Southeast Asia and the World*. New York: Verso.

Anthias, Floya. 1998. Evaluating "Diaspora": Beyond Ethnicity? *Sociology*, 32 (3), 557–580.

Armstrong, John. 1976. Mobilized and Proletarian Diasporas. *American Political Science Review*, 70, 393-408.

Artists Against the Occupation. 2003. *Artists Against the Occupation*. Montreal: MAI.

Atlas Group Archives. n.d. http://www.theatlasgroup.org (accessed February 21, 2007).

Axtmann, Roland. 1997. Collective Identity and the Democratic Nation-State in the Age of Globalization. In Ann Cvetkovich and Douglas Kellner, eds., *Articulating the Global and the Local: Globalization and Cultural Studies* (pp. 33–54). Boulder, Colo.: Westview.

Bakalian, Anny, and Mehdi Bozorgmehr. 2009. *Backlash 9/11: Middle Eastern and Muslim Americans Respond*. Berkeley: University of California Press.

Bammer, Angelika. 1994. Introduction. In Angelika Bammer, ed., *Displacements: Cultural Identities in Question* (pp. xi–xx). Bloomington: Indiana University Press.

Barkan, Elazar, and Marie-Denise Shelton. 1998. Introduction. In Elazar Barkan and Marie-Denise, eds., *Borders, Exiles, Diasporas* (pp. 1–11). Stanford, Calif.: Stanford University Press.

Barth, Fredrik. 1969. *Ethnic Groups and Boundaries: The Social Organization of Culture Difference*. Boston: Little, Brown.

Basch, Linda, Nina Glick Shiller, and Cristina Szanton Blanc. 1994. *Nations Unbound: Transnational Projects, Postcolonial Predicaments and Deterritorialized Nation-States*. Basel, Switzerland: Gordon and Breach.

Beck, Ulrich. 2002. The Cosmopolitan Society and Its Enemies. *Theory, Culture and Society*, 19 (1–2), 17–44.

Bellah, Robert, Richard Madsen, William Sullivan, Ann Swidler, and Steven M. Tipton. 1985. *Habits of the Heart: Individualism and Commitment in American Life*. New York: Harper and Row.

Bhabha, Homi. 1994. The Location of Culture. New York: Routledge.

Boym, Svetlana. 2001. *The Future of Nostalgia*. New York: Basic Books.

Bramdat, Paul. 2001. *Shows, Selves, and Solidarity: Ethnic Identity and Cultural Spectacles in Canada*. The Department of Canadian Heritage for the Ethnocultural, Racial, Religious, and Linguistic Diversity and Identity Seminar, Halifax, Nova Scotia, November.

Brittingham, Angela, and Patricia de la Cruz. 2005. We the People of Arab Ancestry in the United States. *Census 2000 Special Reports*, U.S. Census Bureau (available at http://www.census.gov/prod/2005pubs/censr-21.pdf (accessed January 17, 2011).

Brubaker, Rogers. 1992. *Citizenship and Nationhood*. Cambridge: Harvard University Press.

———. 2005. The "Diaspora" Diaspora. *Ethnic and Racial Studies*, 28 (1), 1–19.

Butler, Kim. 2001. Defining Diaspora, Refining a Discourse. *Diaspora*, 10 (2), 189–218.

Cainkar, Louise. 2009. *Homeland Insecurity: The Arab American and Muslim American Experience after 9/11*. New York: Russell Sage Foundation.

Calhoun, Craig. 2002. Imagining Solidarity: Cosmopolitanism, Constitutional Patriotism, and the Public Sphere. *Public Culture*, 14 (1), 147–171.

Canadian Arab Federation. 2002. *Arabs in Canada: Proudly Canadian and Marginalized. Report on the Findings and Recommendations of the Study "Arab Canadians: Charting the Future."* Toronto: Canadian Arab Federation.

Canadian Museum of Civilization. 2001. *The Lands Within Me*.http://www.civilization.ca/cultur/cespays/pay 2_07e.html (accessed February 21, 2007).

Canadian Multiculturalism Act. 1985. Canadian Minister of Justice. http://laws-lois.justice. gc.ca/eng/C-18.7/FullText.html (accessed January 17, 2011).

Castles Stephen. 1997. Multicultural Citizenship: A Response to the Dilemma of Globalization and National Identity? *Journal of Intercultural Studies* 18:5–22.

———. 2002. Migration and Community Formation under Conditions of Globalization. *International Migration Review,* 36:1143–1168

Castles, Stephen, and Mark J. Miller. 1993. *The Age of Migration: International Population Movements in the Modern World.* New York: Guilford.

Chaliand, Gérard, and Jean-Pierre Rageau. 1995. *The Penguin Atlas of Diasporas.* New York: Viking Penguin.

Chambers, Iain. 1994. *Migrancy, Culture, Identity.* New York: Routledge.

Cheah, Pheng, and Bruce Robbins, eds. 1998. *Cosmopolitics: Thinking and Feeling Beyond the Nation.* Minneapolis: University of Minnesota Press.

Chin, Soo-Young, Peter X. Feng, and Josephine D. Lee. 2000. Asian American Cultural Production. *Journal of Asian American Studies,* 3 (3), 269–282.

Clifford, James. 1994. Diasporas. *Cultural Anthropology,* 9 (3): 302–338.

Cohen, Robin. 1997. *Global Diasporas: An Introduction.* Seattle: University of Washington.

Communication Canada. 2001. *Multiculturalism in Canada.* Minister of Public Works and Government Services.

Conlogue, Ray. 2001. War on Terror: Museum Won't Show Arab Art. *Globe and Mail,* September 26.

Cooke, Miriam. 2002. Beirut Reborn: The Political Aesthetics of Auto-Destruction. *Yale Journal of Criticism,* 15 (2), 393–424.

Cornwell, Grant H., and Eve Walsh Stoddard. 2001. Introduction: National Boundaries/ Transnational Identities. In Grant H. Cornwell and Eve Walsh Stoddard, eds., *Global Multiculturalism: Comparative Perspectives on Ethnicity, Race, and Nation* (pp. 1–25). Lanham, Md.: Rowan and Littlefield.

Cross, Joan, David McMurray, and Ted Swedenburg. 1994. Arab Noise and Ramadan Nights: Rai, Rap, and Franco-Maghrebi Identity. *Diaspora,* 3 (1), 3–39.

Cuccioletta, Donald. 2002. Multiculturalism or Transculturalism: Towards a Cosmopolitan Citizenship. *London Journal of Canadian Studies,* 17:1–11.

Dahab, F. Elizabeth. 1999. Arabic Canadian Literature: Overview and Preliminary Bibliography. *Canadian Ethnic Studies,* 31 (2), 100–115.

Daou, Rita. 2010. Five years on, Lebanon's "Cedar Revolution" wanes. *Daily Star,* February 12.

Davies, Richard. 2000. "Neither Here nor There?" The Implications of Global Diasporas for (Inter)national Security. In David T. Graham and Nana K. Poku, eds., *Migration, Globalisation and Human Security* (pp. 23–46). New York: Routledge.

De Groat, Judith. 2001. "To Be French": Franco-Maghrebians and the Commission de las Nationalité. In Grant H. Cornwell and Eve Walsh Stoddard, eds., *Global Multiculturalism: Comparative Perspectives on Ethnicity, Race, and Nation* (pp. 73–92). New York: Rowan and Littlefield.

De la Cruz, G. Patricia, and Angela Brittingham. 2003. *The Arab Population: 2000. Census 2000 Brief.* U.S. Census Bureau.

Derrida, Jacques. 1992. *The Other Headings: Reflections on Today's Europe.* Translated by Pascale-Anne Brault and Michael B. Naas. Bloomington: Indiana University Press.

Dirlik, Arif. 1997. *The Postcolonial Aura: Third World Criticism in the Age of Global Capitalism*. Boulder, Colo.: Westview.

Dupont, Louis, and Nathalie Lemarchand. 2001. Official Multiculturalism in Canada: Between Virtue and Politics. In Grant Hermans Cornwell and Eve Walsh Stoddard, eds., *Global Multiculturalism: Comparative Perspectives on Ethnicity, Race, and Nation* (pp. 309–336). Lanham, Md.: Rowman and Littlefield.

Eid, Paul. 2008. *Being Arab: Ethnic and Religious Identity Building among Second Generation Youth in Montreal*. Montreal: McGill-Queens University Press.

Farah, May. 2003. Arab Canadians Cry Foul over Early Closure of Ottawa Exhibit. *Daily Star*, September 20.

Fares, Nabile. 1982. *L'état perdu ; précédé du Discours pratique de l'immigré*. Paris: Le Paradou, Actes sud.

Fargues, Philippe. 2004. Arab Migration to Europe: Trends and Policies. *International Migration Review*, 38 (4), 1348–1371.

Fernandez Kelly, Patricia. 2006. A Howl to the Heavens: Art in the Life of First- and Second-Generation Cuban Americans. *The Center for Migration and Development*, Working Paper Series, paper #06-04, Princeton University

Foner, Nancy. 2005. *In a New Land: A Comparative View of Immigration*. New York: New York University Press.

———. 2006. Then *and* Now or Then *to* Now: Immigration to New York in Contemporary and Historical Perspectives. *Journal of American Ethnic History*, 25 (4–5), 741–774.

France Diplomatie. 2008. *Lebanon*. http://www.diplomatie.gouv.fr/en/country-files_156/lebanon_294/index.html (accessed August 1, 2009).

Freeman, Gary. 1995. Modes of Immigration Politics in Liberal Democratic States. *International Migration Review*, 29 (4), 881–902.

Friedman, Jonathan. 1995. Global System, Globalization, and the Parameters of Modernity. In Mike Featherstone, Scott Lash, and Roland Robertson, eds., *Global Modernities* (pp. 69–90). London: Sage.

Gans, Herbert. 1979. Symbolic Ethnicity: The Future of Ethnic Groups and Cultures in America. *Ethnic and Racial Studies*, 2:1–20.

Gilroy, Paul. 1991. *There Ain't No Black in the Union Jack: The Cultural Politics of Race and Nation*. Chicago: University of Chicago Press.

Glazer, Nathan, and Daniel Moynihan. 1970. *Beyond the Melting Pot*. Cambridge, Mass.: MIT Press.

Gualtieri, Sarah. 2009. *Between Arab and White: Race and Ethnicity in the Early Syrian American Diaspora*. Berkeley: University of California Press.

Guiraudon, Virginie. 1996. The Reaffirmation of the Republican Model of Integration: Ten Years of Identity Politics in France. *French Politics and Society*, 14 (2), 47–57.

Gupta, Akhil, and James Ferguson. 1992. Beyond "Culture": Space, Identity, and the Politics of Social Difference. *Cultural Anthropology*, 7 (1), 6–23.

———. 1997. Culture, Power, Place: Ethnography at the End of an Era. In Akhil Gupta and James Ferguson, eds., *Culture, Power, Place: Explorations in Critical Anthropology* (pp. 1–29). Durham, N.C.: Duke University Press.

Haddad, Yvonne Yazbeck. 1983. Arab Muslims and Islamic Institutions in America: Adaptation and Reform. In S. Y. Abraham and N. Abraham, eds., *Arabs in the New World:*

Studies on Arab-American Communities (pp. 64–81). Detroit: Wayne State University, Center for Urban Studies.

———. 1994. Maintaining the Faith of the Fathers: Dilemmas in the Religious Identity in the Christian and Muslim Arab-American Communities. In Ernest McCarus, ed., *The Development of Arab-American Identity* (pp. 63–84). Ann Arbor: University of Michigan Press.

Hall, Stuart. 1990. Cultural Identity and Diaspora. In Jonathan Rutherford, ed., *Identity: Community, Culture, Difference* (pp. 222–237). London: Lawrence and Wishart.

———. 1992. The Question of Cultural Identity. In Stuart Hall, David Held and Anthony McGrew, eds., *Modernity and Its Futures* (pp. 273–316). Cambridge: Polity.

———. 1995. New Cultures for Old. In Doreen Massey and Pat Jess, eds., *A Place in the World? Places, Cultures, and Globalization* (pp. 175–213). New York: Oxford University Press.

———. 1997. The Local and the Global: Globalization and Ethnicity. In Anthony King , ed., *Culture, Globalization and the World System* (pp. 19–40). London: Macmillan.

Hargreaves, A. G. 1995. *Immigration, "Race" and Ethnicity in Contemporary France.* London: Routledge.

Hattab, A. 1985. *Etude socio-demographique sur la communaté Libanaise installée dans le region Parisienne.* Master's thesis, Université Paris V.

Haugbolle, Sune. 2005. Public and Private Memory of the Lebanese Civil War. *Comparative Studies of South Asia, Africa, and the Middle East,* 25 (1), 191–203.

Hayani, Ibrahim. 1999. Arabs in Canada: Assimilation or Integration. In Michael Suleiman, ed., *Arabs in America: Building a New Future* (pp. 284–303). Philadelphia: Temble University Press.

Hechter, Michael. 1987. *Principles of Group Solidarity.* Berkeley: University of California Press.

Heisler, Barbara Schmitter. 1992. The Future of Immigrant Incorporation: Which Models? Which Concepts? *International Migration Review,* 26 (2), 623–645.

Helou M. 1995. Contingency Planning for Systems Evolution after Crisis: Reconstructive Brain Drain Policy-Oriented Implications—The Face of Lebanon, 1975–1994. *Journal of Contingencies and Crisis Management,* 3:149–154.

Hoang, Mai. 2004. Lebanese Filmmaker: Randa Chahal Sabbag. *World Press Review,* 51 (3).

Hockstader, Lee. 1999. Lebanon's Forgotten Civil War. *Washington Post,* December 20, 1999, A24

Hollinger, David. 1995. *Postethnic America: Beyond Multiculturalism.* New York: Basic Books.

hooks, bell. 1991. *Yearning: Race, Gender and Cultural Politics.* London: Turnaround.

Hourani, Albert, and Nadim Shehadi. 1992. Introduction. In Albert Hourani and Nadim Shehadi, eds., *The Lebanese in the World: A Century of Emigration* (pp. 3–11). London: Centre for Lebanese Studies.

Hout, Syrine C. 2005. Memory, Home, and Exile in Contemporary Anglophone Lebanese Fiction. *Critique: Studies in Contemporary Fiction,* 46 (3), 219–233.

Howell, S. 2000. Cultural Interventions: Arab American Aesthetics between the Transnational and the Ethnic. *Diaspora,* 9:59–82

Humphrey, Michael. 2004. Lebanese Identities: Between Cities, Nations and Transnations. *Arab Studies Quarterly,* 26 (1), 31–50.

Hutnyk, John. 2005. Hybridity. *Ethnic and Racial Studies*, 28 (1), 79–102.

Ibish, Hussein, ed. 2003. *Report on Hate Crimes and Discrimination against Arab-Americans: The Post-September 11 Backlash, September 11, 2001–October 11, 2002.* Washington, D.C.: American-Arab Anti-Discrimination Committee.

Ifekwunigwe, Jayne. 2003. The Critical Feminist Auto-Ethnographer. In Jana Evans Braziel and Anita Mannur, eds., *Theorizing Diaspora* (pp. 184–206). Oxford: Blackwell.

Ireland, Patrick. 1996. Vive le jacobinisme: Les étrangers and the Durability of the Assimilationist Model in France. *French Politics and Society*, 14 (2), 33–46.

Issawi, Charles. 1992. The Historical Background of Lebanese Emigration, 1800–1914. In Albert Hourani and Nadim Shehadi, eds., *The Lebanese in the World: A Century of Emigration* (pp. 13–39). London: Centre for Lebanese Studies.

Jamal, Amaney, and Nadine Naber, eds. 2008. *Race and Arab Americans before and after 9/11: From Invisible Citizens to Visible Subjects.* Syracuse: Syracuse University Press.

JanMohammed, Abdul R. 1992. Worldliness-without-World, Homelessness-as-Home: Toward a Definition of the Specular Border Intellectual. In Michael Sprinker, ed., *Edward Said: A Critical Reader* (pp. 96–120). Oxford: Blackwell.

Jones-Correa, Michael. 1998. Different Paths: Gender, Immigration, and Political Participation. *International Migration Review*, 32 (2), 326–349.

Karim, Karim H. 1998. From Ethnic Media to Global Media: Transnational Communication Networks among Diasporic Communities. Transnational Communities Programme Working Paper, WPTC 99-02, University of Oxford. http://reference.kfupm.edu.sa/content/h/h__73711.pdf (accessed January 17, 2011).

Karla, Virinder S., Raminder Kaur, and John Hutnyk. 2005. *Diaspora and Hybridity.* London: Sage.

Karpat, Kemal H. 1985. The Ottoman Emigration to America, 1860-1914. *Inernational Journal of Middle East Studies*, 17, 175–209.

Kastrayano, Riva. 2002. *Negotiating Identities: States and Immigrants in France and Germany.* Princeton: Princeton University Press.

Kearney, M. 995. he Local and the Global: The Anthropology of Globalization and Transnationalism. *Annual Review of Anthrpology*, 24, 547–565.

Kemp, Perg. 1992. The Lebanese Migrant in France: *Muhâjir* or *Muhajjar?*" In Albert Hourani and Nadim Shehadi, eds., *The Lebanese in the World* (pp. 685–694). London: Centre for Lebanese Studies.

Kennedy, Paul, and Victor Roudometof. 2002. *Communities across Borders: New Immigrants and Transnational Cultures.* New York: Routledge.

Khalaf, Samir. 1987. The Background and Causes of Lebanese/Syrian Immigration to the United Stets before World War I. In Eric Hoogland, ed., *Crossing the Waters: Arabic-Speaking Immigrants to the United States before 1940* (pp. 17–35). Washington, D.C.: Smithsonian Institute Press.

Khater, Akram. 2001. *Inventing Home: Emigration, Gender, and the Middle Class in Lebanon, 1870–1920.* Berkeley: University of California Press.

———. 2005. Becoming "Syrian" in America: A Global Geography of Ethnicity and Nation. *Diaspora*, 14 (2–3): 299–331.

King, Anthony. 1991. Introduction: Spaces of Culture, Spaces of Knowledge. In Anthony D. King, ed., *Culture, Globalization, and the World-System: Contemporary Conditions for the Representation of Identity* (pp. 1–18). Minneapolis: University of Minnesota Press.

Klimt, Andrea, and Stephen Lubkemann. 2002. Argument across the Portuguese-Speaking World: A Discursive Approach to Diaspora. *Diaspora*, 11 (2), 145–162.

Kondo, Dorinne. 1997. *About Face: Performing "Race" in Fashion and Theatre*. New York: Routledge.

Kraidy, Marwan. 1999. The Global, the Local, and the Hybrid: A Native Ethnography of Globalization. *Critical Studies in Mass Communication*, 16, 456–476.

Kymlicka, William. 1995. *Multicultural Citizenship: A Theory of Liberal Rights*. Oxford: Clarendon.

———. 1998. *Finding Our Way: Rethinking Ethnocultural Relations in Canada*. Toronto: Oxford University Press.

Labaki, Boutros. 1992. Lebanese Migration during the War: 1975–1989. In Nadim Shehadi and Albert Hourani, eds., *Lebanese Migration in the World: A Century of Emigration* (pp. 605–626). London: Centre for Lebanese Studies.

Laguerre, Michel. 1998. *Diasporic Citizenship: Haitian Americans in Transnational America*. New York: St. Martin's.

Lavie, Samdar, and Ted Swedenburg. 1996. Introduction: Displacement, Diaspora, and Geographies of Identity. In Samdar Lavie and Ted Swedenburg, eds., *Displacement, Diasporas, and Geographies of Identity* (pp. 1–25). Durham, N.C.: Duke University Press.

Lebnan, Karim. 2002. *Itinéraires identitaires chez des immigrants libanais de Montréal: le cas de l'identité confessionnelle*. Master's thesis. Université de Montréal.

Leonard, Karen. 2000. State, Culture, and Religion: Political Action and Representation among South Asians in North America. *Diaspora*, 9 (1), 21–38.

Levitt, Peggy. 2001. *The Transnational Villager*. Berkeley: University of California Press.

Lindsay, Colin. 2007. *Profiles of Ethnic Communities in Canada: The Arab Community in Canada*. Ottawa: Minister of Industry.

Lionnet, Françoise. 1995. *Postcolonial Representations: Women, Literature, Identity*. Ithaca, N.Y.: Cornell University Press.

Lipschutz, R. D. 1992. Reconstructing World Politics: The Emergence of Global Civil Society. *Millennium*, 21 (3), 389–420.

Lipset, Seymour Martin. 1990. *Continental Divide*. New York: Routledge.

Lorenz, Joseph. 1990. *Egypt and the Arabs: Foreign Policy and the Search for National Identity*. Boulder: Westview.

Maalouf, Amine. 2000. *In the Name of Identity: Violence and the Need to Belong*. New York: Penguin Books.

Mahler, Sarah. 1998. Theoretical and Empirical Contributions Toward a Research Agenda for Transnationalism. In M. P. Smith and L. Guarnizo, eds., *Transnationalism from Below* (pp. 64–102). New Brunswick, N.J.: Transaction.

Maktabi, Rania. 1999. The Lebanese Census of 1932 Revisited: Who Are the Lebanese? *British Journal of Middle Eastern Studies*, 26 (2), 219–242

Marienstras, R. 1989. On the Notion of Diaspora. In G. Chaliand, ed., *Minority Peoples in the Age of Nation States* (pp. 119–125). London: Pluto.

Marshal, Susan and Jen'nan Ghazal Read. 2003. Identity Politics among Arab-American Women. *Sociel Science Quarterly*, 84 (4), 875–891.

Marx, Karl. 1852 [1967]. *The 18th Brumaire of Louis Bonaparte*. New York: International.

McCarus, Ernest. 1994. Introduction. In Ernest McCarus, ed., *The Development of Arab-American Identity* (pp. 1–8). Ann Arbor: University of Michigan Press.

Mercer, Kobena. 1994. *Welcome to the Jungle: New Positions in Black Cultural Studies*. New York: Routledge.

Miles, Robert, and Jeanne Singer-Kérel. 1991. Introduction. *Ethnic and Racial Studies*, 14 (3), 265–278.

Millard, Rachel. 2008. *Seven Years after 9/11: Arab Americans and the NYPD*. http://www.jjay.cuny.edu/cmcj/pdfs/NYPD%20Arab%20Americans_article.pdf (accessed March 26, 2010).

Mitchell, T. 1989. Culture across Borders. *Middle East Report*, 149:4–6.

Mohanty, Chandra Talpade. 1991. Under Western Eyes: Feminist Scholarship and Colonial Discourse. In Chandra Mohanty, Ann Russo, and Lourdes Torres, eds., *Third World Women and the Politics of Feminism* (pp. 51–80). Bloomington: Indiana University Press.

Morawska, Ewa. 2008. [Im]migration and Ethnic Research Agendas in Europe and the United States: A Comparison. *The Sociological Quarterly*, 49 (3), 465–82.

Moufarej, Ramzi. n.d. Myriade. http://www.frederiquemusic.com/myriade.htm (accessed January 18, 2011).

Muhana, Elias. 2010. The End of Political Confessionalism in Lebanon? *The National*, March 4. http://www.thenational.ae/apps/pbcs.dll/article?AID=/20100304/REVIEW/703049976/1192/rss (accessed August 17, 2010).

Naber, Nadine. 2000. Ambiguous Insiders: An Investigation of Arab Invisibility. *Ethnic and Racial Studies*, 23 (1), 37–61.

Naff, Alixa. 1985. *Becoming American: The Early Arab Immigrant Experience*. Carbondale: Southern Illinois University Press.

———. 1992. Lebanese Immigration into the United States: 1880 to the Present. In Albert Hourani and Nadim Shehadi, eds., *The Lebanese in the World: A Century of Emigration* (pp. 41–63). London: Centre for Lebanese Studies.

Naficy, Hamid. 1999. Framing Exile: From Homeland to Homepage. In Hamid Naficy, ed., *Home, Exile, Homeland: Film, Media, and the Politics of Place*. New York: Routledge.

Nagel, Joane. 1994. Constructing Ethnicity: Creating and Re-creating Ethnic Identity and Culture. *Social Problems*, 41 (1), 152–176.

Nederveen Pieterse, Jan. 1994. Globalisation as Hybridisation. *International Sociology*, 9:161–184.

Noiriel, Gérard. 1988. *Le creuset français: histoire de l'immigration, XIXe–XXe siécles*. Paris: Seuil.

Papastergiadis, Nikos. 1997. Tracing Hybridity in Theory. In Pnina Werbner and Tariq Modood, eds., *Debating Cultural Hybridity: Multicultural Identities and the Politics of Anti-Racism* (pp. 257–281). New York: Zed Books.

Peffer, John. 2003. The Burden of Global Art. *Rethinking Marxism*, 15 (3), 334–338.

Polak, Monique. 2003. A Community's History. *Montreal Gazette*, January 27.

Portes, Alejandro, and Ruben Rumbaut. 1996. Ethnic America: A Portrait. Berkeley: University of California Press.

Raad, Walid. 1996. *Missing Lebanese Wars*. Archival inkjet prints. Available at http://www.sfeir-semler.de/sites/raad/startraad.htm (accessed February 21, 2007).

———. 1999. *The Dead Weight of a Quarrel Hangs*. Video Data Bank. http://www.vdb.org/smacknacgi$tapedetail?DEAD WEIGHT (accessed February 21, 2007).

———. 2000. *Hostage: The Bachar Tapes*. http://www.vdb.org/smackn.acgi$tapedetail?HOSTAGETHE (accessed February 21, 2007).

Rapport, Nigel, and Andrew Dawson. 1998. The Topic of the Book. In Nigel Rapport and Andrew Dawson, eds., *Migrants of Identity: Perceptions of Home in a World of Movement* (pp. 3–18). New York: Berg.

Richmond, Anthony. 1988. *Immigration and Ethnic Conflict*. Hampshire, England: Macmillan.

Ricoeur, Paul. 1986. *From Text to Action: Essays in Hermeneutics II*. Translated by Kathleen Blamey and John B. Thompson. Evanston, Ill.: Northwestern University Press, 1991.

Ritter, Mitch. 2001. Dirty Linen. *Folk and World Music*, October/November, 59.

Robbins, Bruce. 1998. Comparative Cosmopolitanisms. In Pheng Cheah and Bruce Robbins, eds., *Cosmopolitics: Thinking and Feeling beyond the Nation* (pp. 246–264). Minneapolis: University of Minnesota Press.

Roudometof, Victor. 2005. Transnationalism, Cosmopolitanism, and Globalization. *Current Sociology*, 53, 113–135.

Rowe, Amy. 2010. Heritage Albums and Haflis: Americans in Possession of Lebanese Heritage in Northern New England. In Paul Tabar, ed., Politics, Culture, and Lebanese Diaspora. Newcastle upon Tyne: Cambridge Scholars.

Rushdie, Salman. 1991. *Imaginary Homelands: Essays and Criticism, 1982–1991*. London: Viking.

Rutherford, Jonathan. 1990. A Place Called Home: Identity and the Cultural Politics of Difference. In Jonathan Rutherford, ed., *Identity: Community, Culture, Difference* (pp. 9–27). London: Lawrence and Wishart.

Saab, Jocelyn. 1994. *Once Upon a Time: Beirut*. Seattle, Wash.: Arab Film Distributors.

Safran, William. 1991. Diasporas in Modern Societies: Myths of Homeland and Return. *Diaspora*, 1 (1), 83–99.

Said, Edward. 1978. *Orientalism*. New York: Vintage Books.

———. 1984. The Mind of Winter: Reflections on Life in Exile. *Harper's*, 269 (September), 49–55.

———. 1990. Reflections on Exile. In Russell Ferguson, Martha Gever, Trinh T. Minh-ha, and Cornell West, eds., *Out There: Marginalization and Contemporary Culture* (365–366). Cambridge, Mass.: MIT Press.

Salloum, Jayce. 1994. *This Is Not Beirut*. http://www.vdb.org/smackn. acgi$tapedetail?THISISNOTB (accessed August 19, 2003).

Salloum, Jayce, and Elia Suleiman. 1990. *Introduction to the End of an Argument*. http://www.imdb.com/title/tt0347254 (accessed August 19, 2003).

Sandoval, José Miguel and Mark Stephen Jendrysik. 1993. Convergence and Divergence in Arab-American Public Opinion. *International Journal of Public Opinion Research*, 5, 303–314.

Scholte, Jan Aart. 1996. The Geography of Collective Identities in a Globalizing World. *Review of International Political Economy*, 34 (4), 565–607.

Seidman, Steven. 2011. From the Stranger to the Other: The Politics of Cosmopolitan Beirut. In Janice McLaughlin, Peter Phillimore and Diane Richardson, eds., *Contesting Recognition: Culture, Identity and Citizenship*. London: Palgrane.

Shaheen, Jack. 2001. *Reel Bad Arabs: How Hollywood Vilifies a People*. New York: Olive Branch.

Shalal-Esa, Andrea. 2009. The Politics of Getting Published: The Continuing Struggle of Arab-American Writers. *Al-Jadid*, 15 (61).

Sheffer, Gabriel. 1996. A New Field of Study: Modern Diasporas in International Politics. In Gabriel Sheffer, ed., *Modern Diasporas and International Politics* (pp. 1–15). London: Croom Helm.

———. 1997. Middle Eastern Diaspora: Introduction and Readings. *Middle East Review of International Affairs*, 1 (2). Available at: http://meria.idc.ac.il/journal/1997/issue2/jv1n2a4.html (accessed January 17, 2011).

———. 2006. Transnationalism and Ethnonational Diasporism. *Diaspora*, 15 (1), 121–145.

Silverman, David, and Brian Torode. 1980. *The Material World: Some Theories of Language and Its Limits*. Boston: Routledge and Kegan Paul.

Simmons, Alan. 1999. Immigration Policy: Imagined Futures. In Shiva S. Halli and Leo Driedger, eds., *Immigrant Canada: Demographic, Economic, and Social Challenges* (pp. 21–50). Toronto: University of Toronto Press.

Simon, Patrick. 2003. Personal Communication.

Siu, P.C.P. 1952. The Sojourner. *American Journal of Sociology*, 58, 1, 34–44.

Smith, Dinitia. 2003. Arab-American Writers, Uneasy in Two Worlds. *New York Times*, February 19. http://www.nytimes.com/2003/02/19/books/19WRIT.html?pagewanted=1 (accessed January 17, 2011).

Smith, Robert Courtney. 2005. *Mexican New York: Transnational Lives of New Immigrants*. Berkeley: University of California Press.

Somers, Margaret R. 1994. The Narrative Constitution of Identity: A Relational and Network Approach. *Theory and Society*, 23, 605–649.

Soysal, Yasemin Nuhoglu. 2000. Citizenship and Identity: Living in Diasporas in Post-War Europe. *Ethnic and Racial Studies*, 23 (1), 1–15.

Spivak, Gayatri Chakravorty. 1999. *A Critique of Postcolonial Reason: Toward a History of the Vanishing Present*. Cambridge, Mass.: Harvard University Press.

Statistics Canada. 2008. *Canada's Ethnocultural Mosaic, 2006 Census*. Ottawa: Ministry of Industry.

———. 2009. Visible Minority Population. http://www40.statcan.gc.ca/l01/cst01/demo53b-eng.htm (accessed August 17, 2010).

Sturken, Marita. 1997. *Tangled Memories: The Vietnam War, the AIDS Epidemic, and the Politics of Remembering*. Berkeley: University of California Press.

Suleiman, Michael. 1994. Arab-Americans and the Political Process. In Ernest McCarus, ed., *The Development of Arab-American Identity* (pp. 37–60). Ann Arbor: University of Michigan Press.

———. 1999. Introduction: The Arab Immigrant Experience. In Michael Suleiman, ed., *Arabs in America: Building a New Future* (pp. 1–24). Philadelphia, Pa.: Temple University Press.

Sullivan, Zohreh. 2001. *Exiled Memories: Stories of Iranian Diaspora*. Philadelphia, Pa.: Temple University Press.

Tager, Djénane Kareh. 2004. Defending "Republican Values." *World Press Review*, 51 (3).

Taylor, Charles. 1992. *Multiculturalism and "The Politics of Recognition."* Princeton, N.J.: Princeton University Press.

Thomas, D. 1990. *Immigrant Integration and the Canadian Identity*. Public Affairs and Strategic Planning and Research, Immigration Policy. Ottawa: Employment and Immigration Canada.

Tölölyan, Khachig. 1991. The Nation State and Its Other: In Lieu of a Preface. *Diaspora*, 1 (1), 3–7.

———. 1996. Rethinking Diaspora(s): Stateless Power in the Transnational Moment. *Diaspora*, 5, 3–36.

———. 2007. The Contemporary Discourse of Diaspora. *Comparative Studies of South Asia, Africa, and the Middle East*, 27 (3), 647–655.

Trouillot, Michel-Rolph. 2003. *Global Transformations: Anthropology and the Modern World*. New York: Palgrave Macmillan.

Truzzi, O. 1997. The Right Place at the Right Time: Syrians and Lebanese in Brazil and the United States, A Comparative Approach. *Journal of American Ethnic History*, 16 (2), 3–34.

United Nations Development Programme (UNDP). 2004. *Human Development Report: Lebanon*.

Van Hear, Nicholas. 1998. *New Diasporas: The Mass Exodus, Dispersion and Regrouping of Migrant Communities*. London: University College London Press.

Vertovec, Steven, and Robin Cohen, eds. 1999. *Migration, Diasporas and Transnationalism*. Northampton, England: Elgar.

Waldinger, Roger, and David Fitzgerald. 2004. Transnationalism in Question. *American Journal of Sociology*, 109:1177–1195.

Waters, Mary. 1999. *Black Identities: West Indian Immigrant Dreams and American Realities*. New York: Russell Sage Foundation.

Weiner, Myron. 1986. Labour Migrations as Incipient Diaspora. In Gabriel Sheffer, ed., *Modern Diasporas in International Politics* (pp. 43–74). London: Croom Helm.

Werbner, Pnina. 1997. Introduction: The Dialectics of Cultural Hybridity. In Pnina Werbner and Tariq Modood, eds., *Debating Cultural Hybridity: Multicultural Identities and the Politics of Anti-Racism* (pp. 1–28). London: Zed Books.

———. 1998. Diasporic Political Imaginaries: A Sphere of Freedom or a Sphere of Illusion? *Communal/Plural*, 6 (1), 11–31.

———. 1999. Global Pathways, Working Class Cosmopolitans, and the Creation of Transnational Ethnic Worlds. *Social Anthropology*, 7 (1), 19–20.

———. 2000. Introduction: The Materiality of Diaspora—Between Aesthetic and "Real" Politics. *Diaspora* 9 (1), 1–20.

Westmoreland, Mark. 2009. Post-Orientalist Aesthetics. *Invisible Culture*, Issue 13: "After PostColonialism?" Available at http://www.rochester.edu/in_visible_culture/Issue_13_/westmoreland/index.html (accessed March 3, 2010).

Wihtol de Wenden, Catherine. 1991. Immigration Policy and the Issue of Nationality. *Ethnic and Racial Studies*, 14 (3), 319–332.

———. 1998. How Can One be Muslim? The French Debate on Allegiance, Intrusion, and Transnationalism. *International Review of Sociology*, 8 (2), 275–289.

Winland, Daphne. 1998. "Our Home and Native Land"? *Canadian Ethnic Scholarship and the Challenge of Transnationalism. CRSA*, 35 (4), 555–577.

Yang, Philip. 2000. The "Sojourner Hypothesis" Revisited. *Diaspora*, 9 (2), 235–258.

Younis, Adele. 1995. *The Coming of the Arabic-Speaking People to the United States*. New York: Center for Migration Studies.

Zelizer, Barbie. 2000. *Remembering to Forget: Holocaust Memory through the Camera's Eye*. Chicago: University of Chicago Press.

Zogby, James. 1998. The Politics of Exclusion. *Civil Rights Journal*. Also available at http://findarticles.com/p/articles/mi_m0HSP/is_1_3/ai_66678538/ (accessed March 26, 2010).

Zolberg, Aristide. 2000. The Dawn of Cosmopolitan Denizenship. *Indiana Journal of Global Legal Studies*, 7:511–518.

Index

Citizenship, 9, 102, 122, 190; Canadian, 9, 47; Citizenship and Immigration Services (CIS), 2, 204n18; cosmopolitan, 37–38, 189, 194; definitions of, 9, 107, 110; French, 127; global, 185, 190, 208n8; *jus soli*, 9; requirements for, 8; U.S., 9

Civil society organizations, 100; community, 78, 81; ethnic, 50, 100, 117, 150, 178, 182

Civil war, the, 6, 7, 17, 19, 21, 32, 38, 41, 43, 48, 57, 63, 75, 97, 110, 123, 135, 138–139, 154, 157–158, 164–166, 177, 183, 185, 205n28, 209n5; history of, 171; memory of, 139, 146; remembering, 145–149; representing, 153

Class: background, 2, 19, 30, 47, 59, 63, 77–79, 110, 121, 179, 180, 187; differences, 78, 84, 110–111, 115, 122, 131, 180; position, 19, 147, 179, 180, 184; resources, 64

Colonization, 10, 34, 51, 69; colonial history, 8; French, 31, 52–53, 61, 69; postcolonialism, 167. *See also* Postcolonial

Communal consciousness, 11, 94, 101

Community: Arab, 16, 112; Arab American, 89–90, 100, 103, 117, 205n31, 208n2; Arab immigrant, 47, 117; building, 37; diasporic, 11–13, 35, 45, 91–92, 94, 100, 114–119, 122, 180, 185; ethnic, 11, 34, 44–45, 57, 91, 95, 103, 111, 120, 127, 149, 151, 184; events, 24, 37, 97, 103; global, 38, 121, 135; immigrant, 13, 36, 102, 117, 149; Lebanese immigrant, 42, 149, 150; national, 33, 100, 190; transnational, 38, 108, 165

"A Community of Many Worlds," 20, 27

Context of reception, 4, 8–9, 38, 46, 51, 139, 170, 196

Coptic 54

Cosmopolitan(s) 4; attachments, 64, 108, 126, 134, 172, 189–190, 192, 198; concerns, 38, 119, 135, 164, 168, 187; consciousness, 194; ideals, 14, 173; identification, 27, 35, 76, 80–82, 103, 108, 129, 134, 166, 190, 192, 210n2; meaning of, 189–190; multiple, 194; outlook, 176, 185, 189, 191; status, 165, 172

Cosmopolitanism, 38, 126, 172, 191–192, 195; localized, 188–195; rooted, 190–191; thin, 86, 190–191

Cultural competence, 112, 184

Culture of amnesia, 144–146

Cyprus, 29, 155, 157

Diaspora: concept of, 3, 9, 34, 35, 39, 190, 195–196; definitions of, 10–15, 38–39, 45, 74, 80, 83–85, 92, 94, 100, 116–117, 120, 122, 125, 177, 186, 196, 198, 202n5, 208n7; framework, 4–5, 35, 38, 45, 86, 131, 176, 186, 188, 191, 208n8, 210n3; understandings of, 17, 36, 37, 100, 112, 118, 120, 125, 127, 185, 188, 196, 202n5

Difference, 43–47, 49, 50, 58, 66, 113, 168, 179, 184–185, 190–192, 197–198; among Arabs, 20, 28; awareness of, 2, 17, 50–51, 65, 69, 76, 92, 96, 105, 176; cultural, 23, 30–31, 47, 51, 67, 74–75, 78, 91, 184; ethnic, 26, 43, 51, 58–59, 66, 69, 176, 178, 205n3; political, 67, 70, 81, 184; racial, 4, 21, 66, 67, 182; social, 19, 56, 167

Discrimination, 44, 55, 70, 72–73, 117, 158, 191, 206n4; derogatory comments, 72; ethnic, 73; experiences of, 20, 34, 46, 66, 70, 74, 84, 127; fear of, 8, 23; gender, 119; post 9/11, 20, 34, 204n24; religious, 6

Displacement, 13, 38, 57, 83, 85, 130, 135, 143–144, 154–161, 167, 172–173, 176, 187, 189, 193–195, 197–198

Divided loyalties 93, 102. *See also* Transnationalism

Education, 7, 8, 50–51, 69, 75, 83, 91, 121, 155, 204n19, 205n29; cultural, 105, 153, 184–185; educational programs, 8, 23, 81; French, 30, 61, 64, 69; Western style, 62–63, 78. *See also* Cultural competence

Egypt, 2, 33, 41–42, 89, 118, 201n1, 203n18, 206n3, 208n1; Egyptian government, 1. *See also* Coptic

Emigration, 5–7, 64, 76, 108, 201n1

Ethnic: attachments, 34, 93, 106, 117–118, 125–127, 179, 197; in Canada, 25, 27, 47, 49, 51, 178, 180, 204n19; community,

Host society: Acceptance by/in, 11, 197; belonging to, 84, 104, 120, 131, 133, 157, 161, 171, 179, 184, 189, 197; difference from, 2, 17, 45, 58, 65, 72, 74, 77, 100, 180; incorporation into, 3–4, 140, 143; integration in, 17, 43, 71, 86, 102, 108, 114, 124, 136, 181, 186; interest in, 100, 181; involvement in, 103, 113, 135, 171, 177; lack of belonging to, 61, 70, 80; participation in, 46, 93, 101, 105–108, 113, 122, 124, 130, 152, 162, 172, 188–189

Hybridity, 34, 170, 195; critique of, 170

Identity, 2–5, 15, 18–19, 31, 35–36, 44–46, 57–58, 60, 81, 84, 86, 89, 92–93, 99–100, 105, 113, 126, 128–129, 140, 150, 154–155, 160, 166–167, 178, 180, 182, 184, 187–188, 192–193, 194, 196; American, 66, 69, 85, 182; Arab, 20, 24, 37, 48, 53, 56–58, 67, 69, 72, 79, 84, 87, 89, 90, 110, 150, 179, 182, 184, 207n10, 208n11; aspects of, 26; Canadian, 25–26, 50, 69, 82, 85, 182; choice of, 25, 46, 66, 68, 103, 161, 166, 187, 208n5; communal, 90, 113, 119–120, 186; cosmopolitan, 76, 93, 128, 129, 134, 135, 166, 190, 192; cultural, 44, 57, 85, 86, 154, 186; diasporic, 8, 14, 31, 35, 37–38, 43–45, 59–60, 83, 85, 113, 134, 144, 154, 162, 180, 190, 196, 202n5, 206n4; dual, 24, 80, 102, 108, 112; effect of globalization on, 80–81, 113, 127; essential, 58, 91; ethnic, 3, 8, 14–15, 23–24, 27, 33, 35, 37, 43–48, 50, 52, 55–56, 58–59, 66, 71–72, 83–84, 86, 89, 100, 107–108, 110, 122, 150, 178–179, 181–182, 184, 187–188, 206n4, 207n10, 210n2; exclusionary, 118, 166, 187; French, 8, 32, 69, 205n29; formation/construction, 18, 27, 35, 44–45, 48, 53, 61, 74, 80, 84, 92, 115, 123, 154, 171, 177–178, 180, 183, 187, 191; global, 85, 190, 194, 198; hybrid, 34; immigrant, 35–37, 44–45, 69–70, 85–86, 92, 126, 155, 183, 185, 208n7; Lebanese, 19, 25–26, 42, 52–53, 55–57, 60, 72, 85, 90, 115, 118, 140–141, 143, 150, 167, 179, 181, 186, 192; multiple, 37, 39, 46, 60–81, 85, 93, 96, 152, 168, 189; national, 8, 36, 56, 90, 121, 167, 191, 196, 200n1, 202n11; negotiated, 38, 44–45, 58, 80; political,

57, 69, 117; religious, 56, 73, 110, 205n29; transcultural, 60–80, 85–86; unitary, 48, 60, 81, 86, 186, 188; white, 66, 68, 182

Identification, 21, 25–26, 35, 44–46, 56, 64, 68, 70, 74, 77, 79–80, 82–85, 91, 128–129, 133, 162, 181, 184, 191, 194, 196, 208n5, Arab 56–57, 179, Canadian 69, 182, Cosmopolitan 27, 80, 108, 162, 192, Diasporic5, 13, 37, 45, 60, 113, 128, 210n2, Ethnic 17,43, 46–51, 57–60, 66–67, 122, 171, 178–180, 186, 201n1, French 184, Multiple 38, 61, 82, 85, 133, 171, National 81, Religious, 48, 56–57, 202n11; traditional, 11, 86, 128, 167, 187; transcultural, 61, 79–80, 96, 108

Immigration 9, 37–38, 45, 74, 93, 125, 152, 175; anti-, 36, 45; Arab, 202n11, 203n16; Citizenship and Immigration Services, 2, 204n18; contemporary/global/new, 36, 38–39, 58, 80, 111, 121–122, 127; contexts of, 84, 90, 139; diasporic, 85, 131, 190; in France, 9, 28–30, 32–33, 52, 59, 184; policies, 38; policies in Canada, 23–24, 204n19; policies in the U.S., 8; sociology of, 14; studies of, 3–4, 14–15, 35, 202n5

Integration, 43, 59, 71, 86, 118, 136, 188; contexts, 7–8, 61; desire for, 108; global, 13; in American society, 33; into Canadian society, 25, 27, 182, 183; into French society, 32–33, 54, 57, 65, 107, 183, 205n30; into the mainstream, 114; lack of, 102; patterns of, 38; post-9/11, 17, 22, 34, 183. *See also* Context of reception

Islam, 28, 74, 101, 107, 111, 183, 203n13, 205n29, 207n14

Israeli attacks, 134, 207n15, 208n19; Israeli invasion, 6, 42, 151, 166; Pro-Israeli militia, 19, 209n9

Khater, Akram, 95–96, 182, 185
Kymlicka, William, 4, 23, 47, 204n21

"The Lands Within Me," 152–155, 183
Language, 4, 26, 34, 36, 42, 45, 51, 61–63, 79, 105, 144, 160, 202n5, 203n15; absorption, 3, 33, 91; Arabic, 37, 41, 51, 53; French, 51, 104, 141

On-line media, 116
Otherness, 68–69, 144, 190, 194; other, 20,
    67, 78, 105, 144–145, 203n12; othering, 53
Ottoman Empire, 201n1, 201n2, 202n11;
    Greater Syria, 6, 22, 201n1, 202n11

Philanthropic activities 99, 109, 177
Phoenician(s) 206n5; ancestors, 18, 144;
    heritage, 46
Pluralism, 4–5; contexts of reception, 4;
    ethnic, 4, 5, 14–15, 24, 33–35, 205n29
Political: activism, 55, 109, 140, 194; activ-
    ists, 48, 55, 114–115, 118, 186, 207n17
Postcolonial: analysis, 34, 127, 129, 158–159;
    criticism, 9, 143; identities, 56–57; post-
    colonialism, 167; societies, 142; ties, 183
Postwar, 75, 164, 171; environment, 186;
    politics, 138; reconstruction, 134, 138, 148,
    167, 171. *See also* Culture of amnesia
Public engagement, 37–38, 52, 59, 87, 91, 93,
    95, 105, 114, 124, 129–130, 133, 135, 162,
    167–168, 172, 190; cosmopolitan, 123–124,
    129, 189, 191, 193; political, 60, 101, 104, 177
Public sphere, 4, 33, 61, 87, 91, 108, 124,
    127, 129, 134–135, 145, 171, 188, 190,
    192; diasporic, 162; global, 15, 131, 162;
    transnational, 131

Raad, Walid, 148–149, 209n9
Racial: categorization/classification, 20–21,
    23–24, 66, 68; formation, 20; politics, 66;
    profiling, 22; structure in Canada, 24–25;
    structure in U.S., 4, 20–21, 182
Racialization, 16–17, 20, 28, 67, 182, 203n13
Religious groups: Druze 6, 110, 201n4,
    203n15, Greek orthodox 6, 56, 110, 201,
    203n15, 207n14; Maronites, 6, 19, 41–42,
    48, 53, 55, 60, 74, 110, 115, 179, 183, 201n4,
    203n12, 206n5, 206n9, 207n10, 207n17;
    Sunnis, 28, 41, 43, 63, 67, 109–110, 184,
    201, 203n15; Shiites, 41–42, 56, 110, 147,
    201n4, 207n10
Representation, 133, 141, 143–144, 152, 155,
    160, 171–172, 209n9; in Canada, 44;
    cultural, 133–134, 136, 138, 141–144, 148,
    152–153, 155; diasporic, 172; ethnic, 170;

media, 19–20, 71, 133, 152; modes of,
    138, 141–143, 152, 160, 181; political, 143;
    public, 148; religious, 36
Republican model, 95; French republic, 33,
    178, 205n29
Return, 12, 17, 59, 84–85, 137, 158, 177, 180,
    206n8, 207n11; abandoning/rejecting,
    63–64, 74, 81, 107, 179–180, 193; desire to,
    10–12, 16, 48, 59–60, 66, 84, 94, 104, 131,
    143, 155, 177–178, 180, 207n16; impos-
    sibility of, 12, 48, 51, 55, 59–60, 66, 119,
    179–180, 207n15; myth of, 11–12, 17, 154,
    177, 179, 192, 196, 207n15; possibility of,
    17, 52, 60–61, 84, 207n16

Said, Edward, 55, 85, 93, 111, 144, 155, 175,
    197, 209n1
Salloum, Jayce, 148, 152
Second-generation, 31, 44, 134
Sectarian: conflict, 76, 166–167, 201n3;
    division, 19, 110–111, 115, 135, 145, 147, 180,
    189, 206n6; nonsectarian, 32, 148
Sectarianism, 59, 81, 113, 115, 118, 122, 140,
    187, 207n17
Secular identities, 32, 56–57, 67, 93, 111, 150,
    182, 184, 187
Secularism, 29, 47, 111, 205n29
September 11 (9/11), 16, 17, 19, 20, 22, 27, 28,
    34, 36, 68, 71–73, 152, 178, 181–183, 197,
    203n16, 205n31
Sexuality, 77, 111, 122, 165; homosexuality,
    109, 112
Solidarity, 2, 11, 15, 55, 92, 98–99, 108, 113,
    120–121, 127, 129–131, 135–136, 148, 173,
    178, 185, 193–194, 196; diasporic, 113,
    116, 130, 196, 210n2; ethnic, 4, 11, 12, 101;
    global, 114, 120, 122–123, 127, 129–130,
    161, 173, 185, 193, 195, 196; national, 135;
    transnational, 11, 130, 185
Soysal, Yesmin, 10, 102, 127, 202n5
Stereotypes, 19, 53, 71, 135, 138, 143, 163, 182;
    role of media, 19, 20, 71, 72, 73, 133, 152,
    194, 202n10, 203n16, 204n24

Taif Accords/Agreement, 7, 146
Tölölyan, Khachig, 13, 92, 100, 120, 177, 196

Transcultural: identification, 79–80, 96, 108; identities, 61, 77, 80, 85–86, 93; narratives, 60–61, 85, 159; practices, 86
Transculturalism, 60, 80; features of, 61
Translation, 140–143, 153, 170
Transnational(s), 4, 102, 186, 189; alliances, 14l; attachments, 93, 157, 178, 189–190; communities, 34–35, 38, 83, 92, 99, 101, 108, 117, 131, 136, 165, 196, 208n7; cultural practices, 99, 136, 178, 188; identity, 52, 58, 101, 155; involvement, 38, 86, 93, 108; networks, 117, 162, 210n4; practices, 4, 13–14, 17, 37, 60, 86, 131, 189–190; sentiments 60, 197; solidarity, 11, 130; spaces, 14, 189; tensions, 93; ties, 93, 117, 185. *See also* Divided loyalties
Transnationalism, 4–5, 38, 86, 131, 185, 189, 190; framework, 35, 86; maintaining, 29; studies, 4, 102, 126–127, 136, 185, 191; special registration, 22, 68, 71, 203n18

Visible minorities, 23–24, 47, 69, 182, 204n22

War on terrorism 20; antiwar, 123, 187
Whiteness, 21, 66–68, 182; racially white, 3–4, 20–21, 24–25, 42, 66–70, 77, 178, 182; white identity, 66, 68, 81, 182

About the Author

DALIA ABDELHADY received her PhD in Sociology at the University of Albany. She is a Senior Researcher at the Center for Middle Eastern Studies at Lund University and coordinator of academic research for the Women and Sustainable Growth Inititative created in cooperation with Lund University in Sweden, Zayed University in the United Arab Emirates and Yale University in the United States.